D1474832

ENGLISH
IN TIBET,
TIBET
IN ENGLISH

Self-Presentation in Tibet and the Diaspora

LAURIE HOVELL McMILLIN

palgrave

First published 2001 by PALGRAVE™
175 Fifth Avenue, New York, N.Y. 10010 and
Houndmills, Basingstoke, Hampshire RG21 6XS.
Companies and representatives throughout the world

PALGRAVE is the new global publishing imprint of St. Martin's Press LLC Scholarly and Reference Division and Palgrave Publishers Ltd (formerly Macmillan Press Ltd).

ISBN 0-312-23922-X hardback

Library of Congress Cataloging-in-Publication Data
McMillin, Laurie Hovell, 1962-
      English in Tibet, Tibet in English : self presentation in Tibet and the diaspora / by Laurie Hovell McMillin.
         p. cm.
      Includes bibliographical references and index.
      ISBN 0-312-23922-X
      1. Tibet (China)—In literature. 2. Travelers' writings, English—History and criticism. 3. Tibetans—Foreign countries—Biography—History and criticism. 4. Tibet (China)—Biography—History and criticism. 5. Great Britain—Relations—China—Tibet. 6. Tibet (China)—Relations—Great Britain. 7. Tibet (China)—Description and travel. 8. British—China—Tibet—History. 9. English language—China—Tibet. 10. Autobiography. I. Title.

PR129.C6 M35 2001
820.9'32515—dc21

2001036520

A catalogue record for this book is available from the British Library.

Design by Westchester Book Composition.

First edition: November 2001
10 9 8 7 6 5 4 3 2 1

Printed in the United States of America.

Contents

CONTENTS

CONTENTS

For Tracy Scott McMillin
and for Liam and Jack McMillin

Acknowledgments

$\mathcal{M}$any people have helped me on the long journey that led to this book. James S. Duncan gave me the encouragement to get started, and Donald S. Lopez, Jr. guided the project through to the end. Paula Richman and Len Podis responded thoughtfully to the manuscript at several stages. Jan Cooper, Michael Fisher, Wendy Kozol, Kathie Linehan, and Sandy Zagarell read portions of the manuscript: thanks go to them. The project got underway at Syracuse University; I am grateful to my teachers there: Richard Fallis, Charles H. Long, Susan Wadley, Robyn Wiegman, and the late Agehananda Bharati. Aspects of this book were conceived on the road or around kitchen tables with the help of P. Christiaan Klieger, Tashi Tsering of Dharamsala, Karl Yoder, Eleanor Zelliot, and the late Beatrice and Robert Miller. I thank Joseph Adler, Donald Rogan, and Augusta Rohrbach for their timely questions. And it is safe to say that without my teachers in Wisconsin—Mark Dintenfass, Peter Fritzell, Jack Stanley, and Herbert Tjossem of Lawrence University and Elaine Nelson in Galesville—none of this travel or writing would have happened.

Ruth Amsler, Tsering Dorjee, Tsenshap Rinpoche, and Jigme Risur in Switzerland gave unselfishly of their time and knowledge. I thank Palden Gyatso, Lobsang Ngodrup, Geshe Damdul, and the monks of Drepung Loseling for their visits. The monks of Gajang Dangtse and Sera Me, Sonam of Xigatse, and Sonam Wangdu Numa were generous hosts. David Patt, David Blake of the British Library, Nick Jones, John Olmstead, Tsering Shakya, and Axel K. Ström all gave valuable assistance. I learned a great deal from my students at Kenyon College and Oberlin College, especially from Gordon Fraser, Jason Goss, Megan McDonough, and Brent Werner. Mike Stortz got me to Ladakh, and the friendship of Ellen Sayles and Daniel Gardner sustained me through the writing. Kristi Long and Donna Cherry at Palgrave have been very helpful.

This project has been driven in part by the opportunities to travel and write afforded me by a Thomas J. Watson Fellowship, a Fulbright Fellowship in Buddhist Studies for Sri Lanka, a Syracuse University graduate fellowship, a dissertation fellowship from the National Endowment for the Humanities, a curriculum development grant from Kenyon College, and a Grant-in-Aid from Oberlin College.

My mother and father, Laurena and the late Robert Hovell, have supported me in many ways during my wandering years, as have my siblings, Robert, Debra and Pamela. I am thankful to my children, Liam and Jack, for putting up with a sometimes absent-minded mother and for sustaining and gladdening me every day. And finally, I am deeply grateful to my husband, Tracy Scott McMillin, who read the manuscript at many, many stages, and who was always willing to talk through the ideas that drive and sometimes obsess me. His crazy wisdom and love have made so many things possible.

Preface

When George Bogle visited Tashilhunpo monastery in 1774, the Panchen Lama offered the young Scotsman an astonishing perspective. Peering through the lama's "Camera Obscura," Bogle saw views of London.[1]

The image is striking: Bogle is in what, to England, is a remote corner of the globe, a place widely-known for having been cut off from history. But there, in a monastery in "the land of snows," Bogle sees images of home. Even in 1774, then, Tibet was not a place cut off from the outside world; it was a place that had already encountered Europe, or at least an image of it. When I read this unpublished account of cross-cultural contact in the British Library in 1999, I was aware too that the Tibetans who once seemed confined to "the forbidden land" had now spread themselves around the world. My desk mate at the India Office was a Tibetan who once served on the staff of the library and now made his home in London; across the room was a Tibetan monk in full maroon and gold regalia, perusing the shelves.

These images of England in Tibet and Tibetans in England dramatize one of the convictions that guide this book: Tibet and the West have had a long, complex, and convoluted relationship, a relationship that can be explored, in part, through analysis of English language texts. British colonial presence in India encouraged a relationship and even at times a preoccupation with Tibet unique among Western nations; because of Britain's interest in Tibet, English-language texts have played a key role in larger Western constructions of the place, and have contributed to later American representations of Tibet. English-language texts produced in Britain and the United States have, in turn, had an impact on Tibetan self-presentations of the past 50 years; when Tibetans have opted to tell their life stories in a European language, they have most often done so in English. By focusing on the ways that both British travelers and Tibetan autobiographers have represented themselves in English-language texts, I offer a view of this long-term relationship, which considers how both Anglophone Westerners and Tibetans have been affected by the interaction.

Part One of this study, "English in Tibet," explores the writing of British travelers from George Bogle to Francis Younghusband, that is, from 1774 to 1910.[2] I place these texts within a shifting colonial context and examine how these writers imagine themselves in relation to Tibetan others. Further, by focusing on the textual nature of these accounts, I explore the development of "the myth of epiphany," the notion that travel to Tibet might transform a British traveler. Beginning my study with the manuscripts of Bogle, I consider his shifting understandings of Tibetans, of Tibet, and of himself. I see Bogle as a self-reflective subject whose ability to criticize and reflect on his own situation vis-à-vis Tibetan others is neglected in the shape that British colonialism later takes. From Bogle's texts, I move on to the travel texts of Samuel Turner and Thomas Manning, as well as to the contributions made to Western knowledge of Tibet by Brian Houghton Hodgson, L. Austine Waddell, Helena Blavatsky, and Rudyard Kipling. Finally, I look at Francis Younghusband's *India and Tibet,* the work in which epiphany is finally realized. As I see it, Younghusband's hope for an epiphany in Tibet is a dream from which the English-speaking West has not entirely awoken and has shaped many recent Anglophone accounts of Tibet and Tibetans.

In Part Two, "Tibet in English," I look at a phenomenon of the Tibetan diaspora: the writing of Tibetan autobiographies in English. Tibetan literature has a long autobiographical tradition. Traditionally, Tibetan *namtar* (biography) and *rangnam* (autobiography) focus on the lives of those who have attained "full liberation" within the Tibetan Buddhist system; departing from this formula in both subject matter and narrative forms, the recent wave of Tibetan autobiographies in English includes the life stories of lay men and women, political prisoners, monks without advanced degrees, as well as lamas and teachers of various attainments. The autobiographers whose texts I examine include the Dalai Lama, Jetsun Pema, Thubten Jigme Norbu, Lobsang Gyatso, Chagdud Tulku, Palden Gyatso, Rinchen Dolma Taring, Ama Adhe, and Tashi Tsering. In exploring the production and reception of Tibetan autobiographies, I argue that the making of Tibetan autobiographies in English is inevitably a mixed phenomenon, one that is inextricably intertwined both with Western expectations and with Tibetans' desires to represent their experience. Tibetans who write their life stories cannot keep from sometimes engaging Western representations made of Tibetans, even as they participate in a very Tibetan practice of self-presentation, however transformed and translated.

Parts One and Two do not follow the same methodological or rhetorical strategies but are structured to accommodate the different kinds of stories I tell in each part. While the first part develops a plot line of sorts, the second part performs a variety of readings on selected texts. Nonetheless, the two parts share an interest in the ways in which shifting cultural and historical contexts both enable and limit representations of self and other. Further, some of the ideas explored in the first part inform my work in the second: How have Tibetans dealt with English-language representations of them? How has the dream of epiphany shaped Western reception of these texts? This book is informed by a kind of self-critical hopefulness; in this way I aim to contribute to ongoing discussions about cross-cultural representation as they are worked out in a number of disciplines including English studies, cultural studies, and Tibetan studies.

I come to this topic after long association with and travel among Tibetan communities in India, Nepal, Tibet, Switzerland, and the United States. My initiation into Tibetan Studies, as it were, occurred when I myself was a traveler—an English-speaker among Tibetan peoples. Having pored over Tuesday Lobsang Rampa's *The Third Eye* as a teenager and been intrigued when the Dalai Lama visited my home state of Wisconsin in 1979, I went to a college where Tibet all but fell through the cracks between academic disciplines. While traveling in India on an undergraduate program, I encountered people of Tibetan ancestry for the first time; they were selling sweaters on city streets, offering religious artifacts in exchange for Bic pens at Ladakhi monasteries, and gathering at Buddhist pilgrimage sites. I returned to India in 1984 on a Thomas J. Watson Foundation Fellowship to observe the present shape of Buddhist culture in India, which included that of the Tibetan exiles. Within this framework, I was more interested in seeing how Tibetans lived in exile than in studying texts or meditating. While some Western scholars studied at the Library of Tibetan Works and Archives in Dharamsala or with various lamas, I was more likely to be hanging out in the restaurants in McLeod Ganj, talking with children in rudimentary Tibetan, or going to discos with Tibetan cohorts at Friends' Corner.

These experiences all shaped my sense of Tibetan religion and culture, giving it its particular focus. I had no sense that there was a "pure" Tibetan culture; I was more interested in the ways that Jesus Christ was hailed as a *bodhisattva* in Kopan Monastery's Christmas *puja* near Kathmandu; I was compelled by the way that young Tibetans in Dharamsala called Western Buddhists "*dharma* crazy." I was more interested in the strange cultural phenomenon by which a matron from New York state might believe that she, along with a contingent from Boulder, was actively engaged in bringing the dharma back to Tibet. Such experiences led me to decide not to pursue a graduate degree in Buddhist Studies (where I would have been largely involved in philosophical and philological study of Buddhist texts), even as they alerted me to the ways in which the interactions between Westerners and Tibetans transformed the priorities of both sides. When I did undertake graduate study, my interest was in the history of American and British constructions of South Asia and Tibet and depended on a suspicion of what Edward Said calls the "textual attitude"[3] towards Asian religions and cultures—a skepticism about any claims to presenting and preserving "authentic" or "pure" forms of culture and religion. In recent years I have been particularly indebted to the work of Donald S. Lopez, Jr. and other innovators in the field of Tibetan and Himalayan area studies.[4] Lopez's 1998 book, *Prisoners of Shangri-La: Tibetan Buddhism and the West,* has been crucial to my conception of the project I first began in 1989; Lopez argues that the West's image of Tibet has a particular history and a peculiar trajectory, one at some distance from the lives of Tibetans—from the ways in which Tibetans have *lived out* their history, culture, and religious traditions.[5]

This book, then, is a product of my travels, values, and predilections. It explores the oft-ignored mixedness of Tibetan culture and religion, and engages in an always incomplete effort to be self-reflective. When I look into the mirror the image does not stand still but moves between traveler, writer, teacher, mother, lover, scholar, woman, former farm kid. In the writing of this book I have struggled to maintain the energy as well as the intricacy of those movements; in Part One I use "postscripts" to call special attention to my shifting relationship with the texts and ideas under consideration. In Part Two, these reflections are more integrated into the analysis; even so, I use several postscripts to consider how my travels have connected to those of Tibetan autobiographers. Overall my approach relies on close textual analysis; my strategy is to contextualize selected texts, to see how they are historically situated, to examine how they relate to other texts, and to consider how knowledge about Tibetans and Westerners is produced through cross-cultural exchanges. The limitations of my approach are, no doubt, many; nonetheless, I believe that the advantages of such work lies in its power to make us continually question what we know and how we know it. What do Westerners expect from Tibetans? What do Tibetans expect from the West? What can various self-presentations teach us about an exchange between English-speakers and Tibetans that is now over two hundred years old? By bringing such questions to light I aim not just for the endless play of unsettling conventions and stereotypes (though that's a worthwhile project, too); my hope is that through being so unsettled we might imagine different ways of approaching others and apprehending ourselves.

PART ONE
ENGLISH IN TIBET

CHAPTER 1

The Way to Epiphany

*W*estern travelers have often expected something from Tibet. From James Hilton's *Lost Horizon* (1933) to Jean-Jacques Annaud's *Seven Years in Tibet* (1997), something special is supposed to happen to Western travelers in Tibet. The industry standard for such transformation was set by Frank Capra's film version of *Lost Horizon* (1937) in which the world-weary Conway is bewitched by the peaceable kingdom of Shangri-La. Thus, when Pico Iyer writes about certain magical moments in Tibet in 1988 or Frederick Lenz dreams of spiritual transformation and snowboarding in *Surfing the Himalayas* of 1997, they are participating in a time-honored custom: the myth of epiphany in Tibet.[1] The myth of Tibetan epiphany is so common that it even appeared in a "Sylvia" cartoon in 1996. In this cartoon, the cats, up to their usual tricks, explain the whereabouts of the missing dog by saying "the dog had an epiphany. . . . He left for a more spiritual place. . . . Perhaps he's in Tibet with monks . . . or on an ice floe with penguins." The myth of epiphany is so common that any Anglophone text about travel to Tibet of the past hundred years seems incomplete without one. Tibet without revelation is like France without wine, Africa without lions, Egypt without pyramids.

The word "epiphany" refers specifically to Jesus' manifestation to the Magi and more generally to a manifestation of the divine—to a moment of sudden intuitive understanding. In the late eighteenth and nineteenth centuries, this notion of a flash of comprehension, while deeply connected to Christian notions of salvation and revelation, gained a wide currency in Britain. Evangelism had posited the notion of a transfiguring experience—a rebirth that led one to the Lord. Romantic writers, in turn, took up the hope of transformation and placed it in more secular terms. From there, the trope became an important part of British novels, poetry, and secular biographies.[2] Epiphany, then, was not always integral to Western travelers' conceptions of Tibet. Before the twentieth century, travelers may have wanted many things from Tibet, but transformation was not one of them. By my accounting, the myth of Tibetan epiphany first appeared in an English travel text in 1910. And then it was not produced by someone seeking mountains to climb or *gurus* to enlighten him. Instead, Francis Younghusband was a general of the British Indian army and leader of 8,000 troops; he was in Tibet to negotiate a treaty with the 13th Dalai Lama and to establish British power in Central Asia. When at last the battles and political wrangling were complete, the general looked out over Lhasa and had a life-changing experience. From there, Younghusband's account of his revelation creates a trope and a myth that will shape and influence later representations of Tibet in English.

In a sense Younghusband's epiphany established a horizon, something many travelers have since sought to reach. But because it is in the nature of horizons to recede, this horizon has continued to be glimpsed, discovered, and exposed as mirage—only to be rediscovered elsewhere.

In his 1979 travel narrative, *The Snow Leopard,* for example, Peter Matthiessen has an epiphany—but only after losing one first. Trekking to the Mustang section of the Nepalese Himalayas, which is a culturally Tibetan region, Matthiessen initially feels that he discovers something real and true under the benevolent eye of the Shey Lama and the Crystal Mountain:

> The secret of the mountains is that the mountains simply exist, as I do myself: the mountains exist simply, which I do not. The mountains have no "meaning," they *are* meaning; the mountains *are*. The sun is round. I ring with life, and the mountains ring, and when I can hear it, there is a ringing that we share. I understand all this, not in my mind but in my heart, knowing how meaningless it is to try to capture what cannot be expressed, knowing that mere words will remain when I read it all again, another day.[3]

So it seems that the horizon of epiphany has been found. On his descent back to Kathmandu and "civilization," however, Matthiessen learns that this epiphany was false: "[nothing] has changed; I am still beset by the same old lusts and ego and emotions . . .—that aching gap between what I know and what I am" (p. 298). When Matthiessen acknowledges this false epiphany, a "real"—if less ostentatious—epiphany becomes possible, one better suited to life in the world and his own Shunryu Suzuki-style Zen sympathies:

I leave the tragic sense of things behind; I begin to smile, infused with a sense of my own foolishness, with an acceptance of the failures of this journey as well as of its wonders, acceptance of all that I might meet upon the path. I know that this transcendence will be fleeting, but while it lasts, I spring along the path as if set free; so light do I feel that I might be back in the celestial snows [at Shey]. (p. 301)

By initially criticizing the dream of transformation, Matthiessen, in effect, rehabilitates it. A horizon is found, discovered as false, lost, only to be found again.

A similar play of transformations lost and found appears in Charlotte Watson's 1987 account of travel in Tibet. Here Watson specifically names her desire as one for epiphany:

Travel has curative powers for me, and [after my mother died] I turned to it as a healing drug. I craved a place so distant and so difficult it would take full concentration to survive the present moment, with nothing left for the future or the past. I chose Tibet. I wanted escape and epiphany; I got dust and distraction. In the end, they were almost the same, and I was grateful.[4]

Aware of Tibet's corner on the epiphany market, Watson self-critically examines her desire for transformation. Horizon lost. But in spite of, or perhaps because of, her self-criticism, she gets what she wants—dust and distraction become their own kind of epiphany. Horizon sought, lost, and found.

While recent tales of Tibet have had to reconfigure epiphany in order to rescue it as a dominant theme, earlier stories of travel did not depend on such a trope. Before Younghusband's *India and Tibet,* travelers might be moved, they might get confused, they might even change their minds, but the literary trope of epiphany did not shape their tales. As evidenced in George Bogle's accounts of his travels in Tibet from 1774–75, for example, his expectations towards the land and the people differ vastly from those of Younghusband, Matthiessen, or Watson; his texts suggest quite different ways of imagining what might happen to a traveler there. In the following pages of Part One, I consider selected British texts in order to explore how travelers represent what happens to them in Tibet. How do they imagine their relation to Tibetans? In what terms and tropes do they represent themselves? How do shifting colonial relations affect their understanding of themselves and of Tibetan others? In effect, I offer a textual genealogy of Tibetan epiphany, a way of looking at how texts and ideas are produced by people who write and read within particular historical moments. While scholars such as George Woodcock, Peter Bishop, and Orville Schell have discussed the parade of Western travelers who went to Tibet—and a few have even noted Younghusband's epiphany there—no one has yet explored the lineage of this dream of transformation.[5] And while recent travel writers on Tibet implicitly debunk the myth of epiphany in order to reclaim it, my aim here is somewhat different. I analyze the construction of Tibetan epiphany in order to suggest, through Bogle, a different kind of debunking, a different version of re-enchantment.

CHAPTER 2

The First One There: Bogle's Journey

*E*veryone loves Bogle. That is, among the many European travelers who have gone to Tibet in the past two centuries, Bogle is the favorite of many scholars and Tibetophiles. In 1906, Thomas Holdich noted:

> Bogle was an excellent observer, and possessed the rare faculty of adapting himself to the manners and habits of his hosts, as well as the capability of sharing something of their outlook on the world outside Tibet, appreciating their views and to a certain extent sympathizing with them.[1]

Schuyler Camman commends Bogle's "remarkable sense of observation and [his] great ability to evaluate what he saw."[2] Peter Bishop finds Bogle an agreeable traveler, someone who "was always prepared to use Tibet as a springboard for criticism of Europe."[3] Because of Bogle's character, he *should* be singled out. But I feel that he should also be revisited, reconsidered—or rather, his writings should. While many have admired Bogle, few have treated his account as an open book—as a *text,* with all the complexity such a conception invites. Instead, Bogle's story is treated as a closed case. Part of this results from most scholars' reliance on Clements R. Markham's 1876 edition of Bogle's account.[4] Because of that text, Bogle remains firmly in the past, a solid and coherent figure, a product of his time. By determining him that way, readers can themselves remain comfortable, assured of their own positions.

In the following study I take Bogle's texts as plural; I refer to his manuscripts, letters, and notes, as well as to Markham's edition of his writings.[5] While I am not the first to use these texts, my reading of Bogle's writings seeks out the richness of their textuality, endeavors to explore their contradictions and conflicts, and considers their variety and multiplicity. For even though many have written about him, we are not yet finished reading Bogle. I return to Bogle's texts because their open-endedness bears rereading. I return to his text, but it also returns to me—my reading of it is never quite finished.

BOGLE: THE FIRST ONE THERE

The clerk at the India Office in Blackfriar's, London, plunked down the papers I had requested: file folders, mostly, and a curiously thick package of rolled papers, tied with a string. During his stay at Tashilhunpo monastery near Xigatse, Tibet, George Bogle made over 50 pages of vocabulary notes. In the papers before me, over two hundred years before, he had jotted down the English sounds for Tibetan letters in the U-chen script. There are pages for numbers, parts of dress, abstract nouns, the "surface of the earth," liquids, metals, utensils, animals, insects, adverbs, relations, and government. (In the Tibetan case, this last category includes a word for "transmigration.") On the page for "qualities," he noted no Tibetan equivalents for the words wisdom, wise, folly, foolish, learning, and learned. And tucked among the vocabulary lessons is a moral lesson, evidently translated from the Tibetan:

> A Good Man.—
> Attends the Scruples
> Counts his Beads
> Tells Truth—
> Instructs Ignorant
> Cultivates his Ground[6]

As a fair-minded child of the Enlightenment and servant to the English East India Company (E. I. C.), Bogle might very well be thought to care about what makes a good man. But was this Tibetan definition of the good man also a self-definition—words to live by? Or was it simply a curious artifact, on a par with a Tibetan ritual dagger or the reputed talismanic excrement of the Dalai Lama? And if Bogle used this definition to frame his own self-perception—as in a mirror—what image was thrown back? Outside of home, a traveler frequently locates oneself vis-à-vis another. Speaking languages not one's own, wearing local clothing, encountering the expectations and images of oneself projected by the people one meets along the way: all these combine to revise, undermine, and, in some cases, reify one's notion of oneself.

So in this jotting down of a note: what aspects of himself did Bogle see reflected? What qualities connected him to the "Tibetan good man"? Which images fragmented off, reminding him of the considerable distance between himself and Tibetans? Because even if, as the adage urges, Bogle sought to "instruct ignorance," surely Bogle's conception of ignorance differed from that of the Buddhists he lived among, for whom "ignorance" might refer to a spiritual form of blindness, our human birthright as deluded, grasping, hating beings. And even a company servant and Protestant, who participated in local customs and was not averse to "kow-towing" when the occasion warranted it, might have trouble "counting his beads," clicking off one of 108 beads in a *mala* with each utterance of a *mantra*.

Whether or not Bogle looked into this adage as into a mirror in order to consider his sense of himself, his writings suggest that he was very interested in the image he presented to the world, and in how the world received him. As he writes to his father from Bhutan, "I wish you could have the Honour of seeing my Mustachoes which I have been fostering and nursing with much care ever since I came among these Hills."[7] When Bogle first arrived in Tibet, he was given a set of Tibetan clothes by the Panchen Lama, the articles of which are enumerated repeatedly in his journal and his letters:

> Some days after my arrival the Lama had given me a Thibetian dress, consisting of a purple Sattin Tunick lined with Siberian Fox Skins, a yellow Sattin Cap, faced with Sable and crowned with a Red Silk Tassel, and a pair of red Bulgar hide boots. In this I equipped myself, glad to abandon my European Habit, which was both uncomfortable, and exposed me to Abundance of that troublesome Curiosity which the Thibetians possess in a Degree inferior to no other people.[8]

Bogle's willingness to abandon his "European Habit" and embrace a new self-image suggest that he has changed his thinking along with his clothes. (As he writes to his family in Daldowie, with a new set of clothes and "a pair of whiskers now you would hardly know me."[9]) But at other moments Bogle seems acutely aware of his distance from the Tibetans among whom he lives. Confronted with his physical differences from (and the curiosity of) Tibetans, Bogle notes that at times he feels like a "Specimen," and ponders what Tibetans will deduce from his example. While the out-sized height and girth of Alexander Hamilton,[10] the medical officer who accompanied Bogle, make a good impression on the Tibetans, Bogle notes that the advantage he himself possesses is his "fair Complexion—for although my skin when [it] sits in opposition to [my cousin] Mrs. Moreheads might appear as black as an Africans it gains greatly by Comparison with that of the People of this Country."[11] From moment to moment, then, Bogle shifts from presenting himself in a Tibetan fashion to considering himself as a representative of whiteness.

Many of Bogle's representations of his Tibetan travels have this aspect: at times Bogle connects deeply to the Tibetans he lives among; at other times he retreats into a more familiar and English or Scottish definition of himself. At times Enlightenment values for critique and self-reflection seem ready to undermine his position and threaten his very ability to comprehend himself as anything stable or coherent; and sometimes the same critique just seems conventional, the polite participation in clichéd self-criticism. In many ways, Bogle can be seen as a reluctant servant of the company, in which case he undermines the authority of colonial discourse at the moment. But he can also be seen as playing the role of a reluctant servant of the company, in which case his is a kind of contained criticism that underwrites the colonial project.

BOGLE IN TEXT AND CONTEXT

George Bogle was the first Briton to travel to Tibet, making his journey to the Tashilhunpo monastery of the Panchen Lama in 1774. Unlike the Christian missionaries who traveled to Central Asia before him, Bogle did not go to Tibet in search of long-lost members of the faith or new converts. And unlike the mission led by Francis Younghusband over a century later, Bogle did not seek to conquer. His goals were more modest: he sought a source of gold, trading partners, a route to China; he introduced the potato along the way. Sent by Governor-General Warren Hastings, Bogle was to make contact with the "Teshoo Lama of Thibet," ascertain what goods and services might be traded with Tibet, and help to expand the sphere of influence of the East India Company.

The image of the British colonialist with pith helmet and stiff upper lip, drinking gin and tonics, does not fit the men of the East India Company of Bogle's day. Although changes in the relations between companymen and local people were underway, many colonists of this period wore native dress, learned local languages, and married native women (or kept them as mistresses). One English friend of Bogle's took a Muslim name, and Bogle himself is rumored to have married an Asian woman, perhaps a Tibetan.[12] And unlike the Utilitarians and Evangelicals who would follow them,

Hastings and company did not seek to reform India with what they would term European or English principles. As David Kopf summarizes Hastings' philosophy, he believed that "to rule effectively, one must love India; to love India, one must communicate with her people; and to communicate with her people, one must learn her languages."[13] These languages included Persian for diplomacy, Sanskrit as a key to unlock India's past, and, later, regional vernaculars for ease of communication with the local population. The learning of local languages suggests something of Hastings' conception of the local people: they were not (only) to be managed—they were also people with whom one might converse and learn. And because Hastings' Orientalists felt that people—or rather, adult males—everywhere were capable of reason, the Company could rationally enter into commerce and competition with other rational people in the world. That it took some effort to negotiate the tensions between humanism and commerce, between relativism and colonial expansion, is suggested in Bogle's accounts of Tibet.

The East India Company's opportunity for communication with Tibet came after a series of disputes among various Himalayan powers. The company had been involved in military action with the Bhutanese army at Cooch Behar in 1773. Fearing that company troops would invade this small buffer state north of Bengal, the Gurkha ruler of Nepal, Prithvi Narayan, appealed to the Panchen Lama of Tibet to intervene on behalf of the Deb Raja of Bhutan. The Panchen or "Teshoo" Lama, hoping to stop further battles in the Himalayan region, wrote to Governor Hastings and asked that the British help to preserve peace in the Himalayan states.[14]

At this point in Tibet's political history, the eighth Dalai Lama, Jampel Gyatso, was still a minor, and the Lhasa government was strongly under the influence of the Chinese; Bogle reports to Hastings that "The Emperor of China is paramount Sovereign" over all of Tibet.[15] Nonetheless, residing in the western Tibetan city of Xigatse and some distance from the influence of the Lhasa and Peking courts, the third Panchen Lama, Lobsang Palden Yeshe (1738–1780), wielded considerable influence in southern Tibet and the states south of Tibet. The Panchen Lama's envoys, a Tibetan named "Payma"[16] and the Bengali Hindu Purangir Gosain, arrived in Calcutta in March 1774 and delivered the lama's message in flowery Persian: "As for me, I am but a monk, and it is the custom of my sect, with rosary in hand, to pray for the welfare of all mankind."[17] Asking for peace in the region, he also offered gifts of gold, silver, musk, wool, silk brocade, and gilded leather. Impressed by the gifts and eager for communication, Hastings saw the chance he had been waiting for. Since the Capuchin missions left Lhasa in 1745, Tibet had been effectively closed to Europeans. Not only that, no

Tibetan dignitary had ever initiated contact with a European leader before. Hastings swiftly agreed with the Panchen Lama's requests, made peace with the Deb Raja, and determined to use the opportunity to send an envoy back to Tashilhunpo; in May 1774 George Bogle was dispatched to reply in person, traveling through Bhutan.[18]

In his private commission to Bogle, Warren Hastings charges Bogle with a number of duties, including the standard colonial instruction:

> To keep a Diary inserting whatever passes before your Observation which shall be characteristic of the people, their manners, customs, buildings, cookery, the country, the climate, or the road, &c., or interesting to the Trade of this country; carrying with you a pencil & pocket-book for the purpose of minuting short notes of every Fact or Remark as it occurs, and putting them in order at your Leisure while they are fresh in your Memory.[19]

Bogle responded with energy; he kept a journal, made vocabulary notes (as we have seen), wrote both a long, detailed report of his negotiations, and a general one for Hastings, and did not fail to keep up his correspondence with numerous friends and family in India, London, and Scotland.

In a strict definition of the genre, if we look at the entirety of his *oeuvre,* Bogle's texts are not really travel writing at all, in the sense of a travel *narrative.* They do not comprise a story, exactly; instead, they are writing done *while* traveling. Many of these texts were collected by his family and, nearly one hundred years after Bogle's death, a family representative in Ayrshire, Scotland gave Clements Markham a large box which, as Markham describes it, contained Bogle's "journals, memoranda of various kinds, and on many subjects; numerous bundles of private letters, . . . appointments, minutes of conversations, and official despatches;" these provide the source for Markham's 1876 edition.[20] These texts—or some portion of them—are now collected in the British Library along with the Bogle's official reports and letters he sent to Hastings and his friend David Anderson.[21]

Given that Bogle made copies of many of these texts it is difficult to claim that any are "original;" instead, in these texts, one is offered several versions of Bogle's journey—versions that depart from Markham's representation of Bogle. Although Markham notes that he took care "to keep the author constantly in the foreground and to avoid any sign of editorial intrusiveness," he naturally selected some texts and excluded others in creating a version of Bogle's journey (as I myself do).[22] Writing at a time when knowledge about Tibet was at a premium for the British Raj, Markham, the onetime president of the Royal Geographical Society and Arctic explorer, worked to make Bogle make sense. Notes in pencil on Bogle's manuscripts show some of the changes Markham made; dates of journal entries are excised and replaced by chapter titles, idiosyncratic capitalizations are eliminated, apparent errata are corrected, and updated spellings are provided for Asian places and personages, such as "Teshu" for Bogle's "Teshoo."

In other places Markham's choices suggests something about his own place in colonial history. In a manuscript, Bogle writes: "The people [of Tibet] in general are downright and good humoured, not addicted to yawning as in Bengal, but fond of laughing, dancing, singing, and taking Snuff."[23] Bogle clearly has "yawning," and in this way the passage seems to be about the liveliness and energy of Tibetans. But Markham has changed "y" to an "f" and thus has it that Bengalis are "addicted to fawning."[24] There are no marks on the manuscript for this change: Markham apparently could not read the passage otherwise. This replacement suggests how the British perception of Bengalis has shifted since Bogle's day. For Markham, it is not the laziness of the Bengalis that matters but their duplicity and obsequiousness; from the point of view of colonialists after the rebellion of 1857, Indian subjects of the British Raj were not to be trusted, for the smile they showed you one moment could turn into mutiny the next.

Although he relies largely on Bogle's journals and reports, Markham also uses information from letters in order to string a narrative together (sometimes at the expense of narrative cohesion, as we shall see).[25] Information from other of Bogle's letters is suppressed entirely. For example, it is evident from a letter sent to Bogle by Hamilton, the medical officer who accompanied him to Tibet, that Bogle was suffering from gonorrhea while on his return from Tashilhunpo.[26] Markham may not have thought that this aspect of Bogle's health was relevant to his account of Tibet and Bhutan; including it, however, can give us a different sense of Bogle's well-being as well as his appreciation of the "monastick" life while at Tashilhunpo.[27]

In editing and selecting from Bogle's many texts, then, Markham inevitably creates his own version of Bogle. For Markham, Bogle is a coherent figure, one who is largely in control of his utterances, one with a core of selfhood that assures the consistency and compatibility of a variety of utterances. Writing a century after Bogle, Markham's efforts to make Bogle coherent can be understood as arising out of contemporary ideological concerns: by 1876 the colonial project is both governmental and mercantile. It is organized as a branch of the British government under Queen Victoria, and its smooth functioning depended on the subjugation of both colonizer and colonized to a coherent colonial ideology. But in Bogle's day, the East India Company was a trading enterprise in transition. At that time, the notion of a solid British self, supported by the Orientalist dichotomies of East and West, black and white, backward and advanced, female and male, et cetera, had not yet become hegemonic. Indeed, Britons of the late eighteenth century came to India with intellectual and humanistic aspirations and assumptions that were often at odds with their administrative and commercial commitments.

Instead of being fixed to a single position then, our writer can move: he is able to take up different and contradictory positions with self-reflectiveness and ease. Because of the heterogeneity of colonial discourse, Bogle did not have to be consistent. Bogle's ability to relate in a multiplicity of ways with Tibetan others is also made possible by the generic variety of the texts he wrote while in Tibet. Because genres prescribe modes of address and create subject positions for writers, Bogle addresses various audiences and purposes, goes through moods, changes his mind. While Bogle the man certainly traveled to Tibet, the "I" of his narrative is not heading towards any ultimate ideological or philosophical position; it is not going to any *single* place. Instead, various speaking subjects are going lots of places. The Bogle I "discover"—which arises out of my interests and my particular place in history—is not a coherent author or self but a complex, almost quixotic figure. He both sees himself in the Tibetan other and rejects that identification. He is both revised by his travels and unperturbed. He moves. He returns.

In Bogle's own day, Warren Hastings considered publishing a portion of Bogle's manuscript, and sent a copy to Samuel Johnson in 1775 for his consideration.[28] A few years later, Bogle's elder brother Robert tried to arrange George's papers for posthumous publication; nothing came of that either.[29] Markham published his version of Bogle at the height of British interest in Tibet, but it is tempting to think that had Bogle's account achieved popular circulation a century sooner, Britain's understanding of Tibet might have been considerably different. For Bogle neither demonizes nor fantasizes about Tibetans; he encounters Tibetans largely as people who might be reckoned with. While he was certainly part of a colonialist project, "[f]or Bogle the Tibetan way of life had to be encountered on its own terms," as Bishop notes.[30] Indeed, although Bogle is the earliest of the British travel writers on Tibet, in many ways he is the most advanced: his texts give us a glimpse of his shifting relations to the Tibetans within a particular historical context *before* Tibet becomes a palimpsest of British colonial desires and fantasies. As George Woodcock remarked in 1971, the texts of Bogle and his near contemporaries remind him of nothing so much as "our own" point of view: "I find the pictures evoked by Bogle and Turner and Manning nearer to the real Tibetans, even as they are today, than the fantasies of those who have tried to abstract from the symbolism of Tantric cults a world of chimerical marvels."[31] Through Bogle and company, Woodcock imagines recovering a horizon before the myths take over. But while the return to that unsullied vision—to true, pre-mythical Tibet, to a time before colonialism and the most recent wave of the New Age—is impossible, it *is* possible to read Bogle's texts from the perspective of a post-colonial, postmodern humanist. From that point of view, as I understand Bogle's version of Tibet, it can only come *after* colonialism. Reading Bogle's texts today, even if one sticks only to Markham's edition, a reader with an eye for movement and diversity of expression can retrieve/encounter a complex, decentered subject: Bogle does not come to closure; he is self-reflective and evasive; he recognizes the limits of his knowledge, and still he affirms friendship, cordiality, and the possibility of what some might call "cross-cultural communication." When I look into his texts as into a mirror, they show me where I am (even as I keep moving); they suggest where we are (at the moment). In this way, his texts gesture towards the irrecoverabilty of the past—and in that way reflect the present. Horizons lost and lost again might be found.

TRAVELING AND MOVING

What happens, then, if we let Bogle take us into a land that was not yet known, into a land that was always known? When Bogle first crossed into Bhutan on his way to Tibet, he wrote to his father, George Bogle, Sr.:

> As none of the Company's Servants, and I might also say no European, had ever visited the Country which I was about to enter; I was equally in the Dark as to the Road, the Climate, or the People, and the imperfect Account of some religious Mendicants who had travelled through it, however unsatisfactory was the only Information I could collect.[32]

He is "in the Dark" about the place; he has little to go on. Discontented with the accounts of Catholic missionaries, Bogle makes a space for his narrative so it may fill a gap in European knowledge. Such "space-clearing gestures" would later become standard; a number of travel writers after Bogle reiterate how few have traveled in Tibet and how little is known about the place. Modern readers have long known Tibet as the unknown, but there are "unknowns" that are familiar and others that are truly obscure and threatening.

Bogle's attempts to deal with the unfamiliar can be explored by looking closely at the several rhetorical strategies he adopts in describing what he encounters. One response to his travel experiences might simply be labeled avoidance. While he stays at Tassisudon, Bhutan (Tashichodzong in present day Thimpu) to conduct negotiations and await permission to cross into Tibet, his thoughts are not turned to learning about local customs or interacting with local people. Instead, he is thinking about food—condiments, more specifically. In this letter to Mr. Bayne dated, 27 July 1774, Bogle writes:

> About eight Days ago I troubled you with a few Lines accompanying some different sized Letters, and containing a *strong* and *spirited* application. If you cannot comply with the whole I hope you will with a part, and if not yet gone be so good as [to include] a little vinegar and mustard. When one has nothing to do these Matters come to be of Consequence.
>
> I never was so sensible of this as aboard the Ship. I was a perfect Epicure though God knows it was only in Idea. One morning we spoke with a Swedish Ship just come from [illegible] and bartered some Cheese and Porter for a fine turtle of 500 weight. It lay upon the Quarter Deck some Days, and we devoured it over and over with our Eyes. At last the happy Day came. What Bucketsful of fine Eggs! and what a glorious feast we shall have. We could not eat anything at Breakfast on Account of the Turtle. At dinner there was nothing else to eat. But alas the Son of a Bitch of a Cook, an Aberdeen man, had dressed it in a way that—there is no describing it. Nobody could taste it; even Captain Cheshire was obliged to have Recourse to his namesake the Cheese. . . .
>
> You see how barren this Country is in News when I am obliged to fill up my letters with such a story. If you want to know how I pass my Time you have only to take my Life in Calcutta and capsize it, not forgetting to add about eight or ten Cups of Tea with Butter within a day.[33]

Bored to distraction, Bogle has clearly not yet traversed the proverbial distance between self and other; indeed, his position seems one of retreat and self-preservation, dreaming of a place and a people who care about mustard, who know what kind of uncouth fellow an Aberdeen man can be, who are used to the busy life in the colonial capital. But what kind of travel text is this? He's a Scotsman in Bhutan—the leader of the first Company mission there—but instead of writing about the people of the region, instead of describing the mountains around him, he remembers an earlier sea voyage among countrymen. The unfamiliar is dealt with, for the moment, by escape.

But it's early in the journey. Perhaps such retreat is simply a response to being perceived as different, to feeling like an other among selves. For in another note from Bhutan, Bogle writes: "If there is any pleasure of being gazed at, I had enough of it."[34] While in the first example, Bogle seems cut off from his immediate surroundings, in this one he is all too aware of being in them. In this ironic statement, Bogle takes up a position, if an ambiguous one, vis-à-vis those who look at him. Where does he stand? In an ironic statement, the identity of the speaker is masked and the final truth is ambiguous. The literal meaning of the statement lingers alongside the ironic one, as if to say, "I find pleasure in being stared at," but also, "There *is* no pleasure in being stared at." The philosophical implications of irony, Hayden White argues, involve "a kind of attitude towards knowledge itself which is implicitly critical of all forms of metaphorical identification, reduction, or integration of phenomena."[35] Because of this, the speaking subject and the spoken "I" are not coterminous—the self (wherever it is) is divided.

At other moments, Bogle is better able to tolerate the sense of himself as other, as in the following passage from Tashilhunpo. Here Bogle again finds himself the center of interested observers: "Being the first European they had ever Seen, I had crowds of Thibetians coming to look at me, as they go to look at the Lions in the Tower. My room was always full of them from Morning till Night."[36] He clearly recognizes himself as different from Tibetans, but in this example he renders the scene familiar—he copes with the scene—by figuring Tibetans as Englishmen and himself as the exotic curiosity. Indeed, he treats his visitors graciously: "The [Panchen] Lama, affraid that I would be incommoded, sent me word, if I chose, not to admit them. But when I could gratify the Curiosity of others at so easy a Rate, why should I have refused it. I always received them, and sometimes exchanged a Pinch of Snuff and sometimes picked up a word or two of the language."[37] Perhaps Bogle recognizes in the Tibetans' desire to see him his own desire to look into their lives. For in this case, he is not only a self among others but also an other among selves. Through comparison—a kind of metaphor—Bogle occupies a more comfortable place.

But this comparison of himself with Tibetans takes yet another turn. Bogle had been staying with the Tashi [Teshoo] Lama at Desheripgay outside Xigatse, where the latter resided to avoid a smallpox epidemic. The lama returns to Tashilhunpo with much pomp:

> About two Thousand People were assembled to see and prostrate themselves before his Holiness. . . . From the resting Place, till we arrived at the Lama's Palace the Road was lined on both Sides with Ranks of Spectators. They were all dressed in their Holiday Cloathes. The Peasants singing and dancing. ~ About three Thousand Gylongs [*gelongs,* monks], some with large

pieces of chekered Cloth hung upon their Breasts, others with their Cymbals and Tabours, were ranked next the Palace. As the Lama passed they bent half forwards, and followed him with their Eyes. But there was a look of Veneration mixed with keen joy in their Countenances; which pleased me beyond anything, and was a Surer Testimony of Satisfaction than all the Guns in the Tower, and all the Odes of a Whitehead could have given, one catches Affection by Sympathy, and I could not help, in some Measure, feeling the Same Emotions with the Lamas votaries.[38]

In this passage, Bogle is not being looked *at,* rather he is looking *with* Tibetans. In comparing the Tibetan gesture of veneration for their lama with English ones, Bogle finds the Tibetan custom more satisfactory, perhaps because it relies on numerous individual gestures rather than simply looking on while someone else recites an ode or shoots off a gun. Bogle allies himself with these onlookers, imagines himself in their place—he feels *with* the Tibetans. Although Bogle himself is in the procession, no one cares about him—he doesn't really care about himself in this passage: all eyes turn towards the lama. Bogle's sympathy is especially remarkable given that within a century, such a connection with Tibetans and such reverence for a Tibetan lama would be practically unthinkable for a colonial servant. In Bogle's day, or at least in his journal, the Enlightenment sense of the common nature of humankind wins the day: Bogle is not Tibetan but he can feel like one.

In his general report for Hastings, however, Bogle offers a different view of the same scene, noting only that "the Lama stopped at some Tents about two miles short of Teshoo Loombo. All the world was there, and I was there among the rest. But it was all eating and Ceremony, and no Conversation. We continued our Journey to the Palace, through files of People, and Crowds of Spectators. I accompanied the Lama to his apartment."[39] In this instance, where Bogle's purpose is to report on the progress of his conversations with the lama, Bogle remains tight-lipped about his feelings. Thus, in his attempts to fulfill various duties and to come to terms with the places and people he meets, Bogle shifts—and shifts again. His is not merely a travel of the body, but also a travel in perspective.

A similar movement occurs elsewhere in his journal. Like a horse-rider adjusting his perch on a saddle as he descends a hill, when Bogle first crosses into the unfamiliar territory of Tibet, he shifts several times:

The first object that strikes you, as you go down the Hill into Thibet, is a Mount in the middle of the plain. It is where the People of Paridsong [Phari] expose their Dead. It happened, I hope not ominously, that they were carrying a Body thither as we came down. Eagles, Hawks, Ravens and other Carnivorous birds were soaring about in Expectation of their prey. Every village has a Place set apart for this purpose. I have elsewhere given an account of their custom. ~ There are only two Exceptions to it. ~ The Lamas are burnt with Sandalwood, and such as Die of the smallpox are Buried, to smother the Infection, so that three of the five kinds of Funerals, (and I know of no more) which the Inhabitants of this world use, are known to the people of Thibet.[40]

Bogle begins the account in the second person, or rather, the reader is called on to begin it for him, as the object strikes "you" and "you" descend the hill. He then shifts back to the first person and offers us a glimpse of his own fears: a corpse disrupts their passage—"I hope not ominously." Is it a sign, a bad omen? Bogle then shifts his attention from the corpse to the other living creatures in the scene—the birds of prey. For a Tibetan Buddhist the so-called "sky burial" is a reminder of the cycle of *samsara*, a lesson in non-attachment to the body whose symbolism is inscribed in the *chö* ritual of "cutting," "the visualized dismemberment of the body as an offering to all living beings."[41] For the Scotsman, human corpse-eating birds, however, can be unsettling. But as someone steeped in a belief in the relativism of customs, Bogle soon recovers himself to offer a more descriptive and ethnographic assessment: every village has a place for this purpose, and this is only one of several Tibetan funeral customs. Assuming his composure, Bogle refinds his position as a rational observer who is able to name and categorize Tibetan practices among "the five kinds of Funerals . . . which the Inhabitants of this world use."[42] He knows of no more. The position of the speaker shifts several times in this short passage: at first the reader is rider, as it were; then Bogle becomes an actor in the scene; he is then unsettled and shifts outside the scene to become a commentator on it. I imagine Bogle squirming uncomfortably on his borrowed horse, for just a little further down the road he will lose his place again, mistaking himself for someone else.

His traveling party, led by the Tibetan Payma and including six of the Panchen Lama's servants, had just begun its day's march. "One of Payma's Servants carried a Branch of a Tree with a white Handkerchief tied to it. Imagining it to be a mark of Respect to me and my Embassy, I set myself upright in my Saddle."[43] After they had ridden a bit further, Bogle "was soon undeceived."[44] The Tibetans dismounted near a "heap of Stones" and began a ritual in which they light a fire and make several offerings to the mountain "Tchoomal Harry" [Chomolhari][45]: "[T]he Ceremony was finished by placing upon the Heap of Stones the little Ensign, which my fond Imagination had before offered up to my own vanity."[46] In describing the Tibetan ritual, Bogle, in effect, offers up his vanity and pretension by showing himself as the fool. Of course, such a gesture can be seen as a vintage example of late eighteenth-century irony in the manner of Johnson and Jonathan Swift; in that case, nothing has moved: he is simply repeating a formula. But we could also read this surrender of his own egotism as a Buddhistic gesture, which would be a nice, surprising, radical thing for a colonialist to participate in. We might even take Bogle's self-reflection here as radically self-undermining in a kind of postmodern sense—he realizes that the "self" he thought was being honored does not exist in any stable, coherent fashion. Instead, he has to give up that particular pretension.

But which of these interpretations do we valorize? Which one edges us towards the horizon of transformation? For what does it mean to be self-critical? A number of writers of the eighteenth century used the customs of foreigners—whether "real" or invented—to criticize the hypocrisy and irrationality of customs at home. Voltaire's admiration of the Chinese and defense of Native Americans as well as Swift's portrayal of the civilized Houyhnhnms all served to point out faults in European culture. Similarly, many scholarly essays these days use a self-reflective gesture in which the author attempts to denote his/her own position as speaking subject and the limitations of his/her perspective; but in our day, as in Bogle's time, such self-reflective moves might easily preface "business as usual." (This is a danger of which I am all too aware.) And even Buddhist reflections on the insubstantial nature of the self can become formulaic. When do such self-reflective gestures stop being radical and start being conventional? Is it possible to recover the critical impulse in the conventional gesture? Bogle's multiplicitous texts raise these questions without finally settling on an answer.

In Bogle's account, as Peter Bishop notes, he frequently defamiliarizes European customs by comparing them to those of the Tibetans.[47] In one scene, Bogle wants to shoot game on the way to Xigatse, but his Tibetan guide, Payma, stops him, insisting that it was a serious crime and would scandalize the local inhabitants. "We had many long Debates upon the Subject, which were supported on his Side, by plain commonsensical Reasons drawn, from his Religion and Customs; on mine, by those finespun European arguments, which serve rather to perplex than convince."[48] Here the Tibetan's "commonsensical" arguments are used to comment on European circumlocutions and self-justifications. In a similar manner, Bogle offers a criticism of Europe's pretension to rationality in this account of the Gelukpa monastic system of debate:

> Religion was the Subject of their debates, perhaps the Immortality of the Soul, or the unchangeable nature of Right and Wrong; but my Ignorance of the Language rendered them quite unintelligible to me. They were carried

on with much vociferation and feigned warmth, and embellished with great Powers of action, such as clapping Hands, shaking the Head &c. These Gestures are no doubt very improper and ridiculous, because they are quite different from those used by European Orators, who are the true Standards of what is just and what is graceful.[49]

It is possible to read this passage "straight," that is, in a way that positions Europeans as superior to Tibetans. But that does not gibe with other of Bogle's positions, or his general tendency towards self-criticism. That the statement is ironic is suggested by Bogle's later reconsideration of it in a revised version of his journal. This revision is also in Bogle's hand, but in this text the phrase "because they are quite different from those used by European Orators, who are the true Standards of what is just and what is graceful" has been struck out.[50] These editorial marks suggest that Bogle recognized he was verging into unsettled territory.[51]

Another example of a criticism that is subsequently rethought appears in the same journal. Bogle again criticizes European pretensions when he discusses Tibetans' interest in prognostication and describes how he was frequently mistaken for a "Conjurer;" as he notes, "the Thibetians have great faith in Fortune-telling, which indeed seems to be common to all Mankind, except to our European Philosophers, who are too wise to believe in anything."[52] Here the ironic criticism of European rationalism is apparent: it deprives the world of wonder. The knowledge gained by reason has a price and it is disenchantment. In this passage, Bogle admires not the beliefs of Tibetan religion *per se,* but rather the Tibetans' ability to believe in *something.* That he later felt some misgivings about criticizing European culture in this way is evident in the revised journal; there he crosses out the critical phrase and makes the plain statement "the Thibetians have great faith in Fortune-telling." Bogle is both ready to criticize European values and willing to play it straight for a different imagined audience. It is impossible to say, however, if either version of the journal represents Bogle's "final" account of his trip.

In any case, Bogle's criticism of European customs does not lead him to imagine Tibet as an ideal society; unlike more recent admirers of Tibet, Bogle does not believe that Tibetans preserve the best of human accomplishments in their ancient religion. What Bogle admires in Tibetans (at least some of the time) is that they know how to have a good time, as it were; they are "downright and good humoured . . . fond of laughing, dancing, singing, and taking Snuff."[53] His frequent companions were two nephews of the Panchen Lama, the Pyn Cooshos, who, like Bogle, were in their twenties at the time. As he writes:

[They] used often to come and pass two or three hours with me: I Sometimes went down to their Tent, where we spent the Time in Singing, smoking, drinking Chang, playing upon the Flute or the Guittar, at which the eldest brother is a great adept.[54]

Elsewhere he notes that "the pleasantest Hours I spent, before the arrival of the 'Pyn Cooshos,' were either in my audience with the Lama, or in playing at Chess."[55] This traveler to Tibet is seeking good company, not lofty sentiments. His eye is drawn to the companionable human elements in the landscape.

Bogle's eye for people is suggested by another journal entry. Here Bogle seems ready to follow Hastings' instructions to report on everything; he offers a picture of his apartments at Tashilhunpo: "[A]lthough I have little Success at these sort of Discriptions I must attempt to give Some account of it."[56] He begins well enough: "You enter by a Door formed of one piece of wood painted red," that has this kind of gilding and that kind of hinge. "The Room is about fifty feet long, and thirty broad;" the walls are like this, the windows like that.[57] But then, it seems, Bogle's attention is diverted:

> The floor is Chalky Clay, mixed with small Pebbles, and formed into a Smooth and very beautiful Terass, which by the Labours of a young Gylong, who every Morning gets his Feet upon two woollen cloths, and exercises himself for three or four Hours in Skating about the room, will, in course of fifteen or Twenty years, acquire a Polish equal to the other Floors in the Palace, which are not inferior to the finest variegated Marble.[58]

Bogle's description of the room soon gives way to the irresistible, shaved-head figure who skates about the room, maroon robes flying. For Bogle, the architecture of Tashilhunpo is most interesting as a setting for *human* activity. Similarly, as he writes in a letter to his brother Robert (Robin), "I am generally availed to be present at [daily religious] Ceremonies, in which my chief Amusement is to study the looks and Phisiognomies of his votaries and to observe that veneration mixed with Joy which is generally framed in their countenances."[59] Once again, he looks at people's faces and actions not as signs of their exoticism but as sites of connection and communication. His humanist perspective here departs from that of many Western travel writers to Tibet after him, who disdain and idealize Tibetans by turns.

Bogle's attitude was supported by the goals of the company at the time; as a companyman interested in practical affairs, he follows Hastings' encouragement to learn local languages and studies Tibetan. Unlike many modern day Western scholars of Tibetan Buddhism, Bogle learns colloquial Tibetan rather than the language of religious texts; he is interested in conversation, negotiation, not religion *per se*. And in his ironic way, he reports that the monk who attended him at Tashilhunpo "came to understand my imperfect attempts to speak the Thibet language tolerably well, and [we] used to have long chats together. I grew very fond of him, and he, which showed his Sagacity, took a great liking to me."[60] Bogle's gentle humor in this passage—self-deprecating and self-flattering by turns—suggests his attitude towards his hosts. In this Tibetan's face, Bogle is not looking for a glint of enlightenment but rather the recognition of friendship. Nowhere does he see that better than in the face of the Panchen Lama.

THE MOST PLEASANT MAN

When Bogle went to Tibet and Bhutan, Europeans knew little about the religion of the region. Uncertain as to what exactly he was seeing while among the "Booteas" of Bhutan, Bogle attempts an explanation of notions of rebirth and describes "a multitude of deities whom they represent under the most grotesque Shapes, and with Heads and hands innumerable."[61] About Tibetan religion he writes:

> The religion of the Lamas is somehow connected with that of the Hindoos; though I will not pretend to say how. ~ Many of their Deities are the same; the Shaster is translated into their Language, and they hold in veneration the Holy places of Hindoostan. In short if the Religion of Thibet is not the off-spring of the Gentoos, it is at least educated by them[.] The humane maxims of the Hindoo faith are thought in Tibet. To deprive any living Creature of Life is regarded as a Crime, and one of the Vows taken by the Clergy is to this Effect.[62]

Bogle's descriptions of Tibetan religion would eventually become part of European knowledge of it. But while later scholars focus on Pali and Sanskrit texts, using them to judge the practices of living Buddhists, Bogle does not even have the category "Buddhism."

Given this lack of information, Britons were not sure about the status of the Dalai and Panchen Lamas. Writing of the latter to his father, George Bogle, Sr., in January 1775, the younger Bogle notes: "Teshoo Lama is taken notice of in Bells' Travells,[63] under the name of Bogdu Peinzin. The disrespectful manner however, in which he, and most other writers, speak of the Lamas, appear to me highly unjust; and I may, like Lady Wortley Montague, pretend to Advantages, which no Traveller before me ever possessed."[64] Having stayed in the lama's monastery for five months—"nothing but Priests; nothing from morning to night but the Chanting of Prayers &c. The Sound of Cymbals and Tabours"[65]—Bogle certainly did have advantages that other writers on Tibet lacked. But, unlike many present day Western admirers of Tibetan Buddhism, Bogle is not awestruck. In his report to Hastings and in his letters to his father, Bogle is as apt to consider the lama's political powers as his religious position. As he writes to his father:

> [The lama] is entirely master of his own affairs; he writes and declares Letters; he sees everybody himself, and gives a ready answer to all Representations that are made to him. In conversation he is extremely affable and entertaining.[66] He is very charitable and generous. He is humane to his People, and employs all his Authority in settling his Quarrels which arise, not only in this country; but in the neighboring states. On all accounts he is universally beloved, and is generally allowed to be the best, and the most able Lama, that Thibet ever produced.[67]

Bogle seems aware that his exuberant description of this "Asiatic" leader may offend reigning sensibilities at home; as he continues: "I will make no apology for sending you this account, as I do it in obedience to your commands, and with a view to your entertainment."[68] He offers similar accounts of the lama in the journal he kept for Hastings:

> After two or three visits, the Lama used (except on Holidays) to receive me without any Ceremony—his head uncovered, & dressed only in the red sarge Petticoat which is worn by all the Gylongs, red Bulgar Hide boots, a yellow cloth vest, his arms bare, and a piece of coarse yellow Cloth thrown across his Shoulders.[69]

Such an image may remind readers today of the disarming manner of Tenzin Gyatso, the 14th Dalai Lama. And, just as many Westerners are attracted to the current Dalai Lama's lack of pretension, Bogle is impressed rather than offended by the lama's familiarity:

> He sat Sometimes in a Chair, sometimes on a Bench covered with Tiger Skins. . . . Sometimes he would walk with me about the Room, explain to me the Pictures, make remarks upon the Collour of my eyes, &c. For

although venerated as God's vicegerent through all the Eastern Countries of Asia, endowed with a portion of omniscience, and with many other divine attributes, he throws aside, in Conversation, all the awful part of his Character, accommodates himself to the weakness of Mortals, endeavours to make himself loved rather than feared, and behaves with the greatest affability to everybody, particularly to Strangers.[70]

Evidently impressed by the man, Bogle tries to come to terms with him. But what is the young Scot's position? If there is irony in his assertion that this emanation of the Buddha Amitabha "accommodates himself to the weakness of Mortals," what does such irony signify? Rather than being sarcastic about the lama's presumption of "divinity," Bogle seems to admire the way the lama maintains his humility despite this presumption; he continues: "His disposition is open, candid, and generous. He is extremely merry and entertaining in Conversation, and tells a pleasant Story with a great deal of Humour and Action."[71] This is no pompous king, no vain patriarch—it's a man, a lively, funny, kind man, someone who has made this traveler feel welcome—"one of the most pleasant men I ever saw," Bogle writes repeatedly.[72] As if to check the accuracy of his impressions, Bogle "endeavoured to find out, in his [the lama's] Character, those defects which are unseparable from Humanity, but he is so universally beloved that I had no Success, and not a man could find in his Heart to speak ill of him."[73] So while Bogle doubts that the lama's title alone could make him "God's vicegerent," he is hard-pressed to identify the faults that would make him human. Just who is this fellow? How do we think about a pagan who is "possessed of much Christian charity," a man who "is free from those narrow prejudices, which next to Ambition and Avarice, have opened the most copious Source of human Misery"?[74]

If we are Bogle, we admire and respect him. For while Bogle does not accept the Panchen Lama as a guru or a bodhisattva or an emanation of an enlightened being in the Tibetan Buddhist sense—indeed, Bogle does not have that vocabulary—he can accept him as an "Enlightened" man in the European sense. It would take another century for Europeans to translate Buddhist *nirvana* as "enlightenment," and several more decades for it to be given a positive evaluation.[75] But for Bogle, this Teshoo Lama is a man who has accomplished a European ideal: he has conquered his faults, he is fair to everyone; he is a kind, generous, gentle *human* being who is not *above* this world but whose presence in it ennobles others. In effect, this dignified Tibetan has outdone the Europeans, realizing their best qualities of humility, tolerance, and virtue.

CHANGING PLACES

It is just after this description in his journal that Bogle describes the lama's return to Tashilhunpo and observes again the "veneration mixed with keen joy" that Bogle shared with the Tibetans who greeted him. In that passage, Bogle emphasized his sympathy with Tibetans, his ability to feel *with* them. In another passage, Bogle explains the difference between the "Yellow Caps" (Geluk) and the "Red Caps" (Sakya):

> In times of old there were violent Disputes between them, in which the Yellow Caps got the victory as well by the assistance of the Tartars, as by their superior sanctity. *But as I adhere to the Tenets of this Sect,* and have acquired my knowledge of Religion from them, I will not say here much upon the Subject, lest it should be thought spiteful. I may be allowed however just to mention two things, which must convince every unprejudiced person of the wicked Lives and false doctrines of the Red Caps. ~ In the first place, many of the Clergy marry; and in the next, they persist in opposition to religion and common sense to wear Red Caps.[76]

In this passage, Bogle takes on the role of a Tibetan in order to critique the irrational nature of sectarian disputes—in this case, one that echoes Catholic-Protestant conflicts. In order to take up such a line of criticism, Bogle asserts literally that he himself is a "Yellow Cap" and that he accepts their (irrational) doctrine. Of course, we know that Bogle is not a Buddhist—he couldn't be, could he? And yet, the ironic statement cannot quite cancel out the literal one. The play between the rational perspective, on the one hand, and the religious and "Thibetian" point of view, on the other, throw back a double image of Bogle. Bogle looks into an image of the Tibetan other and imagines his own face there. As in the optical illusion in which a viewer first sees two faces in profile and then sees a goblet, with a blink of an eye Bogle can make the switch: first he is a "Yellow Cap" and then he is a proper Scotsman again. But just as in the optical illusion, in which one can see the ghost image of the faces in the image of the goblet, here, too, the image of Bogle as a Geluk lingers in the mind's eye and changes one's perception of Bogle as Scotsman, as Englishman, as European.

Which is not to say that Bogle thinks he is Tibetan. Indeed, at other less light-hearted moments he declares his suspicion of such a possibility. When the Panchen Lama asks him to write an account of European history, Bogle laments that it "gave me a good deal of Employment and a good deal of Trouble. It was an account of Europe, and I confess I found it a very hard task, for I had to fancy myself a Thibetian, and then put down the things which I had imagined would strike him."[77] And just as Bogle has difficulties imagining himself a Tibetan, he declares himself "unequal" to the task of explaining the finer points of Christian doctrine to the lama. As he writes in his report for Hastings, "I had no mind to attempt an Explanation of the mysteries of the Trinity."[78]

> I told him therefore that according to my Faith God always existed. He observed, Charitably, that we all worshipped the same God but under different Names, and all aimed at the same Object though we pursued different Ways. The answer I gave him was in the same tolerating Spirit: ~ For I am not sent as a Missionary; and after so many able and ingenious Jesuits, dressed in the Habits of Apostles, and armed with Beads and Crucifixes have tried in vain to convert unbelieving Nations, I am not so arrogant as to think that my Labours would be successful.[79]

Bogle is no missionary: the Protestant employee of the company, wearing a purple satin, fox fur-lined *chuba* has different aims, a different self-perception. Getting along with the lama is more important than converting him. Establishing trade ties with Tibet is more crucial than claiming it for Christendom.

While in Tibet Bogle will encounter still other versions of himself and his culture within the confines of the monastery. When Bogle and the Panchen Lama meet at Desheripgay, the lama eagerly shows the foreigner various curiosities given to him by other outsiders. These include the aforementioned camera obscura, a compass of French design, a "Hand Organ," a watch inscribed "Graham's," and portions of the Bible "with written Explanations in the Russian Language at the Top, and Latin ones engraved at the Bottom; also the Heads of the Popes, Emperors of Germany, and Kings from France, which he got from some Russian Pilgrims."[80] Bogle has just attempted to delineate for the lama the differences among the various foreigners that Tibetans call "Frinjiys" (from the Hindustani word for Portuguese, *Farangee*); does the lama see these objects as representations of a generic kind of foreignness, and thus of Bogle himself? (I recall a similar scene in a Tibetan monastery in south India, when a young *tulku* showed me photographs of his European friends, as if I might know them.) How does Bogle receive these items? The Tibetan context renders these objects exotic; in what ways, then, do they reflect Bogle's identity? In another place, Bogle firmly resists having his identity fixed by Tibetan notions of "Frinjiy-ness." As he writes to his sister in London, "I hate to be called Frinjiy—the very sound is pitiful—I have tried very hard to root it out—but cannot brag of any success."[81] This Tibetan label for him fails to capture his identity.

So Bogle moves across texts and genres, identifying as Tibetan here, identifying as European there, taking up still other less secure places—desiring not to be a foreigner, asserting himself as Geluk, refinding himself as European. All these various identifications and disavowals of identity—all this shifting of positions—can lead to trouble. Looking into the face of a burning effigy on *Lo-sar,* Tibetan New Year, Bogle sees something that looks very familiar:

> The Figure of a Man, chalked upon Paper, was laid upon the Ground. Many Strange Ceremonies, which to me who did not understand them appear whimsical, were performed about it; and a great fire kindled in the Corner of the Court, it was at length held over it, and being formed of Combustibles, vanished with much Smoke and Explosion. I was told it was a Figure of the Devil; but am not sufficiently skilled in the Thibetian Mythology to enter into particulars. One thing is certain, it was painted white with regular Features; and whether or no it was intended to represent that Being who "goes to and from upon the Face of the Earth, seeking whom he may devour," I could not help sometimes fancying that it much resembled an European.[82]

The new year's ritual Bogle describes is one through which malignant spirits are banished.[83] Told that the effigy is the devil, Bogle is not sure if the Tibetan devil equals the Biblical Satan.[84] What he does notice is the effigy's whiteness and its regular features—its resemblance to a European and thus to himself. If that particular image is not disturbing enough, Bogle has, in another text, echoed part of the phrase describing the devil—a creature "who goes to and from upon the face of the earth"—in speaking of his siblings and himself. In a letter to his sister, Elizabeth (Bess) from August 1774, he notes that the Bogle children are all "scattered over the face of the earth, and are united only by hope and a tender remembrance."[85] The Bogle siblings, having taken up England's capitalist and colonialist ventures, are dispersed from the family home in Scotland: a brother in sugar in Grenada, himself in the East India Company, another brother in London. In such travel for the sake of profit is a kind of devouring; like the creature who seeks "whom and what it may devour," British colonial ambitions have a consumptive character, as Edmund Burke argued: companymen are like "birds of prey, with appetites continually renewing for a food that is continually wasting."[86] Playing out the metaphor and extending the identification serve to highlight what Bogle's text suggests: Tibet's devil is a

European. In making that connection, perhaps Bogle is only being ironic again, turning the tables on the European image of the pagan as cannibal. But the tone is wrong. Bogle says that he "sometimes" fancies that it "much resembled an European." The uneasy moment in which Bogle recognizes a European face in the white effigy recurs to him. Indeed, he "could not help" having such an idea, compelling as the equation of European with devil—himself with devil—is. The unfamiliar—in this case a Tibetan ritual—is made familiar, *familial,* even; he's met the unfamiliar, and he is it.

Bogle's image of himself fragments and splinters as he encounters the Tibetans. A month after the New Year celebration, Bogle seeks the blessing of the female incarnation, Durjay Paymo (Dorje Phagmo):

> Her Chawa, like the Lama's, is supposed to convey a blessing & and I did not fail to receive it. After making my Presents and obeisances, I kneeled down, and stretching out her arm, which is equal to "the finest Lady in the Lands' ", she laid her Hand upon my Head.[87]

Having decided "to do at Rome as they do at Rome," Bogle readily receives this blessing.[88] His willingness to accept Tibetans as friends, his readiness to rethink the assumptions of his own country, his propensity to take up multiple positions vis-à-vis Tibetans seems to have worked on the man. By the end of the journey, he has some loose ends to tie up.

A journey is a liminal period; in many travel accounts, taking leave is a time to take stock, a time to reorient oneself to matters homeward.[89] On his departure from Tashilhunpo, Bogle makes a number of farewells: official and private ones with the lama, personal ones with the Pyn Cooshos and other friends. He writes some of the accounts of these departures for Hastings, notes others in his journal (which Hastings may also have read), and describes still another farewell in a letter to his sister Bess.

While Bogle's reports for Hastings cover a wide array of topics, in describing these farewells Bogle seems to recall the purpose of his journey. In his description of one farewell meeting, he assures Hastings of the lama's "desire of preserving Peace in the World, and of promoting the Trade of Merchants and the Happiness of Mankind."[90] After he describes his public departure from the lama in which they discuss the possibility of building a Tibetan temple in Calcutta,[91] the capture of musk goats from Tibet, and a chronology of comets in Tibet, Bogle notes that the Panchen Lama "took a Bit of Red Silk, and tying a Knot upon it himself, he threw it about my Neck with his own Hands. I then had my publick leave, but to wait on him again in private."[92]

Having received this public blessing of a *sungdu* [protection cord] from the hands of the Panchen Lama, Bogle meets him several more times privately. In one meeting, Bogle takes care to assure the lama—and Hastings, the reader of the report—that the company's interests are quite distinct from those of

> the Missionary Padres who had been in this country. . . . I repeated to him what I had formerly mentioned, that I imagined they came from Italy, as there were some of that Nation now at Patna, that their Religion differed from ours, and in nothing more than in their intollerating spirit and desire of bringing all the World to their own Opinions, whereas every Religion was allowed in England, and good men of every Faith respected.[93]

In his description of his the final meeting with the lama on April 6, Bogle shows himself assuaging the lama's fears that the English have come to Tibet to spy: "I concluded by telling him that if the Governor had entertained any Intentions that were unfriendly, he never would have sent me into this Country, and that whatever Faults the English might have, all the World knew that Treachery was not among them."[94] Bogle was never one to paint the English as angels, but in this passage Bogle implicitly echoes the prevailing ideology: the English are not the treacherous kind of colonialists, as are, say, the Spanish or Portuguese.[95] And even though the English have faults, Bogle supports the idea of developing trade ties with Tibet—at least in this text. When Bogle returned from Tibet, he clarified this view in his general report to Hastings:

> Although the Teshoo Lama is not entrusted with the actual Government of the Country, yet his authority and Influence appear fully equal to accomplish the Views which you entertain in regard to the Encouragement of Trade. His Passports to Merchants and Travellers are obeyed universally throughout Thibet. He is reverenced by his own People, is respected by his Neighbors, and his mild and pacifick Character seems peculiarly suited to promote Commerce. ~ I found in the Lama, therefore, the readiest Disposition to co-operate with you in removing the Obstacles to a free Trade, and in adopting such measures as might increase the Intercourse between this Country and Thibet.[96]

In this passage, the good man is also a friend of free trade. The shifting definition of the E. I. C.'s project in Asia from one of rampant mercantilism to one of free exchange between trustworthy equals seems to guide Bogle's assessment of the lama. But this is not his final word on the subject.

In his report for Hastings, Bogle's account of his final private meeting with the lama ends with this description:

> Teshoo Lama repeated his Concern at my Departure, the Satisfaction he had received in being informed of the Customs of Europe, and concluded with many wishes for my Prosperity, and that he would not fail to pray to heaven in my behalf. He spoke all this with a look very different from the studied and formal Compliments of Hindoostan. ~ *I never could reconcile myself* to taking a last leave of anybody; and what from the lama's pleasant and amiable Character, what from the many favours and Civilities he had shown me, I could not help being particularly affected. He observed it, and in order to chear me mentioned his Hopes of seeing me again. He threw a Handkerchief about my neck, put his Hand upon my head, and I retired.[97]

In this text, Bogle does not leave out his personal sense of connection to the lama. But it is interesting that the particular way in which Bogle was "affected" is hidden from Hastings and all readers; it is known only to the lama and himself, as it were. The lama gives Bogle the traditional *khata* and lays a hand of blessing on him. Later Bogle would write in his journal:

> Although every thing was ready for my departure, the Lama had already given us our publick audience of Leave. On the morning of the 8th of April I took my last farewell, not without an aking Heart, being strongly attached to him from his Civilities to me, from his bewitching Manners, and from his amiable Character ~ But I am an Enthusiast on this Subject.
> About nine o Clock we mounted our Horses and Set out from Teshoo Loombo.[98]

Talk about long good-byes. Bogle not only takes several leaves of the lama, he writes about these in several different places. But Bogle has still other departures to make.

On March 28, in his journal for Hastings, Bogle notes his sadness at leaving the Pyn Cooshos, the two brothers who had helped to vary "the incipit scene" at Tashilhunpo:[99]

> My Parting with the Pyn Cooshos was a harder Task [than leaving their mother and sisters]. ~ *I never could reconcile myself* to the thoughts of a last farewell, and however anxious I was to return to Bengal and to the world, I could not take leave of my Thibetian Friends with Indifference, and would now find little Satisfaction in repeating the Circumstances of it.[100]

Here Bogle repeats the phrase "I never could reconcile myself," a line that also appears in his description of leaving the lama. The same phrase appears in yet another description of his upcoming departure. In this scene, Bogle anticipates his departure from the lama in a letter to his sister Bess, dated March 10, 1775:

I propose soon to set out from Teshoo Loombo and begin my journey towards Bengal. As the time of my Departure drew near, I find that I shall not be able to bid adieu to the Lama without a heavy Heart. The kind and hospitable Reception he had given me and the amiable Dispositions which he possesses, I must confess have attached me to him, and I shall feel a hearty regret at parting. In spite of all my Journeyings and *wandering over the face of this Earth,* I have not yet learnt to take Leave and *I cannot reconcile myself* to the thoughts of a last farewell.[101]

Really, one might argue, Bogle is too sentimental for this job, for he still cannot reconcile himself. Similarly, the repetition of the phrase "over the face of this Earth" here echoes its use in two other places: his description of the Bogle children's travel—"we are scattered over the face of the earth"[102]—and in his account of the Tibetan devil as European—a "Being who 'goes to and from upon the Face of the Earth. . . .'"[103] Bogle cannot reconcile himself to what comes of such wandering.

Some might argue that Bogle's repetition of these phrases is a sign of a lazy writer, or of a writer who has found a useful phrase, or simply of his sentimentality. But he goes on:

> When I look at the time I have spent among these Hills it appears like a fairy dream. The novelty of the Scenes, and the People I have met with, and the novelty of the Life I have led, seems a perfect Illusion. Although my Days have been spent without Business or Amusement, they have passed on without Care or Uneasiness, and I may set this down as the most peaceful period of my Life. It is now almost over, and I am about to return to the Hurry and bustle of Calcutta.
>
> Farewell, ye honest and simple People! May ye long enjoy that Happiness which is denied to more polished nations; and while they are engaged in the endless pursuits of Avarice and Ambition, defended by your barren mountains, may ye continue to live in peace and contentment, and know no wants but those of nature.[104]

In his letter to his sister Bogle presents himself as a deeply affectionate man. In this text, he shows no desire to establish trade ties with Tibet; he envisions Tibet as an isolated and pristine place—and he wants it to stay that way. Bogle declares his desire that Tibet be left alone—left out of the circle of corrupting commerce and greed, left untouched by English hands. Such a representation departs significantly from his report to Hastings. Bogle cannot reconcile himself and his desires for Tibet. Or rather, he does not.

I am not the first one to notice this passage. Younghusband cites it, as does Bishop. Woodcock's *Into Tibet* begins his book with a selection from it. In the papers at the British Library, a note is written on the back of the folded letter in what appears to be Markham's hand: "Affection for Lama/ a beautiful Letter." Indeed, the fact that Markham included the letter at all is noteworthy, for it departs from his tendency to rely on Bogle's journal and his reports for Hastings. With this passage Bogle inscribes Tibet as a place outside of time, a simple, charming little haven, a predecessor to Hilton's Shangri-La. We are steeped in this myth, and perhaps that is why no critic that I know of has considered this ejaculation in light of other of Bogle's representations. But as I understand things, it is crucial that Bogle writes two versions of his hopes for Tibet. His position on the matter divides into two accounts—one to Hastings, one to his sister. It is as if Bogle must finally come to terms with the ambiguity of his irony, with the multiple positions he has taken up vis-à-vis the Tibetans, with the many images of himself that he has seen and produced in Tibet. He does so not by resolving everything into a single vision but rather by parting ways, by refusing to reconcile and be reconciled. Because he writes two accounts, he need not induce the world and himself to make final sense. His report to Hastings promotes commerce and the letter to his sister abhors it. He leaves it at that.

In larger terms, the conflict in which Bogle is caught also reflects the inconsistencies within colonial discourse of the period. Relativistic humanism can only be wedded to mercantile expansionism with some engineering; Bogle's two versions suggest a conflict within colonial ideology that will need attention soon. For the moment, though, Bogle is allowed to keep his private sentiment separate from his official duty; he can write these two texts. For later colonialists, such as Francis Younghusband, such a split would not be possible; colonialist discourse will demand more of the self.

Of course, Bogle's official representation of Tibet to Hastings as a place ready for commerce had a more immediate and practical impact on E. I. C. policy than his dreams of Tibetan isolation. Based on Bogle's reports to Hastings, trade between Bengal and Tibet was established, Hastings attempted to reunite Bogle and the Panchen Lama for further talks, and also arranged for another mission to Tashilhunpo, this one led by Samuel Turner. The idea of Tibet as a place ready for commerce with the E. I. C. initially won out over Bogle's dream of Tibet as a kind of peaceful haven better left alone, a representation which was only made public in 1876 in Markham's account. By then, the idea of Tibet as an isolated place that must be explored was key to British conceptions of the place, as no Briton had been officially allowed in Tibet for over half a century. Bogle's desire for Tibet's isolation played into nineteenth-century desires for a territory whose virgin status was both forbidden and enticing.

Bogle's "double-talk" (Tibetans call such two-sidedness "*go-nyi,*" literally "two heads")—Bogle's split decision—is not epiphany. Such a trope had not yet become part of travel writing. But what happened to Bogle on this trip? Was he transformed like Brad Pitt's Heinrich Harrer in *Seven Years in Tibet?* Did he finally find his home, like Capra's Conway in *Lost Horizon?* The only option for positing transformation—not a contemporary notion, in any case, at least in this context—is to accept the "self" represented in the letter to his sister as the "real" Bogle. But that is not the only Bogle we have. Rather than transformation, then, we have ambivalence. Rather than closure, we have a refusal to resolve—dissolution, incongruity, movement.

After Bogle returned to Calcutta, he wrote to his friend Anderson and presented yet another view of himself. Because he is connected with Hastings, Bogle's position is threatened when Hastings is deprived of authority by a new E. I. C. council. Bogle is living on the meagerest of incomes. He has no employment, nothing to do:

> I have therefor taken a Garden House in the neighborhood of Calcutta. It is surrounded with Trees like a Hermitage, and I lead the Life of a Hermit. I shun all large Companies I pay few visits and yet, I don't know how it is; but I never was in such credit with the world as I am at this Time. Should you come to Calcutta, and if you will be satisfied with a hearty welcome and plane Fare, I have a Room and a Cott at your Service. I have learned a great deal of Philosophy by my Pilgrimage and we may talk over many things which may not occur to you who are engaged in the ways of men.[105]

His hermit-like existence might be connected to his recovery from illness and travel fatigue, but he seems to have retreated from the world in other ways. This view of Bogle is also suggested by a letter sent to him by Alexander Hamilton; Hamilton shows Bogle back in India, as he worked to complete his report to Hastings:

> I can't help lamenting your situation at Melancholy Hall not only on your own account but from the loss the world is likely to sustain by it; who the deuce would ever think of sitting down to compose anything but Homilies or Elegies by the walls of a churchyard. Let me advise you only to write an account of Thibet funerals while in that Gloomy mansion choose for the rest some spot where you have more pleasing objects in view and where you may now and then enjoy the company of your friends. Ben Johnsons best pro-

ductions were composed when his Bouffet was best stored. I believe the observation would be found just in other works beside those of humour, indeed, I begin to suspect your living at Melancholy Hall has already had some effect on your spirits—"you know I never write news and am little disposed to do it now"—is a paragraph from your letter what am I to conclude from this but that you are got beyond all sublunary matters of this world below your notice. I figure you to myself sitting at a table in a large almost empty hall wrapt up in a Thibet Gown with a fur cap on, here Harvey's meditations amongst the tombs—there Young's night thoughts or our countryman Bunyan's words open before you.[106] Sometimes I see you in the Faranda [veranda] repeating—Beneath those aged thorns that yew trees shade &c. . .[107] God send I may be mistaken but I am afraid if you remain long where you are to find my apprehension verified on my return.[108]

Hamilton presents Bogle as depressed and struggling—and still dressed in Tibetan clothes. If at the start of the journey, Bogle wrote about mustard and cheese, by the end he has assumed the image of a gloomy man spouting poetry, at least in Hamilton's eyes. As Bogle works next to a churchyard, Hamilton imagines him reciting Gray's well-known "An Elegy in a Country Churchyard," the poem he recited when the Panchen Lama asked to hear a bit of English. Bogle once noted that "If ever I forfeit the Company's Service I will turn Facquier [fakir];" Hamilton conjures this ascetic aspect.[109] Having thrown himself and his affections into life at Tashilhunpo, Bogle now retreats. He finishes his report for Hastings. He does his duty. He misses his friends.

Bogle's situation improved when Hastings was restored to power in 1776. In the same year Bogle seems to have abandoned his hermetic ways; he writes to his friend David Anderson that he now lives with [Claud] Alexander and if Anderson should visit Calcutta, "We shall go every night to visit the Ladies."[110] Bogle was eventually put in charge of a trading post at Rangpur. Eager to maintain the strong personal ties established between Bogle and the lama—and hence between the E. I. C. and Tibet—Hastings attempted to send Bogle with the Panchen when he traveled to Beijing in 1779. The arrangements fell through, and Bogle expressed his sentiments in a letter to his brother: "I shall regret the absence of my friend the Teshu Lama, for whom I have a hearty liking, and should be happy again to have his fat hand on my head."[111] The image of Bogle and the Panchen as friends anticipates Kipling's Kim and his Teshu Lama, as we will see, as well as more recent images of friendship between the Fourteenth Dalai Lama and Heinrich Harrer or Richard Gere: a high lama develops a peculiar affection for a Western layman who reciprocates with mutual esteem. But despite Bogle's desire to see the Panchen, they were not to meet again. The lama died of smallpox while in Beijing; by the time the news reached Bengal in 1781, Bogle himself was dead of cholera at the age of 34.

A melancholy state of affairs, but not yet the end of the story. There is a textual legacy to consider. If we read Bogle's text *after* the myth of epiphany has come to dominate popular Western perceptions of Tibet—and we can only do so—we can imagine that, just as in the case of Younghusband, Pico Iyer, or Brad Pitt's Harrer, something special happened to Bogle in Tibet. In that sense, Bogle's texts are only more in a long line of epiphanic texts; his only happen to come earlier. But my aim is not simply to reiterate that myth—not in that way, anyhow. I return to Bogle to reclaim a horizon—which inevitably involves the risk of losing it again. Instead of seeing him as a comfortable character, comfortably epiphanizing, I highlight his ambiguity, his self-reflection, his affection. When I look at his texts, I look for the unsettled. In his texts I see not just that same old story, though that can be read there, too, but also the possibility for criticism *and* movement, criticism as movement. For in Bogle's various writings, he moves; he does not stand still; he reflects. When he encounters Tibetans, sometimes he holds steadfastly to an image of himself as different, sometimes he identifies with Tibetans, sometimes he is willing to rethink his assumptions, sometimes he loses coherence and identity entirely. While at times his self-reflexivity seems a polite participation in literary and intellectual conventions of the day, in that movement between genres and perspectives, in that willingness to rethink is the possibility for rapprochement, for change. The changes—the transformations, even—that might come about through such openness and self-criticism, though, if they are to be anything but conventional, cannot be known in advance. Bogle's is not yet the cliché of epiphany—it is something more unsettled, perhaps even more radical. His movements, I think, can help us to undo the myth. Horizons lost can be re-found, but they have to be continually re-examined, seen as unstable positions and not resting places.

Or at least that is one way to look at it. The danger is in recuperating his text for the same old, same old: Go to Tibet—no—*read* about Tibet—and change your life.

Perhaps the most I can do is plead indulgence for my hope—for my tale, as Bogle did for his, in his note from Bhutan:

> A heavy shower of snow had fallen two days before we left Tasheshijon [Tashichodzong], and the tops of all the mountains were white with it. The Bengalees, when they got up in the morning, were much surprised at the sight of it. They inquired of the Booteas, who told them it was white Cloths, which God Almighty sent down to cover the mountains, and keep them warm. The Solution required, to be sure, some Faith; but it was to them just

as probable as that it was Rain, or that they were afterwards to meet with water hard as Glass, and be able to walk across a River. ~ When different Climes exhibit such incredible Phonomenon to the Inhabitants of other Countries, why should not the accounts of Travellers be treated with Indulgence, and even the adventures of Sinbad the Sailor be read with some grains of allowance.[112]

In this passage Bogle writes relatively about the constructs we unquestioningly accept as truths. In his world snow is a particular kind of frozen water; to those who have never seen it before, and who regularly treat images of deities as living beings in need of food, clothes, and sleep, the white stuff that graces mountains—which are themselves frequently inhabited by deities and spirits—are "white Cloths"—*khatas*—fresh from the hands of a divine being. Bogle's caution here is a kind of lesson in what it means to travel, what it means to represent what one becomes and experiences elsewhere, and what we as readers need to remember. We've got to move too. There may be horizons that we haven't come across yet.

Postscript

Sitting in the India Office in London in 1997 with that sheaf of Bogle's papers, I looked at Bogle's writings as into a mirror, albeit one warped with age. Like him, I traveled to Tibet; I practiced rudimentary Tibetan. Like Bogle, I came to know Tibetans through living among them rather than through reading Buddhist texts. And I too had a hard time saying goodbye. But there the connection trails off. I was sitting in the India Office of the British Library in a hand-me-down lilac-colored maternity dress, feeling my world about to change, my nine-month pregnant belly making people around me a bit nervous. I was an American in London. In less than 24 hours after finishing my work with Bogle's manuscripts, I would go into labor with a boy named Jack. On the last day of having one child instead of two, I copied notes from Bogle's manuscript carefully in pencil, wondered at the way I could just sit there holding the papers that Bogle himself had written over two hundred years earlier—marveled at the travels these papers had undergone, eager to think about what they might mean, eager to write about it all. I pondered what it meant to be American and female writing about these matters. Why have few women looked into Bogle's texts? Was this only men's territory? Should I find a more suitable occupation? And I knew that anything I would want to write would have to wait—there were other tasks to do, tasks that could not be accomplished by thinking or writing but only by surrendering to the movements of this other inside me, this other who was me.

CHAPTER 3

In One Ear: Turner in Tibet

So Bogle's texts are not the place to look for epiphany—at least not in the sense of a single moment of revelation, not in the sense of a "regrasping-of-life scene" in which all becomes clear.[1] This form of epiphany did not gain prominence as a textual convention in secular texts until the mid-nineteenth century, having first been borrowed and refurbished from religious biographies and autobiographies. It is not until the 1910 account by Francis Younghusband, *India and Tibet,* that a full-fledged epiphany appears in a travel text on Tibet. Whereas Bogle's texts refuse resolution—and thus skirt epiphany in the conventional sense—when epiphany appears in Younghusband's account it serves to resolve things. And while the images of Bogle we have explored do not come together to create a unified being, epiphany as it is later expressed serves to make coherent selves.

During the course of the nineteenth century, as the British imperial project is further defined and underwritten by supporting discourses in many fields, the "openings" available to Bogle become increasingly closed—the possibility of remaining an unsettled self fades from the horizon. Because of this, epiphany is not only made possible, it is made necessary. Epiphany helps Younghusband close the gaps opened up by self-reflexivity. Epiphany helps Younghusband justify the imperial project and his participation in it. Epiphany helps the military leader maintain a spiritual life and do his duty at the same time. Tibetan epiphany settles matters.

But before we arrive at Younghusband's climax, there are other texts to consider. The next British traveler to Tibet after Bogle was Samuel Turner, who went to Tashilhunpo in 1783 on the orders of Warren Hastings. Turner's goal was to maintain the channels of communication opened between Bogle and the Third Panchen Lama; in Turner's case, however, he was to meet the Panchen Lama in his newly-reincarnated form, in the body of an 18–month-old child. While Bogle's account lay in manuscript for nearly a century, Turner published an account of his travels in 1800, 13 years after his journey. This book, which enjoyed popularity in English and in translation, is thus the first English travel text on Tibet; nonetheless, Turner himself had access to Bogle's report to Hastings. My analysis of Turner's text considers Turner's relationship to Bogle as well as his representation of himself among Tibetans.

As in Bogle's account, vision is a key sense for Turner, though it functions differently. Often, when Turner looks, he stands apart; he inhabits the position of a "male gazer," one who through his vision and his discourse controls and masters the other, whether the other be a woman, a child, or a colonized subject. In these scenes, Turner's text exemplifies what Charles Long calls "the epistemology of the privileged status of the perceiver," exemplified by a consciousness that assumes preeminence, that drives for mastery, that seeks to impose itself on the world.[2] In that sense, when Turner looks into the mirror of the other, he sees a vision of self—or rather, he works hard to maintain his sense of himself as different from, and even superior to, the Tibetan other. But that is not the whole story. Some of his efforts depend on aural experiences: in these scenes, Turner lends a sympathetic ear to Tibetans and is consequently much less likely to interpret his findings in terms of the reigning colonialist, Romantic, or racialist discourses of the day. The moments in the text where Turner reports on some unexpected aural experience mark points when that coherent image of self becomes unstable. When Turner listens, in other words, something happens to him; he is revised. The world no longer remains the same place. Rather than imposing a view, in these instances Turner seems to be confronted by the world; his subjectivity is apprehended through relation. So much does his sense of himself come to depend on his relation to others that by the time he meets the young Panchen Lama, Turner is practically beside himself. The encounter defies Turner's ability to interpret. In Turner we can read evidence not of epiphany but of the way that this colonial writer is shaken by his encounter with Tibetans in a way that is different from and more radical than conventional epiphany. And, interestingly, when Turner cannot make final sense, he cites Bogle. Bogle, because of his effusive relationship with the Third Panchen Lama, helps Turner to justify his own reaction to his young reincarnation. Although he can offer several commentaries on the encounter, its final significance eludes him: it is excess, unaccountable.

The horizon of epiphany, after seeming to elude my grasp, comes back into view.

SEEING AND HEARING

The ways of seeing evident in Turner's text tend to distance observer from observed, and, in broad terms, are supported by discourses of natural history, of race, and of Romanticism. Turner wrote during a period in which Europe's confidence in its ability to observe and interpret the world was running high. Having taken in enough information, Europeans might stand back, see the world in its entirety, and comprehend its diversity, whether it was expressed in flora or fauna, humans, or the lay of the land. Not unconnected to this plan for a grand vision was the hope for a view of the world that might exalt the spirit, for achievement of what Marlon B. Ross calls "self-possession—a state in which the self has managed to see the world whole, to assimilate both time and space into a vision that is both individual and collective, to assemble all conflicting aspects of the self and put them to creative use, and by doing so to assert the power of the self to engender itself."[3] A discourse of Romanticism which sought out the uplifting, the emotional, and the sublime depended on a particular understanding of the visual, but in this case, what was produced was exhilaration over the apparent order of the world, an order that was understood as connected to and expressive of an order and beauty within the white, European man.

While Romanticism was in its early stages in Turner's day, this drive for an encompassing vision does not present any particular conflict with the goals of the East India Company of the late-eighteenth century. Indeed, only by surveying the situation in Tibet and apprehending the difference between Briton and Tibetan could the E. I. C. establish a political and mercantile relationship with the Tibetans. As a trained surveyor and the first British writer to publish a Tibetan travel tale, *An Account of an Embassy to the Court of the Teshoo Lama in Tibet,* Turner eagerly presents the place to European readers. "My present design," he writes, is "to delineate the appearance of a region, little known, and to mark the manners of the people, as, from an immediate intercourse with them, attracted my observation."[4] Observation need not only refer to the sense of sight, but, especially in the early parts of the narrative, it is the visible that matters to Turner. And thus, whether he is looking at the mountains or at the local people, Turner seems confident that he knows what he sees.

In the case of the Himalayas, these little known mountains offer rewards both to Europe's scientific vision and to Turner personally. As he writes of his approach to a snowcapped range, "The vastness and obscurity of this enormous boundary . . . could not but excite very powerful emotions in the mind; and I look upon the formidable barrier I had to pass with mingled awe and admiration" (p. 9). Turner's response to the mountains suggests the shift within the larger European sense of what mountains mean. As Marjorie Nicolson has argued, by the eighteenth century, visual experience of mountains has become more important than Biblical and classical precedents for interpreting them.[5] And with this new emphasis on vision comes the expectation that the vastness of mountains might symbolize the grandness of human imagination and capabilities. Conversely, bounded views suggest confinement and lack of liberty. Turner's participation in this form of mountain glory is suggested in this passage about mountains and vision:

> And here I cannot help remarking, that something like a feeling of vexation has constantly occurred to me, on coming to the top of every mountain I had yet ascended. While struggling, and almost exhausted with fatigue, there is a spur which yet animates to the last effort; and the mind anticipates, with some delight, the unbounded view with which it will be presented, but how great is the disappointment, when, after all, you see on every side around you, mountains still higher than that on which you stand; whilst all the space that is visible, is that only which intervenes between them! (p. 169)

The eye is the center of this passage, for it is to the eye that the image of the "unbounded view [is] presented." Mountains are valuable because of the negative space they create; in effect, the viewer looks for the most exalted aspects of himself and humankind in the wide open spaces created around and above mountains. If Bogle located himself vis-à-vis Tibetans, Turner looks among the mountains for a particular image of self. Yet, more than seeming like a man who has climbed a lot of mountains in these passages, Turner seems more like someone who has read a lot, who looks at the world for confirmation of the ideas that excite and animate thinking men back in England. The privileged status of the perceiver wins out; the mountains remain the other on which abstractions are hung.

The primacy of vision also shapes many of Turner's descriptions of the people he meets on the journey. Local people offer examples to Turner of the various races into which humankind is divided, each of which is distinguished by particular observable characteristics. Thus Turner describes an official on the border of Bhutan as "a creature that hardly bore the resemblance of humanity; of disgusting features, meagre limbs, and diminuitive stature, with a dirty cloth thrown over his shoulders." The reasons for his ugliness, for Turner, stem from his "impure" racial origin, for Turner declares that "[h]e was of mixed race, between the Bootea and the Bengalees; and it was wonderful to observe how greatly the influence of a pestilential climate, had caused him to degenerate from both" (p. 21). Turner observes, classifies, and pronounces, and thus keeps a manageable distance from these Asian others.

And if these others start to look back and turn Turner into an object, there will be trouble, especially early in the journey. When the Raja of Bhutan attempts to identify similarities between the Bhutanese and the British—the use of woolen clothes, the love of tea and meat and spirits, as well the abhorrence of the "niceties and refined distinctions of the Hindoo"—Turner refuses the identification (p. 74). For him, this is not the proper way to observe and categorize; for him, these visible similarities do not bespeak larger commonalities. Thus he must insist that "nothing can be more different than our habits, and our manners. I had pleasure in recognising a more striking similitude in the products of his country and our own, as well as in the temperance of the climate" (p. 74). Though Turner can look at and judge those he meets, he will not extend the same courtesy to the Raja.

Bogle was not always content to be stared at, as we have seen. But as he adjusted to life at Tashilhunpo, he tended to deal with the look of the other in a different way:

> [C]rowds of Gylongs used, at all hours, to come into my room to see me, or get upon the Leads and look down upon me. . . . I never forbad anybody; and after giving them a pinch a Snuff and indulging them with a look of the chairs &c., which always produced an Exclamation of "pah pah pah, tze tze tze," they used to retire and make way for others. This continued, more or less, all the time I was at Teshoo Loombo.[6]

Whereas Bogle learned to tolerate the stream of onlookers at Tashilhunpo, while in Bhutan, Turner and one of his traveling companions devise a way to deal with the Bhutanese who come to have a look at them. They touch their visitors with a device that produces an electric shock. In a gesture that both serves to entertain themselves and get rid of unwanted pests, Turner gains the advantage of his visitors' twice over and expresses contempt for their curiosity. While elsewhere Turner will declare that "the Tibetians are a very human, kind people" (p. 209), in this relation with the Bhutanese, he demonstrates just how far they are from his consciousness.

So Turner wants to see—but not to be seen. And for Turner, this desire to see is not simply individual voyeurism but is part of a grand scheme to produce knowledge. In one scene, the Panchen Lama's regent asks Turner why the British take on commercial endeavors in far-flung regions of the world. Turner's reply turns his personal curiosity into something of a national trait. The British "system of education," he argues, is

> calculated perpetually to awaken genius, . . . [and] when once roused, and improved, would not suffer their possessors to sit down in listless and inglorious inactivity. Hence it was that numerous branches of respectable families, prompted by curiosity, not less than by a desire of wealth, spread themselves over every region of the universe. . . . Men of learning and science embarked on these occasions, to whom the desire of acquiring and diffusing knowledge, were sufficient inducement to attempt the most hazardous and laborious enterprises. (pp. 277–8)

Turner's own work in Tibet is clearly part of this enterprise, and gives special justification for his desire to look into matters.

Thus when a procession of the newly-reincarnated Panchen Lama is scheduled, Turner wants to see it. "A curious desire, I must own, to be personally witness of so singular a ceremony, induced me to make some effort to be admitted of the party" (p. 249). Bogle had shown himself to be a sympathetic onlooker during the procession of the Panchen Lama to Tashilhunpo. But the officials at Tashilhunpo have their own notions about the importance of vision, and thus forbid Tuner from witnessing this procession. Turner resigns himself to watching the procession from a monastery window.

In all of these processes of looking, Turner participates in a will to mastery that scholars of feminism and colonialism have often noted: to see is to possess, to assert dominance, to claim the privileges of the male gaze. While such attitudes do seem part of Turner's sense of both himself and of the Tibetans he meets, it is not the only way he relates to Tibetan others. While I appreciate the importance of looking for the trope of seeing as mastery in Turner's text (as demonstrated above), I fear that if I only "look for" mastery, that is all I will find. Indeed, as Ashis Nandy and Charles Long have argued, if criticisms of colonialism focus only on the colonizer as a master who imposes his will on his passive, colonized victim, they are bound to overlook the many shifts and struggles that colonial ideology has undergone; furthermore, they are prone to ignore the effects colonialism has had on colonizers. As Long argues:

> [A]ll cultures in the world have experienced colonialism whether as colonizers or as colonized. The former colonized for all sorts of reasons are forced to admit of this situation; the cultures of the colonial powers having relin-

quished their rule have not yet come to terms with the intellectual and theoretical implications of decolonization.[7]

Similarly, Nandy argues that the colonial situation creates a kind of "shaped
culture" that rearranges "cultural priorities on both sides." To fail to recognize
that is to "indirectly admit the superiority of the oppressors and collaborate
with them" by attributing colonizers with a transcendent consciousness
which can impose itself on others without itself being affected in the process.[8]
While Turner certainly does participate in the ideology of the transcendent
consciousness, it is not the only thing that he does; it is not the only way he
is affected by the colonial encounter. One way in which the dominating
effects of vision are undermined in Turner's texts—one of the ways that
Turner seems to be affected—is suggested in his accounts of what he hears
on his travels.

In his accounts from Tashilhunpo, the changes in Turner's point of view
are not sudden but always mixed in with other perspectives. For example,
when Turner first arrives at the young Panchen Lama's monastery, he
writes mostly about the appearance of the place, with its "numerous gilded
canopies, and turrets, and the sun rising in full splendor directly opposite. It
presented a view wonderfully beautiful and brilliant; the effect was little
short of magic, and it made an impression, which no time will ever efface
from my mind." Naturally enough, he stands apart here from the grand
structure in order to look at it, but "[a]t the instant of our entrance, we
heard the deep tone of many sonorous instruments, which were summon-
ing the religious to their morning orisons" (p. 230). Interestingly, when
Turner crosses the threshold, he begins to hear.

If some of Turner's modes of seeing divide subject and object, seer and
seen, the process of hearing allows a different way of relating to the other.
Turner gives the following account of his first night at Tashilhunpo:

> Not long after we had returned to our apartments, I was disturbed on a sud-
> den, by so confused and tumultuous a noise, that I was utterly at a loss to
> what cause, to attribute this alarming uproar. At length I was informed by my
> attendants, the Goseins, that it was only the Gylongs at their *pooja,* or reli-
> gious exercises, and I could not possibly refuse to give them ample credit for
> their zeal. (p. 243)

Unable to observe the event, Turner is momentarily confused; he cannot
name or categorize the phenomenon. He has to rely on his ears to give him
information on a people and a religion that are as yet little known to Europe.

But given aural evidence of Tibetan religion, Turner is driven to see it. Having heard the monks' ceremonies, Turner longs to look into their "gorgeous temples":

> From the first day of my arrival at Teshoo Loombo, I was extremely desirous of viewing the interior of some one of those magnificent edifices, in the midst of which I had taken up my abode, and which continually excited my curiosity by the profuse and costly ornaments bestowed upon their outside. (p. 255)

Turner's emphasis on vision here is underscored by a vocabulary of desire and excitation. The colonizing eyes that long to collect the world give him a way to think of and interpret the visual. But because the Tibetans at Tashilhunpo are suspicious of Turner's desire to peek into matters, Turner is forced to turn his ear to the subject. Some of what he hears he can interpret easily enough:

> The frequent recurrence of solemn sounds from a variety of deep toned instruments, after short pauses of profound silence; the low hum of invocation, during both night and day; and occasionally the more vociferous clamour of crowded congregations, joined with a full choral band; left me no room to doubt, that I was close to the scene, of some of the most solemn and mysterious ceremonies of their religion. (p. 255–6)

Turner is driven to interpret what he hears but has to beware lest his curiosity overstep the bounds the Tibetans have set up:

> I lost little time in endeavouring to ascertain the truth of my conjectures; but I trod upon tender ground. Any indication of extraordinary curiosity, even in the common affairs of life, was sufficient to raise, in an instant, an host of suspicions, against which, I should have been compelled eternally to combat; and religion, especially among a people so bigotted to its forms, was a subject to which I adverted, with still more scrupulous caution. (pp. 256)

Turner's drive to see raises Tibetan suspicions, suspicions which he understands not as a reaction to his curiosity but as one of the traits of bigotted and insular Tibetan religion.

Unable to freely observe the monks and their ceremonies, Turner is forced again to rely on what he can hear. He notes that 2,500 monks convene to proclaim

> aloud the attributes and praises of the Supreme Being; a service which was performed with a vehemence of vociferation perfectly astonishing, and, as

I thought, altogether inconsistent with the decorum of a well regulated assembly.

The object of this solemn meeting, as far as I could collect, was for every individual present to repeat, and enforce with all his powers of utterance, the praises of the Deity; and we need not wonder that from such a congregation, who had attained by long practice to a Stentorian strength of lungs, there should arise the most surprising discord, the very counterpart of that which is produced by the vociferations of an enraged and hostile multitude. But all this was, in fact, nothing more than a pious token of the most ardent zeal, a sort of contest for the palm, a struggle, which should do the highest honour to his supreme and tutelary gods. (p. 256)

It is worth noting that in these accounts Turner fails to name the deity being praised, choosing instead the generic terms "Supreme Being" and "Deity," terms that more closely connect the Tibetans' "wholly other" with those of European Deism. But for Turner the sounds he hears can only be "discord"—that word again—though, as he listens further and considers, Turner changes his mind from this first impression. Noting that religious rituals at Tashilhunpo "are always accompanied by music" (p. 257), Turner goes on to suggest that, altogether, Tibetan religion seems to lead to mercy and peace, if also to naïveté. "Placing their sole reliance in the mediation of the sacred Lama, the immaculate viceregent of the Supreme, they imagine, that he covers them with the broadest shield, from the encroachments of others; and the benign influence of his doctrines teaches them to be benevolent, and humane to all around them" (p. 257). Turner clearly stands apart from Tibetan religion here to judge it. While L. Austine Waddell and Younghusband will make similar claims about Tibetan religion over a century later—Tibetan Buddhism takes advantage of compliant lay men and women—at this point in the colonial project, such sentiments mean something other than they will later. When manipulated properly, such attributes bode well for continued intercourse between Bengal and Tibet.

But even if Turner is driven to a kind of mastery over Tibet, what he hears convinces him "that [he] was in the midst of men, who made religion the sole business of their lives" (p. 257). This movement towards trusting the ear rather than the eye seems to affect his later interpretation of one religious ceremony (probably the celebration of Tsongkhapa's birthday) that he is allowed to observe. In this ritual he notes that a visual symbol— Turner calls them "general illuminations," which are probably butter lamps—is used differently in Tibet from in England. At home, he notes, such illuminations suggest joy, whereas in Tibet they denote melancholy, awe, and respect. Contemplating the relativity of custom here, Turner notes how much the effect of such a display "depends on a previously declared design." Meaning, in that case, does not reside in the symbol; meaning is shaped by symbolic systems which are themselves culturally constructed, we might say these days. But whereas previously Turner had judged the sound of Tibetan ritual clamorous and inappropriate according to English standards, this one strikes a chord in him:

> The darkness of the night, the profound tranquillity and silence, interrupted only by the deep and slowly-repeated tone of the nowbut, trumpet, gong, and cymbal, at different intervals; the tolling of bells, and the loud monotonous repetition of sentences of prayer, sometimes heard when the instruments were silent; were all so calculated, by their solemnity, to produce serious reflection, that I really believe no human ceremony could possibly have been contrived, more effectually to impress the mind with sentiments of awe. (p. 319)

How does Turner move from the position of the external, judging observer to someone who "really believes" that this ritual expresses something accurate and even universal about the human sentiment of awe? Has an epiphany happened while we weren't looking—or listening? Not at least as Turner writes it. Not a literary epiphany, in any case. But something is shifting.

The movement in Turner's text is not simply from looking to hearing. Throughout the text he continues to look and hear. And it would be wrong to suggest that when Turner looks he only strives to master and when he listens he is only confronted by a kind of radical otherness. As the text proceeds, Turner both sees and hears; Turner both masters and attends, is both confident and confused, settled and unsettled. By the time Turner meets the young Panchen Lama, he is not only receptive, he is also a little disoriented.

Turner is only granted an audience with the toddler lama at the end of his stay, and it is worth looking at the encounter at some length. For it is in this section of his long monograph that Turner gazes upon the emanation of Amitabha, a Buddha to come; it is in this section that Turner makes use of Bogle.

MEETINGS WITH REMARKABLE MEN (AND BOYS)

Before Turner goes to Terpaling to see the 18–month-old lama he must first bid adieu to Tashilhunpo. Bogle had had difficulty leaving the place, and Turner seems similarly moved. Servants of the company from this period customarily engage in local rituals such as bowing and kow-towing without reservation; such cultural relativism lubricates the larger goal of mercantilism. When he leaves Tashilhunpo, Turner participates in a ritual that expresses something of his personal feeling towards this place and appears to be more than a perfunctory performance:

> I could not . . . bid adieu to the place, till, in conformity with the custom of these regions, I had bound a white silk scarf round the capitals of each of the four columns, that stood within the apartment I occupied. I stopped not, to examine nicely, the obligations of this ceremony. If it were meant as a tribute of gratitude, it was certainly due to the comfortable accommodation this dwelling had afforded me. If it were the solemn designation of a long farewell, it equally accorded with my state of mind. (p. 329)

Whether or not Turner's account draws directly from Bogle's account of taking leave, the farewell sentiment expressed in both texts sets up a precedent for later travelers to Tibet and their texts. And Turner's genial participation in this ritual gesture prepares us for his encounter with the lama.

Turner's description of his meeting with the lama unveils slowly. First he carefully describes the arrangement of the room, the people in it, and the throne on which the small lama sits. Then Turner, who wears English dress as requested by the lama's father, notes that he "advanced, and, as the custom is, presented a white pelong scarf and delivered also into the Lama's hands, the Governor General's present of a string of pearls, and coral, while the other things were set down before him" (p. 333). Turner's escorts then proceed to prostrate themselves before the lama, who receives their gestures "with a cheerful look of complacency."

> His father then addressed me in the Tibet language, in words which were explained to me by the interpreter; he said that "Teshoo Lama had been used to remain at rest until this time of day, but he had awoke very early this morning, and could not be prevailed upon to remain longer at his repose, for added he, the English gentlemen were arrived, and he could not sleep." During the time we were in the room, *I observed that the Lama's eyes were scarcely ever turned from us,* and when our cups were empty of tea, he appeared uneasy, and throwing back his head, and contracting the skin of his brow, continued to make a noise, for he could not speak, until they were filled again. He took some burnt sugar out of a golden cup, containing some confectionary, and, stretching out his arm, made a motion to his attendants to give them to me. I found myself, though visiting an infant, under the necessity of saying something; for it was hinted to me, that notwithstanding he is unable to reply, it is not to be inferred that he cannot understand. However, his incapacity of

answering, excused me many words, and I briefly said, that "the governor General, on receiving the news of his decease in China, was overwhelmed with grief and sorrow, and continued to lament his absence from the world, until the cloud that had overcast the happiness of this nation, was dispelled by his re-appearance and then, if possible, a greater degree of joy had taken place, than he had experienced of grief, on receiving the first mournful news. The Governor anxiously wished that he might long continue to illumine the world by his presence, and was hopeful that the friendship, which had formerly subsisted between them, would not be diminished, but rather that it might become still greater than before; and that by his continuing to shew kindness to my countrymen, there might be an extensive communication between his votaries, and the dependents of the British nation."

The little creature turned, *looked stedfastly* [*sic*] *towards me,* with the appearance of much attention while I spoke, and nodded with repeated but slow movements of the head, as though he understood and approved every word, but could not utter a reply. (pp. 334–5, emphasis added)

In this passage, the lama is attributed with marvelous powers of aural comprehension; his eyes are turned on Turner, and under that gaze, the Englishman produces a remarkable speech (or rather, in this account of being under that gaze, he produces a remarkable text of his speech). Whereas before Turner had shunned the gaze of Tibetans and longed to see for himself, in this scene he accepts the gaze as—if not a blessing—then as a compliment. And what is more stunning here is that, in this passage, Turner accepts the young lama before him as the incarnation of his predecessor—the reappearance of the lama Bogle met, who had made promises of friendship with the E. I. C. Are his remarks here simply a cynical strategy to further Anglo-Tibetan relations? Do they echo the Persian-style compliments of Moghul India? Or might the excessiveness of Turner's compliments, remarks which Turner oddly calls "brief" (p. 334), suggest that something else is going on here? For just as Turner feels compelled to speak to a young Tibetan who neither knows English nor can talk, he seems compelled to say something about the way the young boy captured his attention.

That Turner recognizes the excess of his own discourse is evident in several places in the text. Immediately following this passage, Turner suggests that some may find his words "trivial" or even "preposterous" (p. 335). But there is a precedent for such behavior in the writings of George Bogle. When Turner declares the good character of the previous Panchen Lama, he refers to Bogle:

Teshoo Lama's whole character . . . so powerfully excited the admiration of Mr. Bogle, as to have drawn from him this enthusiastic, but sincere expression: "I endeavoured to discover in him some of those defects, which are inseparable from humanity; but he is so universally beloved that I had no success, and not a man could find in his heart to speak ill of him." (p. 338)

Bogle was certainly impressed by the Panchen Lama. The interesting thing is, though, that Bogle's words were all about this lama's predecessor. Bogle's effusive text cannot fully account for Turner's behavior before this young incarnation. Turner goes on to claim Bogle not only as a gracious and generous man but as a possible model for all emissaries of the company:

> That the effect produced on the mind of the Lama, by a disposition and manners perfectly congenial with his own, was great and powerful, cannot excite our surprise. Indeed, towards whatever object it was directed, the patient and laborious exercise of the powers of a strong mind, in my predecessor, Mr. Bogle, was always accompanied by a most engaging mildness and benevolence, which marked every part of his character. I am thoroughly aware of the very favourable impression, which these amiable qualities left behind them in the court of Teshoo Loomboo; and this circumstance, whilst it reflects the highest honour on that judgment, which, free from the bias of partial considerations, could select its agent with such nice discrimination, places, at the same time, in the strongest point of view, the salutary influence of conciliating manners, in men, who are employed as agents, or ministers, to independent states; to those more especially, among whom the British character is imperfectly understood, or entirely unknown. (p. 339)

In Bogle, Turner finds justification for his own gentle, conciliatory, and perhaps even obsequious behavior before "the sacred little man," as Graham Sandberg called him.[9] For it is on this child that all of Hastings' hopes rest. Given the weakness of the Lhasa government, Turner suggests that the most the E. I. C. can do is wait for the Teshoo Lama to attain his majority and then insist that he recall his previous friendship with Hastings and the British. Turner carefully notes how the E. I. C. might take advantage of the Tibetan system of reincarnation; in his report to Hastings he argues:

> [T]he new Lama will be taught to recur to the connections of the former Teshoo Lama as one of the strongest marks that can denote his identity, and facilitate his acceptation. And here I ground my presumptions built upon the tenets of their faith, which is the basis on which their government itself is constructed. (p. 378)

In the official report, at least, this polite participation in local customs, this acceptance of the toddler as the reincarnation of the Teshoo Lama can be seen as creating very useful political effects.

But if the child is to be understood as the reincarnation of the previous Teshoo Lama, then it may not be lost on Turner that he is, if not Bogle's incarnation, then his stand-in. In Tibetan Buddhist tradition it is common that relationships between gurus and disciples continue down lines of incarnation. Thus, for example, the present Gonsar Rinpoche was once the student of Geshe Rabten; the mature Gonsar Rinpoche is now the teacher of the young Rabten incarnation. Bogle never formally accepted the Third Panchen Lama as his teacher, of course, but, in some ways, Turner takes up Bogle's position vis-à-vis the young lama. Perhaps the discerning eye of the young lama sees something in Turner and he in him. Indeed, this connection seems to be confirmed by Tibetan members of the lama's household, who are compelled to remark on "how extremely fortunate it was, that the young Lama had regarded us with so very particular notice" (p. 337). The eye of the other has turned on Turner, and by that point in the journey—or least in his narrative of it—he is ready to bask in that gaze.

Indeed, the coming together of eye and ear in Turner's account may be signaled by his response to the song later offered by the "handsome" mother (p. 336) of the Panchen Lama: "I am not ashamed to own, that the song she sung, was more pleasing to my ear, than an Italian air" (p. 343). Of course, by suggesting that there may be something to be ashamed of in preferring a Tibetan song to an Italian one, Turner registers something of his own discomfort with this feeling. Similarly, throughout the rest of the account Turner will repeatedly return to the question of his response to the lama. In the final lines of his report to Hastings he continues the apology:

> As the meeting was attended with very singular and striking circumstances, I could not help noting them with most particular attention; and though the repetition of such facts, interwoven and blended as they are with superstition and folly, may expose me to the imputation of extravagant exaggeration, yet I should think myself reprehensible in repressing them. (p. 379)

Turner is aware that from an outsider's point of view, his account may seem ridiculous, superstitious folly. But for Turner, that is not the whole story. And although he risks being laughed at for including impressions that he himself is hard-pressed to fully understand, he feels the need to express them: "I should think myself reprehensible in repressing them." So he leaves it at that; his bit of effusion, his plain gaga-eyed attraction to the lama are left without further explanation. Writers of the later colonial period will be pressured to make complete sense of their experiences among the non-Europeans they would govern. But at this point, Turner, like Bogle, does not make everything make sense. The scene remains in excess, as it were, protruding like the foldout in flowing Tibetan script within Turner's book. (Recorded there is a letter to Turner and a list of Tibetan words in the U-chen script including *Om mane padme hung* and Panchen Rinpoche.)

In this excess, in his failure to make sense, we might say, lies Turner's salvation. But not his epiphany. Perhaps this strange account offers evidence of a consciousness of the other, rather than a consciousness that impinges on the other. Perhaps this account looks back to us, as it were, confronts us as other, and helps to rattle our interpretive frameworks. But if I force Turner's account into a single vision, whether that of racism, colonialism, romanticism, or Tibetan epiphany, I risk falling into the very dichotomies and simplification that my criticism aims to undo. If I try to keep Turner at arm's length—he's a bad guy, I'm nothing like him—I claim for myself the kind of moral superiority, absolution, and purity that has perpetuated colonial discourse in many forms. If I don't let Turner unsettle me and those colonizing dichotomies, I may not be listening.

Postscript

On my first night in a Tibetan monastery, Gajang Dangtse in Mundgod, south India, I was stirred from my room by a great whirring noise—a hurricane, a boiler about to explode, a great thunderstorm. In fact, it was nothing but the monks at evening assembly.

I could hear pretty well back then. At present, though, my concern with hearing in this chapter might seem ironic, seeing that I am a person with one deaf ear. I was just back from two years traveling among Buddhist and Tibetan communities abroad when my ear started to hurt. Diagnosed finally as a fungal infection, this malady had to be treated by pouring acid into my ear. Such a treatment was excruciating, out-of-body painful. I was studying Tibetan language in Madison, Wisconsin at the time, and I would show up to class with a cotton ball in my ear. (*Amchi chin pa yin pe?* my teacher would ask: Did you go to the doctor?) It was then that the constant ringing began, perpetual crickets buzzing in my head. Back in Dharamsala soon after, the eardrum blew, precluding forever the chance of actually hearing Tibetans well. Four operations later I don't hear in stereo. I've learned to depend on lip-reading. I misunderstand consonants. If I sleep on my good ear I can't hear my kids crying, the phone, sweet nothings—not anything.

CHAPTER 4

Manning's Sentimental Journey

While Bogle and Turner might have had interesting trips, their accounts of their journeys do not yet culminate in epiphanies. This "failure" to epiphanize is due not to some defect in their psychological make-up but rather to the historical lack of textual models and cultural conventions that make such transformation possible, among other factors. In their day, such momentous internal movements were not yet part of secular travel. One might expect to be educated, one might reflect on one's home culture, one might return with some interesting artifacts and information, but one did not yet expect from secular journeys a kind of spiritual revelation. But even as Bogle and Turner traveled to Tibet, a movement was already underway that would help to make such revelations possible: the Romantic refashioning of the journey/pilgrimage motif. As M. H. Abrams argued in 1971, so-called Romantic writing reinterpreted standard Christian concepts within a new frame of reference; as he notes, Romantic writers undertook "to save traditional concepts, schemes, and values which had been based on the relation of the Creator to his creature and creation, but to reformulate them within the prevailing two-term system of subject and object, ego and non-ego, the human mind or consciousness and its transactions with nature."[1] Because Christian concepts and frames of reference were deeply embedded in linguistic, cultural, and literary forms, Romantic writers frequently ended up translating and transposing certain concepts such as "revelation" and "pilgrimage" to the realm of the "secular," thus paving the way for secular epiphany.

The impetuses for the shift from Christian to secular frames of interpretation are multiple, but some dimensions of Romanticism were themselves inspired by the Orientalist works of such scholars as William Jones and

H. T. Colebrooke; Jones's "discovery" in 1788 that Sanskrit was related to European languages had a profound impact on European self-perception, at least in academic circles. Both in England and in Germany, Jones's translations of the Hindu *Puranas*—and his version of an omnipresent, all-pervading "Spirit of Spirits"—helped reconfigure the conception of the divine and its relationship to the self, while translations of the *Bhagavad-Gita* in the early nineteenth century would captivate scholars and writers as far from India as England and the United States. These shifting visions of divinity and humanity would shape the attitude of the next British traveler in Tibet.

Thomas Manning's 1811 account of his travels to Tibet hardly comprises a full-blown Romantic text; instead, it is made up of a series of entries that do not finally amount to a narrative, let alone a coherent vision of the world. Nonetheless, Manning produced a text that shows signs of shifts in the conception of the self, travel, and the colonial project. Unlike Bogle and Turner, Manning did not travel to Tibet on behalf of the East India Company; instead he was a solitary traveler, a sojourner on his way to China. Thus, despite the fervor that would accompany later travelers to Tibet, Manning was hardly interested in the place. Avowed Sinophile, Manning reached Lhasa as part of his scheme to travel to the Chinese capital of Beijing. Traveling without official sanction, he spent time in the Tibetan capital—the goal of so many travelers after him—before finally being ousted by Manchu officials. In 1811, the E. I. C. was disinterested in his journey, but the Raj reversed this position 60 years later, when its hunger for knowledge of Tibet acquired particular urgency. For between Turner's 1784 journey and 1903, when Younghusband invaded, Qing dynasty policies forbade foreign travel in Tibet. During a period when Europe set out to explore every inch of the globe, Tibet was off-limits, unaccounted for—a region inaccessible to Britain both practically and intellectually. Within this milieu, the texts of Bogle and Manning acquired a certain prestige; these writers, at least, had been to Tibet. Markham published their accounts in one volume in 1876.

When I ponder Markham's pairing of Bogle and Manning, I cannot help but be struck by the coming together of two Tibetan travelers who were adventurous not only in their physical exploits but also in their thinking. The incomplete, unfinished, and unedited nature of their texts offers glimpses of travelers who are willing to move in their thinking, travelers who will not be pinned down. This may be what Bishop means when he says that Turner's text is more restrained and formal than Bogle's, which, in Bishop's eyes, "anticipates the dawn of the Romantic era": there's a liveliness in both Bogle's and Manning's accounts—an aliveness to the world.[2] While Bogle was more reflective about such shifts, the episodic shape of

Manning's writing shows him in a variety of seemingly quickly changing moods, contradictory positions that are never resolved within the body of the manuscript. As in my reading of Bogle, I am interested what these shifts suggest about Manning's conception of Tibet and his varying attitudes towards Tibetans.

Like Bogle, Manning had few textual precedents for his understanding of Tibet. He did not have access to Bogle's account, but was probably familiar with Turner's book. Like that 1800 document, Manning's manuscript is punctuated by an encounter with a high lama—in Manning's case, the young Ninth Dalai Lama. And like Turner before him, Manning is quite moved by this meeting. But while Turner is pressed to make sense of this encounter for Warren Hastings and the East India Company, Manning has no such blatant political pressure on him. Rather, his interpretation of this meeting is largely framed by a Romantic orientation, one which emphasizes the importance of human emotion, one in which the divine springs from among the things of this world. Because Manning's journal was published it contributed to the intertextual knowledge gathered by writers such as Kipling and Younghusband after him.

Because he is seemingly self-motivated, single-minded, and iconoclastic (at least as far as his own culture was concerned), Manning's story at times resembles that of a Romantic questor, a secular kind of pilgrim, a figure that was beginning to take shape in English life and letters. Manning's behavior before the young Dalai Lama is all the more remarkable because he starts off his journey with little interest in Tibet at all, inclined instead to understand Tibetans by means of a Sinophilic discourse that describes the Tibetans as barbarians. Over the course of his journey, Manning comes to revise his high estimation of things Chinese; in effect, he moves from strict adherence to a discourse of Chinese superiority to a more Romantic discourse on the value of human emotion, which, in his case, embraces many Tibetans. In Manning's case, then, even if there is not epiphany, there is movement.

As in the case of Bogle, what we have of Manning's text are fragments, sifted by Markham, and, in my case, read with an eye for movement and reflection. In his text, there is no grand story of revelation and change; instead, there are the almost daily jottings of a traveler who is little concerned with the consistency of his vision. Despite—and perhaps because—of the text's fragmentary nature, they suggest that something happened to Manning in Tibet. While Manning does not have a single moment of revelation that changes his sense of himself and the world, his text does suggest that travel within Tibet does something to him; or rather, his account of his travels, framed as it is within available discourses, suggests a shifting relation between the British traveler and alien Tibet. In this way, these fragments suggest Manning's participation in larger plot structures provided by Orientalism and Romanticism.

TO CHINA THROUGH TIBET

Even before Manning left England for the East, he had developed a burning interest in China. Unable to study Mandarin at home, he moved to Paris, where Chinese studies were more advanced. French writers had done much to promote the glorification of China. Voltaire had expanded on the reports of European traders and missionaries to China to imagine a country ruled by morality and law; his *Esai sur les moeurs* of 1756 emphasized the positive aspects of Jesuit reports and represented China as a noble civilization. Such a positive evaluation was not confined to France; in *Citizen of the World,* Oliver Goldsmith invented a Chinese character who, on his travels in England, could not help but remark on the superstition and buffoonery of his English hosts. Tibet, on the other hand, was still ill-defined for Europe. A few fragments in Marco Polo, rumors of Prester John, some vague notion of a place ruled by a pope-like figure—these were almost all that Europe had to go on until the publication of Turner's account in 1800.

Manning seems to have sought something personal and ideal from traveling to China; this is suggested by a letter from his friend, the essayist Charles Lamb, in which he begs the would-be traveler to give up his plans. Arguing that Manning has been misled by travelers' accounts to expect wonders from his journey, he writes:

> Believe me, . . . there are no such things. 'Tis all a poet's invention. A horse of brass never flew, and a king's daughter never talked with birds. These are all tales. Pray try and cure yourself. Take hellebore. Pray to avoid the fiend. Read no more books of voyages, they are nothing but lies.[3]

Manning was not dissuaded, and in 1806 he set sail on an East India Company ship bound for Canton.

Once in Canton, Manning's attempts to travel to Beijing were repeatedly frustrated by the restrictive travel policies of the Qing dynasty. Seeing no other alternative, he sailed for Calcutta where he hoped to enlist the aid of the E. I. C. No such aid was forthcoming—perhaps due to lack of interest in the project, perhaps due to Manning himself. For this traveler clearly did not ingratiate himself to employees of the E.I.C. Among Company officials, the eighteenth-century style accommodation to local customs as well as Hastings' style of Orientalist relativism were being replaced by an insistence on the value of Anglicized customs and mores. Manning, with his taste for the exotic, with flowing "Tartar robes" of his own design and an unfashionably long beard, failed to win allies when he criticized the impracticality of the displaced Britons' insistence on wearing English dress in India. From his own report, Manning observed to Company men:

> [H]ow lucky it was the Russians had no settlement [in Calcutta], for their fur dresses would be an intolerable nuisance to them. The person to whom I addressed it could not say, "Oh, they would leave them off," because they would be aware that I should say, "No more than you your neckcloth."[4]

As if to put further distance between himself and the Anglifying companymen, Manning acquiesced to Hindu forms of ritual while in Calcutta, visiting Hindu temples and prostrating himself before their images.[5] No wonder then that Manning, disguised in his approximation of a Hindu holy man's garb, departed India for Lhasa without Company sanction, with only his Chinese servant to help him on his way.

Trained in Chinese language and culture as well as in a European belief in the excellence of Chinese civilization, Manning initially reads Tibetans as an uncouth and grimy people. Early in the journey, he remarks that the "politeness [of the Chinese], even in the common soldiers, forms a contrast with the barbarians of this place."[6] Comparing Chinese to Tibetan houses, Manning notes:

> These [Chinese] post-houses, though from the barrenness of the country they are miserably furnished, yet compared with the ordinary Tibet men's houses, they are elegant and comfortable. The Chinese are really civilized, and do not live like cattle; and it is a comfort, after having lodged in smoke and dirt with the native animals of Tibet, to take shelter in a Chinaman's house, where you are sure of urbanity and cleanliness at least. (p. 242)

Part of Manning's alliance with things and people Chinese may be a result of his training; unable to speak with Tibetans, he takes on a "Chinese-centered" view of them by default. But when Manning is allowed to interact with Tibetans on his own terms, he gains a different impression and shows that he is willing to change his mind. While staying overnight in a Tibetan house, Manning notes the "pleasant faces, and great kindness of manners" of his Tibetan hosts (p. 246). Later, after the owner brings him and his servant some hot coals to warm their room, Manning writes:

I was sorry I could not talk with him. As for using the medium of my servant, who spoke bad Tibetan fluently enough, it would have been to no purpose. His impertinent, insolent manner did not at all harmonize with ours. I was vexed and pained to see him encroach upon their kindness, and imperiously demand their services. . . . Though I could not speak, I tried to express by my manners and countenance that their kindness was not thrown away upon me; and as in these cases there is undoubtedly a great sympathy, I trust they partly understood my sentiments. (pp. 246–7)

Manning's servant—who is referred to by the Persian and Urdu term "*munshi*" or "scribe" throughout—does not represent all Chinese for Manning; Manning is aware of the Catholic convert's idiosyncrasies, his indifference and lack of affection as well as "his sublime crossness" (p. 231). Appalled by his servant's behavior, which comes perhaps from the same discourse of Chinese superiority to Tibetans to which Manning himself is often inclined, Manning's feelings for his fellows win out.

But Manning's affection for individual Tibetans does not translate into love of the country. Manning loves the *idea* of China, but he has no corresponding emotion for the concept of Tibet. As Manning nears Lhasa, the city that would preoccupy Western travelers later in the century, he remarks indifferently: "As there was no use in hurrying now [to meet Chinese officials], we proceeded calmly on" (p. 255). When, nearly a century later, Younghusband arrived in Lhasa in 1904, he waxed ecstatic about his first glimpse of the gilded roofs of the Potala, The Dalai Lama's palace: "The goal of so many travellers' ambitions was actually in sight!"[7] But Manning, the first Briton to see the place, is fairly nonchalant about it all and compares it with the Vatican:

As soon as we were clear of the town, the palace of the Grand Lama presented itself to our view. . . . As we approached I perceived that under the palace on one side lay a considerable extent of marshy land. This brought to my mind the Pope, Rome, and what I had read of the Pontine marshes. (p. 255)

Christian missionaries in Tibet had earlier noted a similarity between the signs of Tibetan religion and their own; Manning makes a similar comparison between the Vatican and Lhasa, but ultimately such a likeness has little personally emotive power for the secularized Englishman. There is, nonetheless, some grandeur to the palace: it is "a majestic mountain of building" with a "magnificent effect" (p. 256).

In comparison to the Potala, which "exceeded [his] expectations," the city of Lhasa "far fell short of them:"

There is nothing striking, nothing pleasing in its appearance. The habitations are begrimed with smut and dirt. The avenues are full of dogs, some growling and gnawing bits of hide which lie about in profusion, and emit a charnel-house smell; others limping and looking livid; others ulcerated; others starved and dying, and pecked at by the ravens; some dead and preyed upon. (p. 256)

Instead of reading such signs as material proof of Tibet's barbarity, however, Manning figures them as dream-like:

In short, everything seems mean and gloomy, and excites the idea of something unreal. Even the mirth and laughter of the inhabitants I thought dreamy and ghostly. The dreaminess no doubt was in my mind, but I never could get rid of the idea; it strengthened upon me afterwards. (pp. 256–7)

Clearly, Lhasa was not the home of opulence and wonder suggested by some European accounts of the East. Its "meanness" and grime seem to alienate Manning from it. But interestingly, Manning does not come to any conclusions about the barbarity of the place from these perceptions. As he suggests, he does not really *see* the town at all; his alienation from it leads him to create a dreamy image of the place. Upon his departure from Tibet, George Bogle had described his time in Xigatse as an episode from a "fairy dream," "a perfect illusion."[8] In Manning's case, he places the dreaminess not in Lhasa but in his own mind.

Later writers would make much of Tibet's mysterious and otherworldly qualities, lingering on its dreamy qualities. If there is any romance of this scene, however, Manning quickly undercuts it; his next entry begins not with some declaration of wonder but the plain assertion that on their first morning in Lhasa [O]ur first care was to provide ourselves with new hats" (p. 258).

In Lhasa, disguised as a "priest" and doctor from India, Manning is not averse to kow-towing to Chinese officials. He does such things because he wants to. But Manning often resists living up to other people's expectations. Loathe to follow custom for custom's sake, he is averse to doing anything he does not *feel* like doing. Because he wants to, he bows down before Tibetan officials, even if such an act jeopardizes his position with the Chinese representatives of the emperor, or *ambans,* in Lhasa. But the moment he feels expected or required to perform some action, he is likely to refuse. Faced with Tibetan prayer wheels outside a temple, for example, Manning responds:

I do not know whether it was expected of me to twirl these machines. I certainly never did all the time I was in Tibet; for though I am a great conformist in certain ways, take me in another line and I am a most obstinate non-conformist, and would sooner die than swerve a little. (pp. 253–4)

Though Bogle and Turner had participated in local customs for the sake of diplomacy, changing values within the E. I. C. led many of Manning's contemporaries to frown on such respect for local images and customs. Manning seems to resist performing local rituals—at least in this case—for a different reason: his participation in such actions must be based not on diplomatic expediency but on his own inclination. Without sympathy, without proper emotion, such rituals can only be empty.

Given Manning's resistance to doing rituals for rituals' sake, his behavior before the young Dalai Lama is especially significant. The first Briton to lay eyes on a Dalai Lama does not describe or dramatize the arrangements that would bring him to the Potala palace in his diary; one day he is just there, in disguise, before the seven-year-old Lungtok Gyatso:

> I presented my gifts, delivering the coin with a handsome silk scarf with my own hands into the hands of the Grand Lama and the Ti-mu-fu.[9] While I was ketesing [curtsying, perhaps doing prostrations in the Tibetan manner], the awkward servants contrived to let fall and break the bottle of lavender water intended for the Ti-mu-fu. While I seemed not to observe it, though the odiferous stream flowed close to me, and I could not help seeing it with the corner of my eye as I bowed down my head. Having delivered the scarf to the Grand Lama, I took off my hat and humbly gave him my clean-shaved head to lay his hands upon. (p. 265)

Manning had begun his journey with an indifference and even a distaste for Tibetans. But here, like Bogle and Turner in front of the Panchen Lama, Manning is respectful before the young incarnation. And like his predecessors in Tibet, Manning lingers on the "Grand Lama's" charming human attributes:

> The Lama's beautiful and interesting face and manner engrossed almost all my attention. He was at that time about seven years old: had the simple and unaffected manners of a well-educated princely child. His face was, I thought, poetically and affectingly beautiful. He was of a gay and cheerful disposition; his beautiful mouth perpetually unbending into a graceful smile, which illuminated his whole countenance. Sometimes, particularly when he had looked at me, his smile almost approached to a gentle laugh. No doubt my grim beard and spectacles somewhat excited his risibility, though I have

afterwards, at the New Year's festival, seen him smile and unbend freely, while sitting myself unobserved in a corner, and watching his reception of various persons, and the notice he took of the strange variety of surrounding objects. (pp. 265–6)

In terms similar to Turner's, Manning praises the young lama's fine manners, gentle humor, and acute perceptiveness. Before this princely child, the scruffy Manning is humbled. He does not assume his superiority—indeed, he has to work to measure *up* to the lama. When the lama asks about his journey to Lhasa, Manning returns the "proper answer:"

I said I had had troubles, but now that I had the happiness of being in his presence, they were amply compensated. I thought of them no more. I could see that this answer pleased both the Lama and his household people. They thus found that I was not a mere rustic, but had some tincture of civility in me. (p. 266)

Recognizing that the Tibetan may not immediately credit him with manners, Manning is eager to give the right answer, one that will both prove his good breeding and please the lama. Apparently, at this point, his feelings are commensurate with his actions. He responds to the lama emotionally:

I was extremely affected by this interview with the Lama. I could have wept through strangeness of sensation. I was absorbed in reflections when I got home. I wrote this memorandum, "This day I saluted the Grand Lama! Beautiful youth. Face poetically affecting; could have wept. Very happy to have seen him and his blessed smile. Hope often to see him again." (p. 266)

In this passage, Manning does not focus on the regal position occupied by the Dalai Lama. It is not his position as "god-king" that impresses Manning; instead, he emphasizes the young lama's inspiring human qualities—his graciousness, his beauty, his smile. The romanticized poetry of his face stirs something within the traveler. This something, however, is not epiphany—it is a mood, a feeling, which, while it does make him more sympathetic to a Tibetan does not lead him to reveries about the altered state of his own soul.

Neither does it make him sympathetic to Tibetan religion in general. In the passage above, Manning's response to the lama has less to do with the lama's position within the Tibetan hierarchy than it does with his divinely human qualities. In effect, Manning disconnects the lama's status as religious leader from his affection for him. (I am reminded of some contemporary Westerners' inclinations to adulate the present Dalai Lama as a holy man apart from his position within the Tibetan hierarchy.) Manning's affection, however, does not lead him to take on the religion of the lama as his own. Sticking to a more Enlightenment view of things, he chooses to rely on a more relativistic and individualist approach, one underwritten by contemporary intellectual currents in England.

Thus, faced soon after with multiple-armed images, prayer wheels, and throngs of pious Tibetans, Manning remains unmoved. While visiting the Jokhang temple Manning does not want to participate in the action; instead, like a tourist, he asks for explanations. His Chinese servant encourages him to show some respect to the images—after all, he is posing as an Indian doctor, and his failure to participate may arouse suspicion. But because Manning has no feeling for these "saint images," he can only stand and observe (p. 290). As a reply to his *munshi*, Manning writes:

> I had no more objective to bowing to the image than he had to a paper, a roll or other missive coming from the Emperor. When I entered the temples in Bengal, if there were natives about, I always made a salaam. All religions as they are established have a mixture in them of good and evil, and upon the whole they all perhaps tend to civilize and ameliorate mankind: as such I respect them. As for the common idea that all the founders of all religions except our own were impostors, I consider it a vulgar error. I have expressed this opinion long before I visited Lhasa. (p. 291)

It is not that he is against religion, or even against performing other peoples' rituals: in this entry, it is the tendency of religions to claim their unique access to the truth that disturbs Manning. When he can be relativistic about religion, that's fine; but if he is asked to assent to the ultimate validity of any particular creed, he will resist. Doubting Christianity's sole claim to the truth in Enlightenment fashion, Manning believes in the potential of divinity on earth—among humans and in one self. His multiple and diverging responses towards Tibetan religion, like Bogle's, express something of Europe's shifting and multiple understandings of Asian others.

Though he resists Tibetan Buddhist ritual, Manning's admiration for the Dalai Lama is indicative of a larger shift in his evaluation of Tibetans. By the end of the journey, Manning reorients his thinking about the relationship between Tibetans and Chinese and his position within both groups. The Chinese officials have come to doubt his identity as a Hindu holy man and doctor and are threatening to oust him. Suspecting that the Chinese do not recognize him as an equal, Manning allies himself with Tibetans who are also subject to the capricious will of the Chinese *ambans* in Lhasa. Rather than simply accepting the Chinese discourse of the bar-

baric Tibetan, Manning comes to understand its relativity. Changing his earlier tune, Manning notes that because the Chinese see Tibet as an uncivilized outpost, they send their worst officials there. Such a policy

> no doubt displeases the Grand Lama and Tibetans in general, and tends to prevent their affections from settling in favour of the Chinese government. I cannot help thinking, from what I have seen and heard, that they would view the Chinese influence in Tibet overthrown without many emotions of regret; especially if the rulers under the new influence were to treat the Grand Lama with respect, for this is a point in which these haughty mandarins are somewhat deficient, to the no small dissatisfaction of the good people of Lhasa. (p. 274)

For Manning, the Chinese are alien rulers in Tibet whom Tibetans might be happier without. And just as Tibetans are subject to their despotic rule, he finds himself at the mercy of Manchu officials.

Manning is accused of illegally entering Tibet and thus violating the Qing dynasty policy. Faced with the prospect of execution for his crime, Manning applies an English notion of justice and rights to offer a criticism of Chinese modes of power; this criticism allies him with Tibetans who are similarly subject to what Manning feels is an arbitrary and unbending Chinese authority:

> I never could, even in idea, make up my mind to submit to an execution with firmness and manliness. The sight of the despotic pomp of mandarins at Canton, where I was perfectly secure, has almost turned me sick. What I read of their absolute power, not only in China, but in various Asiatic countries, has always appalled me. I put myself in imagination into the situation of the prisoner accused; I suppose myself innocent; I look round, I have no resource, no refuge; instruments of torture, instruments of execution are brought by florid, high-cheeked, busy, grinning, dull-hearted men; no plea avails; no kind judge to take my part, as in England, but, on the contrary, because I am accused (and perhaps by my judge) I am presumed guilty. They harshly and inequitably examine, not to discover whether I am guilty or not, but in order to force out the conclusion that I am guilty. I am before evil-minded men, void of conscience, who proceed according to the forms and violate the spirit of justice. . . (pp. 278–9)

Despite some European tendencies to glorify Chinese order and morality and his own earlier willingness to praise Chinese civilization, Manning, as the accused, shifts his point of view. He now sees the Chinese *ambans* as devoid of morality, law, and compassion:

> If one is before a generous-minded man, who is wantonly exercising his power, one may appeal to what is noble in his nature, and excite a flame that will dissipate his malice and dark suspicions; but these evil-minded men, who outwardly are perfect politeness, and inwardly are perfect selfishness, have no touchwood in their heart; nothing for the spark to catch hold of; one may as well strike fire against the barren sand as appeal to their hearts. (p. 279)

True barbarity seems not to reside in the outward signs of grime and dirt but rather in the semblance of civility that covers an evil heart. For Manning, there is no kindness, no humanity in the Chinese *ambans;* their politeness and civility only serve to disguise their selfish and evil nature, and this darkness is structured, in turn, into their system of justice. Whereas, in Manning's view, an English court could account for and respond to his very human plight, the Chinese allow no emotion to color their adherence to the letter of the law.

Manning's earlier idealization of all things Chinese has been revised, supported in part by Orientalist notions of the Orientalist despot and the English notion of protected freedoms and rights. His account of the despotic nature of Chinese law and his characterization of the Chinese as evil serves to elevate both Tibetans and himself as victims. As Lopez describes it, the tendency to demonize the Chinese, rooted in nineteenth-century images of the Oriental despot, persists in the tendency to imagine China as allied with "the powers of darkness" and Tibet as connected to "the powers of light."[10] While the methods of coercing confessions and torturing victims employed by both Qing dynasty official and Communist functionaries may be real enough, the interpretations of them, whether offered by Manning or by contemporary supporters of Tibet, almost inevitably fall into dichotomizing and racist discourses. The conflict then is translated into manichean terms: good versus evil, light versus dark, God versus the devil, civilized versus uncivilized.

Despite Manning's view of his predicament, however, he is not executed for entering Lhasa without permission; he is only forced to return the way he came. No doubt Manning's humiliation and frustration at not reaching Beijing contribute to his sorrowful leave-taking, but his entries focus on his departure from the Dalai Lama and his regent:

> April 6. I took leave of the Grand Lama with a sorrowful heart. I said I would tell my king (Governor of Bengal) that I was well-treated. His heart rejoices. I thank the Grand Lama, and promise that if afterwards a Lhasa man comes to Bengal it shall not be forgotten. I take leave of Ti-mu-fu. Sorrowful. Receive presents. . . . Make up things. Rather sorrowful. (p. 294)

Bogle was "particularly affected" upon his departure from the "Teshu" Lama; Turner's departure also arouses his emotion. Manning seems similarly moved. After this entry, Manning effectively suspends journal-keeping altogether; all that follows of the outward journey is a record of dates and overnight stops. The lack of elaboration of the return journey places departure as the final event in the account; it is almost as if Manning could say no more. In terms of the narrative, the departure is neither a conclusion nor a culmination—the account is too unstructured for that. Nevertheless, the heartfelt departure remains the last event on the books—a turning point, a farewell.

So what happens to Manning in Tibet? He had begun his journey with an attraction towards things Chinese and an indifference towards the Tibetans. Although he is willing to use the colonial apparatus whenever it can aid him in his travels, Manning has no desire to uphold the values of the E.I.C. Indeed, as his time in Calcutta suggests, he tries to distance himself from colonial culture. Instead of extracting wealth from the "Orient," he is more concerned with experiencing the unique civilization of China. Classically trained, willing to think relatively about European customs, Manning depends upon European constructions of "the East" gleaned initially from textual sources. Once in Tibet, however, Manning is confronted with the distance between what he has learned and what he sees. While he does not abandon his admiration for Chinese culture, it is modified by his experience. As the journey proceeds, his encounters with individuals help to revise his views; a discourse of human affection and emotion that seeks society and exchange with others displaces his attraction to the Chinese. Self-motivated and self-defined, Manning strives to make "his own" meaning, and increasingly tries to listen to the dictates of his emotions—or rather, he increasingly interprets his experience through a discourse of feeling. Tapping into a Romantic discourse about the possibility of divinity in the human, Manning finds himself attracted to the young Dalai Lama—not as an abstracted or generalized Tibetan, but as a mannered and beautiful individual. By the end of the journey, Manning expresses a sympathy for the Tibetans who, like himself at the moment, are subject to the mean spirit of the *ambans*. Over the course of the journey/journal, Manning alters his interpretive schemes. In this way, his position vis-à-vis the Tibetans shifts. Indeed, in that sense, the world shifts a bit for Manning.

But sympathy is not epiphany. If we focus on the textual nature of epiphany, it is clear that the unfinished nature of his account precludes any such outcome. The epiphany, if there was one, is not written—not textualized; it could only be read between the lines. In this way, there is something

Bogle-like in his movements, his unwillingness to be pinned down, his refreshing propensity to contradict himself, to change his mind, to resist.

Readers of Manning's text in 1876 were probably little concerned with his reflective agility; for them, Manning offered a view of Tibet, fragments that contributed to the European effort to chart, describe, and interpret the far-flung parts of the globe. For those readers, Manning was the first of the gate-crashers, an eccentric whose quirky account might be rehabilitated for the colonial and intellectual cause.[11] As Lopez argues, in the nineteenth century, "Tibet was . . . an object of imperial desire, and the failure of the European powers to dominate it politically only increased European longing and fed the fantasy about the land beyond the Snowy Range."[12] Colonial Britain did what they could to gather knowledge about the place, seeking out details concerning Tibet's geography, botany, strategic position, culture, and religion. Indeed, while Bogle, Turner, and Manning could say little about the intricacies of Tibetan Buddhism, the work that would untangle and represent that tradition began in earnest in the nineteenth century as Western scholars turned their attention to that curious object, Tibetan religion. Focusing largely on the texts of the tradition, these figures created representations of Tibet and Tibetan religion that both draw on Bogle and Turner and contribute to the later construction of Tibetan epiphany.

Postscript

As I have suggested, Manning's criticisms of Chinese power in Tibet anticipate contemporary criticisms of Chinese human rights' violations in Tibet. Similarly, Manning's run-in with the Chinese authorities in Lhasa is a kind of precursor to later foreigners' encounters with the law. Unlike Manning, when I first went to Tibet in 1985, at the age of 23, I was not at all inclined to idealize the Chinese I met there. My inclinations were all the reverse. I had a hard time separating my disdain for the policies of the Chinese government from Han Chinese citizens: all Chinese were to blame, in my mind, and I fixed on the numerous fights I saw in Lhasa between Tibetans and Han Chinese, the apathetic attitudes of Chinese store clerks, and the profound social distance between Chinese and Tibetans I witnessed all over the country. On my second journey to Tibet in 1987—having had my own epiphanies and become a staunch pro-Tibet activist—I carried political literature written in Tibetan from Dharamsala. I gave some of this literature to a group of monks at Tashilhunpo. This was a mistake: in such a situation, even a dissident would be forced to turn me in, as anyone else in the group could be a collaborator. Sure enough, later in the day I was picked up in the market by a Chinese policeman, escorted to the police station, and questioned through Tibetan interpreters: Didn't I know Tibet was part of China? Didn't I know that pro-independence literature was illegal? Didn't I know that the Dalai Lama was a reactionary? After having my passport confiscated, I was made to stay in Xigatse. I could remain in my hotel but had to return to the police station every afternoon for three days so I could be questioned by a Chinese-speaking policeman and his two Tibetan interpreters. I was sure that I would be deported. But the policeman's manner of questioning allowed me some leeway: he tended to ask a series of questions. After they were laboriously translated, I would answer the most innocuous one. Or, drawing on the current Chinese policy of separating the Dalai Lama's political status from his power as a religious figure, I ventured, "Since these texts are written by the Dalai Lama, aren't they just religious literature?" And I played the stupid American tourist (an easy task, since I was one)—"I thought since his photo was legal, his writings would be too." Eventually, I was made to write a lengthy self-criticism and confession; my passport was returned to me, and I was free to go on to Lhasa.

The Tibetan man, Sonam, in whose hotel I was staying at the time, had been imprisoned for 20 years. When he first learned I knew a little Tibetan—and before I got in trouble—he quietly led me in to see his elaborate altar room. Then, the next day, when I was taken to the station in a police jeep, Sonam peeked out from the shadows of his doorway. He was afraid, I think, that I would turn him in. His altar room was perfectly legal by that time, and yet there was that fear—the fear of quixotic Chinese law. After several days of agonizing in which I fancied I learned something about the fear Sonam felt, the police returned my passport. I boarded the bus for Lhasa. I'm sure that Sonam was glad to see me go.

CHAPTER 5

Barbarian Translations and Impure Forms: Hodgson, Waddell, Blavatsky

Neither Bogle nor Turner could count Tibetan religion as an instance of Buddhism, but the work that would eventually describe, name, and classify the thing that most Tibetans practiced was already in its formative stages. As we have seen, Orientalists in the late eighteenth century began formal study of Indian religion and language, locating the truth of Indian religion in written documents rather than in current practices; for them, texts provided evidence of a by-gone Hindu Golden Age. Although they focused on what later came to be known as Brahmanism and Hinduism, even then Buddhism was an area of interest. Positing similarities between the living religions of Siam, Burma, Ceylon, Tibet, and China, European scholars in the early nineteenth century began to classify various practices, beliefs, and texts as part of the religion of Buddha or Buddhism.[1] By the 1830s, Europeans understood Buddhism as defining the religious beliefs and practices of most of Asia. As Philip Almond notes in *The British Discovery of Buddhism,* during this period, Buddhism became "an object" for Western scholars; it took "form as an entity that existed over and against the various cultures which [could] be perceived as instancing it, manifesting it, in an enormous variety of ways."[2] For the Orientalists, texts were the basis of this entity; texts provided a standard against which diverse practices and customs could be measured. With this value for scripture as the source of authentic, stable, and pure Buddhism, British scholars turned to the case of Tibetan religion. Two British scholar-officials are of special note for their work in this field: Brian Houghton Hodgson and L. Austine Waddell.

The attempt to be comprehensive in Hodgson's work is evident from the title of his collected studies: *Essays in the Languages, Literatures, Religion of Nepal and Tibet Together with Further Papers on the Geography, Ethnology, and Commerce of those Countries.* Trained at the College of Fort William in Calcutta, Hodgson conducted his researches on Tibet from Nepal, where he acted as assistant resident, postmaster, and resident of Kathmandu between 1820 and 1842. Forbidden to travel to Tibet, Hodgson turned practical difficulty into methodological directive and argued that texts were the best source for the study of Buddhism.[3]

For Hodgson, Sanskrit texts represent the pinnacle of Buddhist thought. He writes: "Buddhism arose in an age and a country celebrated for literature [India]; and the consequence was, that its disciplines were fixed by means of one of the most perfect languages in the world (Sanskrit), during, or immediately after, the age of its founder."[4] In a kind of scholarly fundamentalism, Hodgson suggests that later translations and commentaries only distort an original and self-evident perfection. So confident is Hodgson in the superiority and authority of Sanskrit texts to Pali versions, vernacular translations, and to lived religion that he declares his desire to "separate Buddhism *as it is* . . . and Buddhism as it ought to be."[5] The irony is that Shakyamuni Buddha himself probably spoke the vernacular Magadhi, and the earliest Buddhist texts were probably not written in either Sanskrit and Pali but in the vernacular Prakrit.

But for Hodgson, Sanskrit is a lofty and pure tongue. (That no living Buddhist community spoke Sanskrit as its mother tongue may have contributed to his sense that contemporary Buddhism was impoverished). Echoing William Jones's work, Hodgson finds Sanskrit comparable to Greek in that both are "capable of giving a soul to the objects of sense, and a body to the abstractions of metaphysics" (p. 66). Through Sanskrit, he argues, scholars may discover "very many things inscrutably hidden from those who were reduced to consult barbarian translations from the most refined and copious of languages upon the most subtle and interminable of topics" (p. 110). Discrediting the research of Alexander Csoma de Körös, a Hungarian scholar who studied Tibetan language and texts, Hodgson argues that Csoma de Körös's "attainments in Tibetan lore have been comparatively useless" (p. 65) because he has relied on "Tibetan translations of my Sanskrit originals" (p. 66).[6] Dubious of the authenticity of vernacular translations, Hodgson notes:

> [W]hoever will duly reflect upon the dark and profound abstractions, and the infinitesimally-multiplied and microscopically distinguished personifications of Buddhism, may well doubt whether the language of *Tibet* does or can adequately sustain the weight that has been laid on it. (pp. 66, emphasis in original)

For Hodgson, Tibetan texts are "barbarian translations" (p. 110); indeed, it is remarkable to him "that literature of any kind should be . . . so widely diffused as to reach persons covered with filth" (p. 9).

Despite Hodgson's conviction that "documentary is superior to verbal evidence" and his suspicion of those scholars who "prate about mere local rites and opinions," he maintains that local informants can be of some use for study: "[W]hatever may be the general intellectual inferiority of the orientals of our day, let us not suppose that the living followers of Buddha cannot be profitably interrogated touching the creed they live and die in" (p. 100). But this profitability too resides in their association with the *texts* of Buddhism; living Buddhists guard against the complete degeneration of their religion "by the possession and use of original scriptures, or of faithful translations of them, which were made in the best age of the church" (p. 100).

Hodgson participates in a larger Victorian tendency to create an ideal textual Buddhism with which scholars judged the practices of living Buddhists. As Almond argues, "[T]hose who saw Buddhism in the East in the second half of the [nineteenth] century could not but measure it against what it was textually said to be, could not but find it wanting and express this in the language of decay, degeneration, and decadence."[7] In effect, Hodgson and others like him sacralize the texts that seem to comprise Buddhism—canonize them: texts become the source of the sacred truth about Buddhism, a truth to which Europe has privileged and seemingly unprejudiced access. Edward Said uses the term "textual attitude" to describe the Orientalist preference for "the schematic authority of a text to the disorientations of direct encounters with the human."[8] By the middle of the nineteenth century, Western scholarship had thoroughly integrated the textual attitude such that, in Almond's words:

> [T]he Buddhism that existed "out there" was beginning to be judged by a West that alone knew what Buddhism was, is, and ought to be. The essence of Buddhism came to be seen as expressed not "out there" in the Orient, but in the West through the West's control of Buddhism's own textual past.[9]

Hodgson's desire to "fix" Buddhism—by locating it in texts and in the Sanskrit language—serves to wrest Buddhism from Asians and give it to Europe. Hodgson sees Buddhist practice—the historical and cultural forms of Buddhism as it is lived out in symbolic and ritual forms by living human beings—as necessarily degenerate and inferior. For Hodgson, we might say, the really good Buddhism is a dead Buddhism, a corpse/corpus, which European scholars might preserve and position to their own liking. Such an orientation would profoundly shape later European understandings of Tibetan religion.

The value for textualized Buddhism is also part of L. Austine Waddell's influential study of 1895. *The Buddhism of Tibet, or, Lamaism* strives to differentiate authentic Buddhism from what Tibetans actually do, which in Waddell's eyes is to (mistakenly) institutionalize reverence for lamas.[10] Because Tibet was officially off-limits to European travelers, Waddell, like Hodgson, had to conduct his researches in Tibetan religion from border regions, in his case, Darjeeling and Sikkim. From there he could read what was available and conduct original, primary research. For departing from Hodgson, Waddell was expressly concerned with what Tibetan Buddhists actually practiced— going so far as to purchase a monastery in Darjeeling where he could undertake his investigations. He writes, "[R]ealizing the rigid secrecy maintained by Lamas in regard to their seemingly chaotic rites and symbolism, I felt compelled to purchase a Lamaist temple with its fittings; and prevailed on the officiating priests to explain to me in full detail the symbolism and the rites as they proceeded."[11] Despite this interest in practice, however, his work begins from the notion that real Buddhism lies in texts.

Waddell's purpose in his massive study is to exhaustively represent Tibetan Buddhism to English readers. With section headings that include items on history, doctrine, monastic institutions, buildings, mythology, gods, rituals, sorcery, festivals, plays, and popular lamaism, Waddell strives to present to Britain a kind of encyclopedia of Tibetan Buddhism. To this end, he quotes Bogle and Turner verbatim for several pages in his chapter "Hierarchy and Reincarnate Lamas." The quoted sections include descriptions of the Panchen Lamas encountered by these eighteenth-century travelers, and Waddell makes few comments on the excerpts. There are long sections from Markham's edition of Bogle which include physical descriptions of the lama as well as the passage in which Bogle attests to the lama's admirable human qualities:

> For although venerated as God's vicegerent through all the eastern countries of Asia, endowed with a portion of omniscience, and with many other divine attributes, he throws aside in conversation all the awful part of his character, accommodates himself to the weakness of mortals, endeavours, to make himself loved rather than feared, and behaves with the greatest affability to everybody, especially to strangers.[12]

Waddell ends his quotation of Bogle with the passage in which Bogle observes the behavior of the monks gathered to see the Panchen Lama return to Tashilhunpo; Bogle declares that he felt "the same emotions with

the Lama's votaries" and confesses that "I never knew a man whose manners pleased me so much, or for whom, upon such a short acquaintance, I
had half the heart's liking."[13] For Waddell these passages are useful for their
depiction of the lama; he appears not to take issue with Bogle's affection
for the holy man. As Waddell presents them, these passages simply suggest
Bogle's kindness and sentimentality and not the ambiguity and contradiction that mark Bogle's texts.

When Waddell turns to Turner's text, he is more inclined to judge the
material, declaring Turner's account of his meeting with the infant lama
"remarkable" and quoting the strange passage in which Turner, through an
evocation of Hastings, seems to accept the Tibetan notion of reincarnation:
as he writes, the governor-general was overwhelmed with grief until "' the
cloud that had overcast the happiness of this nation was dispelled by his
reappearance.'"[14] For Waddell what matters is not so much how these lamas
are represented but that their representations can furnish information for
his exhaustive study. In his desire to be comprehensive, to gather all that is
known about Tibet, Waddell must cite Bogle and Turner, but he does so in
a relatively uncritical fashion. The quotes are used to simply present "the
facts" about the two lamas they met; one does not get the impression that
Waddell was in any way moved by these accounts to rethink his own relation to Tibetans. For Waddell Tibetans are people to be studied, their religion something to be discussed, analyzed, and critiqued, but neither
Tibetans nor Tibetan religion are things that one would want to use in any
direct way for one's own spiritual or intellectual life.

Waddell makes his attitude towards Tibetan religion clear on the first
page of his study:

> To understand the origin of Lamaism and its place in the Buddhist system, we
> must recall the leading features of primitive Buddhism, and glance at its
> growth, to see the points at which the strange creeds and cults crept in, and
> the gradual crystallization of these into a religion differing widely from the
> parent system, and opposed in so many ways to the teaching of Buddha. (p. 5)

For Waddell, the history of Buddhism is the story of a downward spiral
from the Buddha's original lofty teachings. By the time Buddhism reaches
Tibet it is an "impure form . . . covered with foreign accretions and satu-
rated with so much demonology" (p. 29). After this, "the distorted form of
Buddhism introduced into Tibet . . . became still more debased" (p. 15).
What scholars today might interpret as the inevitable adaptation of Buddhism to existing cultural, political, and historical contexts, Waddell is
inclined to read as an ugly syncretism: "Primitive Lamaism may . . . be

defined as a priestly mixture of Sivaite [*sic*] mysticism, magic, and Indo-Tibetan demonology, overlaid by a thin varnish of Mahayana Buddhism. And to the present day, Lamaism still retains this character" (p. 30).

In its texts, nonetheless, as Waddell sees it, Tibetan Buddhism still preserves "much of the loftier philosophy and ethics of the system taught by Buddha himself" (p. 30); but these admirable aspects are compromised by the practices of the lamas who jealously keep this knowledge hidden from lay men and women. Waddell contends that the laity has

> fallen under the double ban of menacing demons and despotic priests. So it will be a happy day, indeed, for Tibet when its sturdy over-credulous people are freed from the intolerable tyranny of the Lamas, and delivered from the devils whose ferocity and exacting worship weigh like a nightmare upon all. (P. 573)

In this Protestant criticism of the power of priests, Waddell reasserts Europe's authority to preserve and define "true" Buddhism as a moral and atheistic creed, one with a systematic and ethical if largely pessimistic philosophy. Thus when Waddell looks into contemporary Buddhist practice, he cannot find even a hint of familiarity; only through projecting an idealized, ancient, pristine form of Buddhism could Waddell and other European scholars construct an image they could value. In other words, if one knows how to read them, texts can show one the truth about Buddhism—one might even glimpse one's ideals there. But if one looks at the living practitioners of Buddhism, they simply fail to measure up.

Postscript

That Waddell succeeded in creating a landmark text is suggested by the numerous reprintings it has undergone. That his book has also been influential in Tibetan self-understandings is suggested by a story told to me by Beatrice Miller, the late anthropologist of Tibet. When a young Tibetan prepared to leave his home in Darjeeling to study in the West, his father presented him with a copy of Waddell's book, with the advice that he should know something about his own religion.

UNBELIEVABLE TRAVELER

Waddell's work helped to put Tibet on the map. As an ostensibly scholarly and "objective" work, his 1895 book was designed not for those who wished to become Tibetan Buddhists but for those who wished to comprehend it as an interesting foreign, and sometimes repugnant, object. But before his volume came out, the work of Helena Petrovna Blavatsky appeared with quite a different emphasis. For unlike the work of the scholars, Blavatsky was expressly interested in what Asian religions (as well as Egyptian religion, the occult, spiritualism, and other esoteric systems) might do for her and her followers personally and spiritually. Thus, before Waddell purchased a Tibetan monastery, Blavatsky and Henry Steele Olcott had named their Manhattan apartment "The Lamasery." Before Waddell compiled his monumental tome on Tibetan religion, HPB (as she was widely known) had used Tibetan religion as one of many ingredients in her own esoteric philosophy. The nebulous, encompassing Theosophical teachings created by Blavatsky drew on the vagueness of knowledge about Tibet and invested the place with mystery and exoticism; Waddell himself was not immune to its charms.

Madame Blavatsky was born in the Ukraine in 1831, cofounded the Theosophical Society in New York in 1875, and claimed, long before Harrer, to have lived in Tibet for seven years. Among her many adventures, this trip to Tibet proved to be most important both for her spiritual quest and the development of Theosophy. For in Tibet, Blavatsky claimed to have met Master Morya and other *"mahatmas"* (Sanskrit for great souls); while not themselves Tibetan, Blavatsky contended that these mahatmas continued to send her messages after she left Tibet, sometimes through dreams and visions, and often through notes which seemed to materialize from nowhere. Blavatsky's relationship with these masters capitalized on and compounded Tibet's mystery, and, at the same time, enhanced Blavatsky's own charisma.

There is reason to doubt that Blavatsky ever traveled to Tibet; similarly, many doubt the authenticity of her occult knowledge. While some assert that Blavatsky was a medium for higher powers, others see her as a plagiarist; scholars have detected over two thousand items lifted from one hundred books in her *Isis Unveiled.* But for the purposes of tracing the trope of epiphany, it does not matter if she traveled to Tibet at all—it matters that she *claimed* to have gone there. By collecting and inventing esoteric knowledge on Tibet, Blavatsky added another dimension to Europe's view of Tibet: Tibet as the home of mystery and the occult. And while she left no account of epiphany as such, her claim to have entered into a program of occult initiation there enhanced the image of Tibet as a place one could go to be transformed. That her book, *The Secret Doctrine,* included what appeared to be an endorsement by the "Tashi" or Panchen Lama can be read as either her debt to Bogle's account or a sign of her authenticity.[15]

Despite the uncertainties about Blavatsky's travels and sources, her texts and personality influenced later travelers in and writers on Tibet. A query made by Waddell, for one, attests to his familiarity with her purported association with mahatmas in Tibet; while on the Younghusband Mission to Tibet in 1904, he asked the Ganden Tri Rinpoche about them. Waddell reports that "this Cardinal [the Thirteenth Dalai Lama's senior tutor], one of the most learned and profound scholars in Tibet, was, like the other learned Lamas I have interrogated on the subject, entirely ignorant of such beings."[16] Rudyard Kipling also knew of Blavatsky, noting in his autobiography, that while in India:

> At one time our little world was full of the aftermaths of Theosophy as taught by Madame Blavatsky to her devotees. My Father knew the lady and, with her, would discuss wholly secular subjects; she being, he told me, one of the most interesting and unscrupulous impostors he had ever met.[17]

If Kipling doubted her spiritual claims, he was not himself immune to the charms of Tibet. Like Blavatsky's *The Secret Doctrine,* Kipling's novel *Kim* uses the figure of the "Teshoo Lama," even as it draws on Bogle's account and, finally, offers epiphany.

CHAPTER 6

Kipling's Kim, Lamas, and Epiphanies

Neither a study of Tibetan religion nor another Tibetan travel account, Rudyard Kipling's novel *Kim,* published in 1901, tells the story of an orphan of Irish descent on the loose in India and follows the travels of young Kim and his sidekick, a Tibetan lama; the travel motif that shapes the novel culminates in the dual, though diverging, epiphanies of both wayfarers. In this fictional coming-of-age story, Kipling draws on available knowledge on Tibet for his portrayal of the lama. In creating the character of the "Teshoo Lama," for example, Kipling uses for his modest monk the title of the second highest incarnation of the Gelukpa sect, described by Bogle and Turner and cited by Blavatsky. His portrayal of the lama seems to draw specifically on the Markham's edition of Bogle's writings, but because Kipling does not cite sources (naturally enough for a work of this sort), it is as if the novel has swallowed Bogle whole.[1] Kipling's book also accepts the textual attitude portrayed in the works of Hodgson and Waddell. Further, the novel significantly uses the trope of epiphany to solve a question of colonial identity. In this way, once epiphany has come into close proximity to a Tibetan character, it will then travel along when the figure of the lama transfers yet again into Younghusband's account.

To first consider the import of the textual attitude towards Buddhism: the novel describes the religion of some hill people as "an almost obliterated Buddhism, overlaid with nature-worship fantastic as their own landscape, elaborate as the terracing of their tiny fields."[2] Figuring Tibetan Buddhism in Waddell's demonizing terms, Kipling refers to Tibetan ritual dances (*cham*) as "devil-dances" and notes the "horned masks, scowling masks, and masks of idiotic terror" used for such rituals (p. 197). Similarly, *thangkas* representing various fierce protective deities are characterized as "fiend-embroidered draperies" (p. 197). To Britons schooled in benevolent images of Jesus and Mary and steeped in the notion of pagan idolatry, such figures can only suggest the worship of dark forces. All in all, such seemingly demonic representations seem to offer support for the view of Buddhism offered by Hodgson and Waddell: various Tibetan excrescences have obscured the dignified Buddhism gathered and translated in European texts.

As if acknowledging these textual sources, Kipling displays a collection of European books on Buddhism in the opening pages of the novel. In the Lahore museum, a building the lama takes for a temple of sorts, the curator shows the Tibetan monk "a mound of books," the physical manifestations of "the labours of European scholars, who by the help of these and a hundred other documents have identified the Holy Places of Buddhism." Kipling's lama is sufficiently reverent before the eminent pile, and his comments on Tibetan religion further ally him with the European criticism of Tibetan superstition: "For five—seven—eighteen—forty years it was in my mind that the Old Law was not well followed, being overlaid . . . with devildom, charms, and idolatry" (p. 56). The lama's estimation of living Buddhism, which corresponds with many European's view of it, elevates him, as does his disdain for elaborate ritual, his humility, and his determination to seek out the truth for himself.

Suggestions of Bogle's influence on Kipling's novel can be found in such small details as Kipling's description of the lama's hat as "a gigantic sort of tam-o'-shanter" (p. 52); Bogle had written that "the Servants and peasants wear horizontal caps made of Locks of Sheeps' wool, died yellow. They are like the Scotch Bonnets, but much larger."[3] But it is especially in the representation of the Teshoo Lama that Bogle's influence can be read. Curiously, in all the critical work on *Kim*—and there is plenty these days— I have encountered no mention of the importance of accounts of the historical Teshoo Lama (or Lamas) for Kipling's lama. Like Bogle's Teshoo Lama, Kipling's lama is dignified, compassionate, kind, and affectionate towards his Anglo friend. Bogle's lama and Kim's lama both occupy important positions in the Tibetan hierarchy, but somehow manage to preserve their modesty. Kipling's lama, like Bogle's, is dignified, soft-spoken, and devoted to his white companion. Both lamas also have a practical side: Kipling's lama can undertake negotiations with Christian clerics and arrange for Kim's educational expenses; Bogle's Third Panchen Lama can deal effectively and fairly with almost any political or economic situation he encounters. And like the Teshoo Lamas met by Bogle and Turner, Kipling's lama has a certain usefulness in colonial machinations. Finally, in the relationship between Kim and his lama there are echoes of the guru-disciple relationship I mentioned in the discussion of Turner. Of course, neither Bogle nor Turner ever designated the relationship as such, but the Tibetan framework provides a productive way to look at these relationships.

With Bogle and the Third Panchen Lama, the Tibetan held the senior position. Turner seems to take Bogle's place in the next Anglo-Tibetan encounter, but here, the usual relationship between the elder man and the younger is confused; Turner bows down before the lama, but he also exercises a certain colonial power over him. The relationship between guru and disciple in the novel *Kim* is also ambiguous. In Buddhist terms, the lama would clearly occupy the place of guru and superior; such a perspective is signaled in the novel by Kim's designation as "*chela,*" or disciple. But within a colonialist framework, Kim, as a white boy/man, is ultimately superior to the Asian lama, despite his age; thus, the lama is deceived in thinking Kim is his disciple in a religious sense, for Kim's devotion to the lama is largely that of a good friend. Indeed, from the novel's point of view, without Kim as protector, without the paternal arm of imperialism, the lama, with his pacifist and innocent ways, could hardly survive. As an Indian character in the novel sums up the situation: "[I]f evil men were not now and then slain it would not be a good world for weaponless dreamers" (p. 100). The lama, despite his presumption that Kim needs him as a teacher, actually depends on the young boy, who guides and protects him.

But Kim also loves the lama and needs something from him. As in the texts of Bogle and Manning, it is especially in scenes of departure that this love and affection are expressed. When Kim leaves the lama to go to St. Xavier's school, his sad farewell echoes Bogle's sorrowful departure from Tashilhunpo. Kim cries, "I have no friend save thee, Holy One. . . . [H]ow shall I ever forget thee?" So attached is Kim to the lama that he almost forgets who he is: "'But whither shall I send my letters?' wailed Kim, clutching at his robe, all forgetful that he was a Sahib." After reciting a proverb on the illusory nature of desire, the lama replies: "'Go to the Gates of Learning. Let me see thee go . . . Dost thou love me? Then go, or my heart cracks'" (pp. 170–1).

On his departure from the Panchen Lama, Bogle was also moved. In writing both to his sister and to Warren Hastings, Bogle emphasized his reluctance to leave. He felt "a hearty regret at parting"[4] and writes that ". . . what from the Lama's pleasant and amiable character, what from the many civilities he had shown me, I could not help being particularly affected [on my departure]."[5] When Turner departed from Tashilhunpo he enacted a ritual of departure; he then turned with an open heart and mind to meet the young Panchen Lama. In *Kim* too the affection between the white boy and the lama becomes heightened on departure. As Kim turns his attention to matters elsewhere and the duties expected of him there, the tension between his allegiance to the lama and his birthright as a white man are heightened. If Bogle failed (or refused) to resolve this tension when he left Tibet, Kim, like Younghusband after him, must make sense of it; he does so through epiphany.

Throughout the novel, both Kim and the lama search for something: the lama for his river and the spiritual revelation it portends, and Kim for an answer to such questions as "Who is Kim?" (p. 166, p. 233) and finally "[W]hat is Kim?" (p. 331). These parallel searches culminate in the final pages of the novel: the lama finds his river and, in a moment of revelation, Kim finds his way in the world. But because Kim's regard for the lama is based on friendship and not discipleship, his epiphany at the end of the novel is not through Buddhism, the lama, or through any expressly religious practices or affiliation. It is essentially a secular epiphany that reinserts him into the world. How is such an experience possible? What is the legacy of this secular revelation? And on what notion of self does the epiphany depend?

As I have noted, tropes of epiphany and the secularized revelation of the divine gained prominence in the nineteenth century, having shifted to secular texts from Christian biographies to Romantic accounts of flashes of intuition in poetry. By the late nineteenth century the idea of secular revelation had become a common trope in novels, poetry, and secular biographies. The literary epiphany is evident in such *fin de siècle* British novels as Charlotte Bronte's *Jane Eyre,* George Eliot's *Middlemarch,* and Henry James's *A Portrait of a Lady.*[6] And, interestingly, a moment of secular revelation also structures Kipling's own autobiography, prepared for publication posthumously by his wife, Caroline Balestier. In *Something of Myself,* Kipling recounts how his "seven years' hard" labor in India was rewarded by a revelation of sorts.

It happened one hot-weather evening, in '86 or thereabouts, when I felt that I had come to the edge of all endurance. As I entered the empty house in the dusk there was no more in me except the horror of a great darkness, that I must have been fighting for some days. Late at night I picked up a book by Walter Besant which was called *All in a Garden Fair.* It dealt with a young man who desired to write; who came to realise the possibilities of common things seen, and who eventually succeeded in his desire. What its merits may be from today's standpoint I do not know. But I *do* know that that book was my salvation in sore personal need, and with the reading and re-reading it became to me a revelation, a hope and a strength. I was certainly, I argued, as well equipped as the hero and—and—after all, there was no need for me to stay here for ever. I could go away and measure myself against the doorsills of London as soon as I had money. Therefore I would begin to save money, for I perceived that there was absolutely no reason outside myself why I should not do exactly what to me seemed good. For proof of my revelation I did, sporadically but sincerely, try to save money, and I built up in my head—always with the book to fall back upon—a dream of the future that sustained me.[7]

This passage portrays the secular and worldly nature of Kipling's revelation as well as the important role a book—a novel—played in that epiphanic moment. A secular text offers the young man guidance—it presents a version of secular faith. The terms "salvation" and "revelation" have shifted from an expressly religious context and now give meaning to a life devoted to writing, to a life concerned with "common things seen," to life in the world. And although it is fictional, the text Kipling reads is seen as telling something of the truth; the novel as a genre has acquired a crypto-religious status, conforming to Thomas Carlyle's dicta that it provide readers "'edification,' 'healing,' guidance,' and 'a divine awakening voice.'"[8] In Kipling's version of himself, the budding novelist emerges from his reading with a new direction. Besant's novel provides not only—or not even—a structure for his life; the epiphanic moment gives a structure to Kipling's account of that life. Kipling is able to make sense out of his life through an established interpretive framework; a textualized "enlightenment" gives his (textual) self coherence.

Creating a coherent textual persona was not a priority for Bogle, as I have argued. Throughout his texts we see him continually move, take up various positions and points of view, change his mind, and contradict himself. Bogle's relationship with Tibetan others oscillates between utter indifference, to self-reflection and even to self-revision. In his day, the difference between European self and Asian other is still under negotiation. But by the late nineteenth century, the difference between self and other has become increasingly fixed, supported as it is by a wealth of knowledge and colonial lore that delineates the utter alterity of the Asian other. Such an assertion of difference, however, does not come without a struggle.

The tendency of colonial ideology to dichotomize the colonizer and the colonized was often belied by participants' experience of that relation; as Nandy argues, given the "shared culture" created in colonialism, as a child Kipling himself was prone to identify with Indian culture as much as with British. The young, India-born Kipling spoke Hindustani with ease, was dark-skinned, and in his earliest years was raised largely by Indian servants with whom he entered into easy exchanges of intimacy. (Nandy describes a scene in which Kipling as a child was visiting a farm with his parents: "[H]e walked away holding the hand of a[n Indian] farmer, saying to his mother in Hindustani, 'Goodbye, this is my brother.' ")[9] From this early identification, Kipling was thrust into public school life in England, where he learned to internalize manichean colonial ideology; as Nandy notes:

> [H]is oppressive English years inevitably gave Kipling the message that England was a part of his true self, that he would have to disown his Indianness and learn not to identify with the victims, and that the victimhood he had known in England could be avoided, perhaps even glorified, through identification with the aggressors, especially through loyalty to the aggressor's values. (p. 68)

The disowning of Indian-ness and the assertion of a coherent English self comes at a cost, however: the inability to confront the Indian parts of himself and thus the loss of a significant part of his development and formative identity. In this way, Nandy suggests, Kipling becomes "the English counterpart of the type he was later to despise: the bi-cultural Indian babu" (p. 67). Or, to return to the metaphor of reflection, Kipling becomes the mirror image of the hybridized "native" so despised by colonial ideology; he becomes a "bi-cultural sahib" (p. 69) who is forced to deny the very fundamental ways in which his experience has been shaped by exchange and contact with the colonized.

The question of identity is also a significant one for Kim, and much of the novel is devoted to his dawning realization that despite looking, talking, and living like a "native," he is nonetheless a white man and should act like one. Thus twice in the novel Kim verges on an important revelation, only to fall short of it. But just as Kipling despairs and is repaired, by the end of the novel, Kim too suffers and is cured. As in Kipling's account of his own life, the character Kim experiences a physical version of a dark night of the soul. After this collapse, he is tended by Indian women who feed and massage him:

> And the two of them, laying him east to west, that the mysterious earth-currents which thrill the clay of our bodies might help and not hinder, took him to pieces all one long afternoon—bone by bone, muscle by muscle, ligament by ligament, and lastly, nerve by nerve. (p. 324)

After this, Kim sleeps for 36 hours and then is fed with fresh and home-grown food. This description of physical rejuvenation (whose minute description invites this reader to fantasize a similar renewal) is worth look-ing into further. Kim's healing takes place along the axis from East to West, and in this moment, at least, seems to span that polarized world of Orien-talist, manichean difference.[10] Indeed, upon his recovery Kim thanks the Indian woman who tended him, calling her "mother." In what might be read as Kipling's acknowledgement of his own Indian roots through Kim, Kim is, in effect, born again. This physical rejuvenation is a precursor to Kim's epiphany. For after this scene of healing, Kim is urged to "Get up and see the world!" (p. 327) and eventually concurs that it is true: "I must get into the world again" (p. 331).

But Kim is not quite ready for the world, as his recovery from this phys-ical collapse precipitates a psychic confusion: once outside, he becomes "unable to take up the size and proportion and use of things." The nature of his disorientation is expressed in mechanical terms: "[H]is soul was out of gear with his surroundings—a cog-wheel unconnected with any machinery, just like the idle cog-wheel of a cheap Beheea sugar-crusher laid by in a corner." When the solution to this difficulty arrives, when, that is, the epiphany comes, it arrives "of a sudden," and "with an almost audi-ble click he [feels] the wheels of his being lock up anew on the world with-out." With this revelation, roads, houses, cattle, and people become things that are "all real and true—solidly planted on the feet—perfectly compre-hensible—clay of his clay, neither more nor less" (p. 331). Unlike the *chakras* of Kundalini and other yogas, when Kim's (cog-) wheels line up, they lead to the embracing of samsara rather than its transcendence.[11] Kim's secular revelation places him securely within both the things of this world and the colonialist machinery. In the final pages Kim's destiny is finally settled, and even the lama—in his way—admits it. "[N]ow I under-stand that the boy, sure of Paradise, can yet enter Government service, my mind is easier" (p. 334). Kim's epiphany provides the answer to his ques-tions of identity: he will work in the world, within the colonial apparatus. The horizon of epiphany is found at last.

After his realization, Kim gets up and walks to a banyan tree, where he embraces "the hopeful dust that holds the seeds of all life," and collapses, with "his head powerless upon [Mother Earth's] breast" (p. 332). The Bud-dha also found enlightenment under a tree, but while he called on the earth as his witness that he would not stray from his determination to attain lib-eration, Kim embraces the earth as real and ultimate. In effect, Kim embraces the cycle of birth, growth, and decay that some forms of Bud-dhism seek to transcend.

The nature and significance of Kim's epiphany is further emphasized by its contrast with the culmination of the lama's search. When the lama finds his river and thus the end of his search, his realization is first narrated by those who recognize only its physical manifestation. The earthy Sahiba begs the question: "[To] go roving into the fields for two nights on an empty belly—and to tumble into a brook at the end of it—you call you *that* holiness?" (p. 325, emphasis in original). While Kim's epiphany is dramatized in the physical and active terms valorized by the novel, the lama describes his own revelation in increasingly abstract language:

> Yea, my Soul went free, and wheeling like an eagle, saw indeed that there was no Teshoo Lama nor any other soul. As a drop draws to water, so my Soul drew near to the Great Soul *which is beyond all things* . . . By this I knew the Soul had passed beyond the illusion of Time and Space *and of Things*. (p. 337, emphasis mine)

In describing the lama's epiphany, Kipling seems to rely more on Vedantic notions of *moksha* rather than on Buddhist notions of nirvana, where the lama's individual soul has the chance to unite with a universal soul, or *atman;* this is a view of things fundamentally denied by Buddhism. And in the lama's case, even this realization is incomplete, for the old monk says that he turned away from this absorption into the sacred in order to be with Kim: "I pushed aside world upon world for thy sake" (p. 338). The lama's realization, with its near-transcendence of the world of things, contrasts markedly with Kim's, for Kim does not push the world away; he takes it up. And as a newly-made man of the world and not of the spirit, Kim can only understand the lama's revelation in physical terms. He finds it marvelous that the lama abstained from food for two days; told about how the lama discovered his river, Kim can only ask, "Wast thou very wet?" (p. 338). The divergent epiphanies emphasize what was already evident: while the lama once sought escape from the "Wheel of Life" and its sufferings, Kim cannot keep his eyes and affections from it. From the lama's perspective, "this a great and terrible world" (p. 242). Kim, in his attachment to the lama, cannot help but revise this estimation: "[T]he Holy One . . . is right—[it is] a great and *wonderful* world" (p. 273, emphasis mine).

With this epiphany, Kim's break from the lama seems complete, which is not to say that the friendship is over but that Kim has come to recognize his utter difference from the lama. Throughout the novel the question of Kim's identity has been complicated by his ability to pass for a native, to speak the vernacular, and to assume the guise of almost any Indian he liked; by the end of the novel, Kim's understanding of his own relation to these guises is fixed. In effect, he comes around to the narrator's perspective in the novel's first page: "Though he was burned black as any native; though he spoke the vernacular by preference, and his mother-tongue in a clipped uncertain sing-song; though he consorted on terms of perfect equality with the small boys of the bazar; Kim was white—a poor white of the very poorest" (p. 49). Any questions Kim might have had about his identity vis-à-vis the lama or the locals is now cleared up. He may be able to mimic them, but he is always other to them. When he looks into them as into a mirror, he recognizes his complete difference. Epiphany, in effect, asserts the insularity and enclosed nature of the colonial self.

As I have suggested, Kipling's *Kim* depends on available knowledge on Tibetan religion, including the work of Bogle, Turner, and Waddell; from other genres, Kipling's novel adopts the structure of epiphany. While Bogle's texts do not come from a single vision, and as such, do not present a solid, unified character, epiphany brings coherence to Kim's self and closure to the novel. The different kinds of selves and resolutions that appear in these texts are not just due to the different genres in which they appear, however; they are also connected to the needs of colonial ideology. By Kipling's day, when the stability of colonialism was threatened by both Indian resistance and British critiques of imperialism, the need to deny exchange between colonizer and colonized was increasingly enforced. By Kipling's day, the need to create a coherent, internalized self which is inscribed as something altogether different from the colonized has become a cornerstone of colonial ideology, a kind of desperate clinging to "the illusion of permanence," as Francis Hutchins calls it.[12] As Nandy has argued, the myth of colonialism as something *done to* the colonized by colonial masters is a story that has been perpetuated both by nineteenth century colonialists and would-be critics of colonialism today. Such a vision denies and elides the ways in which the colonizers were also transformed by the colonial encounter. If we follow Nandy's perspective, epiphany can be seen as a surrogate vision of transformation, put forward to cover over the less flattering and less edifying forms of transformation colonialists had to go through—the transformations of which they were not master, the transformations that allowed them to deny the full humanity of other people, the transformations that forced them to cripple their own impulses to compassion, rapprochement, and self-reflectiveness and created in them what Nandy, echoing Forster, calls "the undeveloped heart."[13]

We have seen how Bogle's texts—in report form and in Markham's edition—influenced some of those which came after it. Kipling's popular novel, in turn, would become part of the ideological and textual baggage carried by members of the Younghusband Mission who traveled to Tibet in

1903 and 1904. Through Kipling's depiction of a Tibetan lama and through his use of epiphany to solve a colonial dilemma, the stage is set for secular epiphany in Tibet.

Postscript

My own brush with epiphany took place when studying on an undergraduate program to Pune, India. While on break, I traveled with my friend Mike to Leh, Ladakh on the Tibetan plateau. Tucked in a corner of the Himalayas, accessible by gravel roads with hairpin turns and marked by the debris of previous accidents, Ladakh had succulent blue skies. When we dozed in the afternoon we could hear farmers—men, women, kids—cutting and threshing grain; their songs rose and fell like a calliope.

Like other tourists in Ladakh, we made the rounds of the Buddhist monasteries, puzzled over a wheel of life portraying the realms of rebirth painted outside a monastery wall, tried to count the thousand arms of Avalokiteshvara. At one monastery, Mike traded a monk a Bic pen for a mani stone. On the street, Ladakhi ladies wore gigantic turquoise headdresses and sold radishes as big as my arm. They smiled openly, unlike the more close-faced women on the Deccan plateau. Mornings we were served fresh-baked flat bread and homemade apricot jam. Afternoons we strolled the markets of Leh. And the whole time I was there I felt like I'd come home. I wanted to call out to women, "Hello, Auntie!," or to men, "Where are you going, my uncle?" It was then that I fell in love with Tibetan culture with all the infatuation of first love and with all the certainty my 20–year-old heart could muster. All was designed to elicit joy. And yet I was so afraid. Afraid I would be wrong, afraid I would lose who I thought I was. I got my ticket out early and retreated to the plains.

CHAPTER 7

Younghusband: Arrivals and Departures

t the start of chapter 2, I imagined Bogle looking into a Tibetan adage as into a mirror, judging how his own image fit with the Tibetan prescription for a good man. When I look at the beginning of Younghusband's *India and Tibet,* I can imagine a similar kind of mirror gazing: Younghusband begins by pondering Bogle, how the younger man related to Tibetans, what he was able to accomplish, and what kind of man he was. And tucked into the book is an image of the young Scot: an oval portrait of Bogle, framed in what appears to be gilt, gazes out from the pages of the first chapter. While Younghusband—like his readers—probably looked *at* the picture, there is a way that the representation can also be imagined as showing one's own likeness in a mirror. It's not an easy trick: the image is flat, the reproduction poor. It takes some creativity to imagine what Bogle might have looked like, how his earthly features might have been transposed to this flat mask with fluffy brown hair. The frame of this image, however, encourages such imagining, working as well for a portrait as for a looking glass.

In his biography, *Younghusband, The Last Great Imperial Adventure,* Patrick French ponders an image of Younghusband he found in the India Office and which is included on the back of the dust jacket.[1] In this one, Younghusband, in Central Asian garb, stares out from the photograph in a cluster of several similarly exotically-cloaked men, his glance piercing, his demeanor proud and forthright. Although the group setting makes such imagining difficult, what does it feel like to look into Younghusband's eyes as if they were one's own? For even if I, as a Westerner, would hold these colonial figures at arm's length, othering them, I have to recognize what I share with them. I'll admit it: there is a part of me whose *wanderlust* thrills to the thought of traveling in Central Asia a century ago, a part of me whose passions are stirred by names of the places he passed through—Gilgit, Kashmir, the Mustagh Pass; my own travels in India and Tibet were fueled by a desire to be in a place totally different from what I knew—a place completely "not-home." Even now the dream of traversing the Gobi on camel, of trekking in the hills above Dharamsala is not unseductive. But then I sit back, a woman, married with two children, whose face is more likely to be reflected in the screen of a computer monitor than a mirror, and have to smirk. There is so much about Younghusband to push away. There is so much about him that seems to force itself on one.

Unlike Bogle or Manning, Younghusband (like Turner, and even like me, I suppose) intended for his work to be published. While Manning and Bogle never pulled their work together into an emplotted narrative, Younghusband (like Turner and me) was compelled to. As in this book, Younghusband's first several chapters deal with the work of Bogle, Turner, and Manning. And as in my project, Younghusband's narrative is shaped by his epiphany on the Tibetan plateau. Given these similarities, one might well ask, do we take the same route to the end of the story? Do our accounts differ in significant, structural ways? And does it matter that Younghusband does not figure his epiphany as his climax? For him, the story is one in which he is justified. For me, it is a race to epiphany.

If there are superficial similarities in how Younghusband and I begin our work, our purposes differ widely. After apologizing for the length of his book, on the first page Younghusband announces his intentions:

> The whole forms one connected narrative of the attempt, protracted over 137 years, to accomplish a single purpose—the establishment of ordinary neighbourly intercourse with Tibet. The dramatic ending disclosed is that, when that purpose had at last been achieved, we forthwith abandoned the result.[2]

For Younghusband, Bogle is the start of the story of which he himself is the culmination. Bringing diverse material into one volume, Younghusband's hefty text includes historical accounts, travel stories, minute details of laborious negotiations, a romantic epiphany, and justification for both the Younghusband Mission and the imperial project more generally. But does the "whole" form "one connected narrative," as he suggests? French writes:

> With hindsight the book is more remarkable for what it leaves out than what it includes, although it does have important information on Younghusband's

own attitude to the Tibet question. There are few insights into his personal feeling, and he felt unable to mention his battle with General Macdonald, or what he saw as his betrayal by the British government.[3]

French projects a complete text of self-presentation for which *India and Tibet* is only the stand-in. Exploring the story at hand, I find a heterogeneous text, and pull apart the narrative that Younghusband weaves together in order to see how it works, to see what other texts and ideas enable it. My goal is not to simply condemn Younghusband as a colonialist and romantic, for he has given us Tibetan epiphany; he has shaped our understanding of Tibet and travel in fundamental ways. As imposing, quirky, and distasteful as Younghusband sometimes is, his book *India and Tibet* is worthy of a Bogleian reading, one that is self-reflective and self-critical; one that moves. (I wonder if I can really do this. I'm so eager to get to the epiphany, to get to the end. And when I first started working on his writing 12 years ago it was easy to see how wrong he was. To "other" him was pure joy.)

So to begin his story: as is suggested in the quotation above, Younghusband figures Bogle's mission as the beginning of the narrative to which his work is the conclusion—a conclusion eventually retracted by the powers that be. Thus, much of chapter one works to display the similarities between Younghusband and Bogle on the one hand and Viceroy Curzon and Hastings on the other. Younghusband valorizes Bogle for his good nature and his ability to negotiate with the Tibetans. But writing at a time when easy liaisons between Britons and locals were severely frowned upon, and perhaps mindful of Bogle's relationship with an Asian woman, his "illegitimate" children, and his tendency to sympathize with Tibetans, Younghusband is careful to note, "His letters to his father and sisters show him to have been a man of the strongest home feelings, and his conversations with the Tibetans indicate that he was a man of high honour and strict rectitude" (p. 8). Younghusband has nothing but praise to heap on the young agent, and Hastings is similarly heralded for his forward-looking policy. But more than their personalities, Younghusband envies the possibilities afforded these industrious men: unlike himself and George Curzon, who are shackled by a chain of command that stretches clear from Tibet to London, Bogle and Hastings were given free rein to act on the spot, to seize an advantage when they saw one, rather than having to phone home to ask permission first (p. 11). Indeed, Younghusband imagines that Bogle's and Hastings's ability to act is what defines their personalities and their public reception, while agents like Younghusband and Curzon, despite their best intentions, are hampered by the dolts and fools around them and then chastised for what they are thus unable to accomplish.

From Younghusband's perspective, Bogle's diplomatic gifts helped to initiate a relationship with the Tibetans that was in turn carried on by Turner—only to be allowed to waste and wither by an unseeing government. According to Younghusband, by 1903 Anglo-Tibetan relations had gone almost completely sour, having been especially undermined by the Chinese and the Russians. This is a deplorable situation, for instead of being some far-flung place, remote from British interests, Younghusband argues that Tibet is integral to British-Indian interests. Not only do many fail to realize that India and Tibet share a 1,000–mile border, "[s]till less have they appreciated that this contact between the countries means intercourse of some kind between the peoples inhabiting them, even though it has to be over a snowy range" (p. 3). In a manner that anticipates contemporary discussions of "border-crossing" and "contact zones,"[4] Younghusband goes on to relate the many ways Tibetans and Indians have interacted:

> At other times, again, the intercourse has been of a more pacific kind, and intermarriages between the bordering peoples and interchanges of presents have taken place. In a multitude of ways there has even been intercourse between Tibet and India. . . . And, as I shall in due course show, the Mission to Lhasa of 1904, was merely the culmination of a long series of efforts to regularize and humanize that intercourse, and put the relationship which must necessarily subsist between India and Tibet upon a business-like and permanently satisfying footing. (p. 3)

In the passage above, Younghusband uses the term "intercourse" to describe several kinds of relations between Indians and Tibetans: the relations of trade, of culture, and of marriage. While it may seem sophomoric to emphasize this repeated use of the term intercourse (this from a man who, upon his wedding, agreed with his wife to remain celibate, a vow apparently later retracted), I note it because such a trope is common to colonial descriptions of imperial invasion.[5] For example, in his account of the Younghusband mission, Waddell, chief medical officer and archaeologist to the Mission, uses metaphors of sex and courtship to describe the British invasion of Tibet. In the opening pages of *Lhasa and Its Mysteries* he claims:

> [N]ow . . . the fairy Prince of 'Civilisation' has roused [Lhasa] from her slumbers, her closed doors are broken down, her dark veil of mystery is lifted up, and the long-sealed shrine, with its grotesque cults and its idolised Grand Lama, shorn of his sham nimbus, have yielded up their secrets, and lie disenchanted before our eyes.[6]

In this story, the virginal beauty with her hymen-like shrine is proven, upon penetration, to be grotesque and over-rated: she is shaven like a whore; her charms prove false.

Waddell describes Britain's penetration of Tibet through a conventional and violent version of heterosexual intercourse; indeed, as many feminist critics have noted, such tropes of sexual penetration (foreplay-penetration-climax) parallel the conventional narrative structure of introduction, rising action, and climax. Younghusband's own narrative is shaped by this same plot structure, punctuated by its penetration of the forbidden city and an effusive ejaculation on the Tibetan plateau. (Indeed, my own work in Part One bears signs of such a plot structure, leading as it does to a kind of culmination in Younghusband.)

But let me return to the main track. Eager to draw parallels between Bogle's mission and his own, Younghusband has to overlook some significant historical differences, as Alastair Lamb points out in his introduction to the 1985 version of *India and Tibet* (p. viii). Younghusband's representation of Bogle is designed to reflect on his own energy, commitment, and good heart. By quoting Bogle's famous farewell address to the Tibetans, Younghusband likens Bogle's "warm-hearted and affectionate feelings to the people of Tibet" to his own feelings about the place:

> Farewell, ye honest and simple people! May ye long enjoy the happiness which is denied to more polished nations; and while they are engaged in the endless pursuits of avarice and ambition, defended by your barren mountains, may ye continue to live in peace and contentment, and know no wants but those of nature.[7]

I find it interesting that Younghusband does not comment on this passage. I read it as contradicting Bogle's suggestions elsewhere that the E. I. C. should profitably pursue trade ties with Tibet and thus as thoroughly undercutting any dream of imperial advancement; in this way, it is also an implicit indictment of the Younghusband Mission. Younghusband, it seems, sees no such criticism. To him, apparently, Britain is not one of the "more polished nations" which are guided by "avarice and ambition." Indeed, when he looks into Bogle's exclamation, Younghusband may read exuberance, affection, and love, even, but not, presumably, a criticism of the colonial ambition that drives both him and his narrative. The passage, however, remains on the books, as it were, a bit of excess (as in Bogle's texts, and in Turner's), which in this case pulls against the direction of Younghusband's narrative.

If Younghusband allies himself with Bogle in chapter I, his aim in chapters II and III on Turner and Manning respectively is not to delimit the history of Tibetan exploration but rather to show how Britons had earlier established relations with Tibetans and how they subsequently let them languish. For this reason, in discussing Turner he makes no mention of Turner's performance before the young Panchen Lama but, instead, he underlines the Tibetans' interest in relations with the British: "The Regent assured Turner of the firm, unshaken attachment which the Tashi Lama had entertained for Mr. Hastings to his latest breath" (pp. 28–9). In his discussion of Manning, Younghusband notes something of the traveler's eccentric character and quirky diary. Given Manning's unofficial status, it comes as a bit of a surprise that Younghusband would mention him at all, but as Younghusband notes, even such a "meagre record . . . showed that an Englishman, with delicacy of touch and with a real sympathetic feeling towards those among whom he was travelling, could find his way even into the very presence of the Dalai Lama in the Potala itself" (p. 39). He ends the chapter by noting that after Manning no Briton was able to travel to Tibet. But rather than go on to discuss the many European attempts to explore Tibet, Younghusband states that his aim is to consider efforts to "regularise and foster intercourse which already existed with its people" (p. 41). It is communication that matters to him, relation, interaction. One might say that much of the rest of the book is his personal version of that story—how to get Tibetans to listen and negotiate. It is a tedious story, with many lost opportunities, affronts, and misunderstandings, punctuated by several bloody battles. Indeed, a flip reader might even say that, after the battles are over, a good two hundred pages of the book could simply be summarized by the sentences, "[The Tibetans] repeated the usual requests that we should not go to Lhasa. I reiterated my usual statements that we must go there" (p. 249).

The ostensible reason for the Younghusband Mission was to settle a border dispute with Tibet, though both Curzon and Younghusband were convinced of Russian encroachment in Tibet and wished to assert British power. Along the way, other reasons for pushing on to Lhasa are produced—the imprisonment of two British Indian citizens, the killing of some yaks, the need to negotiate with no less a personage than the 13th Dalai Lama himself. Younghusband led 8,000 troops over the Tibetan plateau and engaged in battles with the ill-equipped Tibetan army at Phari, Tuna, and Gyantse, before finally going on to Lhasa where, because the Dalai Lama had fled to Mongolia, Younghusband negotiated a punishing treaty with the Regent and the Tibetan assembly (*Kashag*). This treaty provided for new trade marts in Tibet, a large indemnity to be paid over 75 years, and the occupation of the Chumbi valley until the indemnity was paid; it also forbade the Tibetans from having dealings with any foreign powers other than Britain. The terms of the treaty were later revised, and Younghusband was berated for having taken matters into his own hands. It is after this humiliation and his return to England that Younghusband turned his hand to the writing of *India and Tibet*.

THE UNTOLD STORY

Much of Younghusband's book is a repetitive story of stubborn Tibetans and ever-diplomatic Brits, a story so tedious at times that I sometimes wonder why the reading public took to it so. Three other volumes from the Younghusband Mission already preceded his—Waddell's *Lhasa and Its Mysteries,* Perceval Landon's monumental *The Opening of Tibet,* and Edmund Candler's *The Unveiling of Lhasa.* But this is the story from the man who gave his name to the debacle, the man who was nearly disgraced by the whole affair. This is the story from the man himself. Or so it seems.

French had noted that *India and Tibet* is more interesting for what is *not* in it than what *is* in it. One of the most important omissions, French notes, is that while Younghusband was in Tibet and engaged in serious diplomatic and military decisions, he not only undertook a life-threatening visit to the Tibetan camp at Guru, he was also engaged in a serious spiritual search. As French writes:

> In a revealing private note written some years later, he admits that meditation on Walt Whitman's *Leaves of Grass* occupied much of his attention: "Important as was the task upon which I was engaged, I all the time thought it of very minor consequence in comparison with the great main deeper interest of my life in which I was absorbed."[8]

As French notes, Younghusband's musings on the spiritual life also included discussion of the existence of life on other planets, the "subliminal self" that was able to separate from the body, as well as consideration of the many religions he had encountered in his travels. (French suggests that Younghusband's spiritual investigation gave him a kind of holy fervor that was frequently taken as military fortitude and vigor by his troops.)[9] Just how Younghusband used *Leaves of Grass* in this search is not clear, though Whitman's celebration of an all-embracing self in "Song of Myself"—"I celebrate myself and sing myself,/And what I assume you shall assume,/for every atom belonging to me as good belongs to you"—seems to have had some impact on his representation of his epiphany, as we will see.[10]

Younghusband's spiritual explorations in Tibet were only an interlude in what had been a long search and a future avocation. Younghusband was an admirer of the Romantic poets, and his early excursions into the Himalayas were influenced by the English poets' reveries in the Lake District and the Alps. As French argues, "Mountains, and the Himalayas in particular, were to form an essential dimension in Younghusband's spiritual theories: his ideas combined the Romantic tradition of Wordsworth, Byron, and Coleridge with Hindu and Buddhist faith in sacred mountains."[11] By 1891 Younghusband's contact with this version of nature mysticism, his acquaintance with various world religions, and his immersion in theories of evolution combined to give him grave doubts about institutionalized Christianity. In addition to his love for Wordsworth and Byron and his reading of Charles Darwin, Herbert Spencer, Charles Dickens, John Lubbock, and Leo Tolstoy, Younghusband also dabbled in European works on Asian religions; George Seaver notes that Younghusband took a book by Annie Besant to Tibet and Monier Monier-Williams's *Buddhism* to Kashmir.[12] Engaged in an individualized quest, Younghusband wrote in his diary while posted in Gilgit in Central Asia in 1894, "I think I have had from time to time the feeling that I was born to recognise the divine spark within me. . . . I shall through my life be carrying out God's Divine message to mankind."[13] While Younghusband would continue to work out the exact details of his spiritual beliefs and mission throughout his life, his investigation of other religions continued. While posted in Indore in 1903, for example, he undertook a systematic study of the *Bhagavad-Gita* (published in English translation in 1785) and also perused works on Vedanta, which Vivekananda had begun to popularize in the West.[14] After his work in Tibet, Younghusband would go on to found several ecumenically-oriented religious organizations; as head of the Royal Geographical Society, he would even transform mountain-climbing, particularly that of Everest and the Himalayas, into a kind of quasi-spiritual mission.

As is suggested by the examples above, Younghusband was thirsty for religious experience, and, from his perspective, existing religious institutions could only get at part of that experience at best, and, at worst, stifle it completely. As Whitman writes in "Song of Myself":

> I do not despise you priests, all time, the world over,
> My faith is the greatest of faiths and the least of faiths,
> Enclosing worship ancient and modern and all between ancient and
> modern . . . (Stanza 43)

For Whitman, real experience had to be wrestled from life; it could not be meted out in rituals or memorized by a "llama" [sic]. It had to be won by daring individuals. In his life and work Younghusband valued individual spiritual experience, and when this was combined with a textual attitude towards Tibetan religion á la Waddell and Hodgson, with anti-Buddhist sentiments from Monier-Williams, and with criticisms of Tibetan Buddhism from a recent book by the Japanese Buddhist Ekai Kawaguchi, Younghusband could only see the absolute otherness of Tibetan religion. When Younghusband looks at Tibetan religion, then, he can only see alterity, difference; he is closed to it. As he writes, "The religion of the Tibetans is grotesque, and is the most degraded, not the purest form of Buddhism" (p. 247).

Tibetan Buddhism is off-limits for Younghusband's personal search. Nonetheless, as I have argued in my discussion of *Kim,* the notion of a secular epiphany has by Younghusband's day gained considerable cultural currency. The coexistence of these two trends—an adherence to Victorian attitudes towards Tibetan religion and Younghusband's own spiritual ambition—creates a tension, certainly, but also a space through which Younghusband's awakening on the Tibetan plateau bursts. In order to contextualize it, let me further consider Younghusband's representations of Tibetan religion.

DEGRADED RELIGION AND EXALTED EXPERIENCE

As I have suggested, some of what Younghusband knew of Buddhism came from the work of Monier Monier-Williams, a French Sanskritist who held the Boden Chair of Sanskrit at Oxford. As Charles Long notes, Monier-Williams was selected for this position instead of Max Müller because his work coincided with that of the donor, Lieutenant-Colonel Joseph Boden of the East India Company. As Monier-Williams wrote in his manifesto for the chair:

> Had I found plain instructions that the electors of the University were to search throughout Europe for the man most likely to secure a world-wide reputation for the Sanskrit Chair, I confess I should have hesitated to prosecute my design. But Colonel Boden thought more of aiding, by means of Sanskrit, the diffusion of Christianity in India than of promoting in all parts of the globe the fame of the Professorship.[15]

A similar missionary spirit is evident in Monier-Williams's 1889 *Buddhism, In Its Connexion with Brahmanism and Hinduism* (which Younghusband carried to Kashmir in 1891). Here Monier-Williams confidently declares the superiority of Christianity and European civilization over that of Asia. Monier-Williams writes, for example, that most Indians "are so enfeebled by the debilitating effect of early marriages, and so deadened by the drudgery of daily toil and the dire necessity of keeping body and soul together, that they can scarcely be said to be capable of holding any definite theological creed at all." Thus, instead of concerning themselves with "the nature of a Supreme Being," most Indians worry about caste, local deities, and folk legends. In Monier-Williams's estimation, Tibetans are no better, their "Lamism" being a "form of Buddhism which, although based on the Hina-yana and Maha-yana of India, is combined with Shamanism, Shiva-worship and magic"[16] (pp. 4–5). Not only is Tibetan Buddhism a bastardized creed, as it is for Waddell, its institutions are uniquely designed to preserve the power of the monastic hierarchy. Monier-Williams suggests that the *tulku* system of reincarnation was designed by "some shrewd Head Lama" to circumvent the problem of succession among celibate monks.[17] Thus, when Younghusband carried the volume into Central Asia, he possessed not a how-to book on Buddhist philosophy and meditation; instead, he transported a denigrating discussion of Buddhism, one which depended on the textual attitudes inscribed in European studies of Buddhism.

Such attitudes towards Buddhism played an official role in the Younghusband Expedition in the figure of L. Austine Waddell, the attending expert on Tibetan Buddhism. While at one point Younghusband offers Waddell to Tibetan negotiators as an example of the Britons' tolerance of other religions (p. 240), Waddell's distrust of the Tibetan clergy matches Younghusband's own. Younghusband writes that the monks "were a dirty, degraded lot, and we all of us remarked how distinctly inferior they were to the ordinary peasantry and townsmen we met. The monks, as a rule, looked thoroughly lazy and sensual and effete" (p. 266). Stranded on the plateau waiting for representatives from Lhasa with whom to negotiate, Younghusband writes:

> Captain O'Connor [his translator] reported that the whole demeanor of the Lhasa monks, who were the men who really guided the destinies of Tibet, was impracticable in the extreme. They made no advance in civility . . . and they adopted the high tone of demanding our withdrawal. (p. 150)

This estimation of the Tibetan clergy contrasts with Bogle's more modulated assessment of the monks at Tashilhunpo. For Waddell and Younghusband, these degenerate monks oppress laymen and women, who continue to be portrayed in terms more aligned with Bogle's as forthright, sincere, and good-natured. Waddell had argued that Tibet's "sturdy incredulous people" were weighed down by "intolerable tyranny of the Lamas."[18] Younghusband views the monks as similarly obstructive:

> The disposition and manners of the Yutok Sha-pé [a lay government official] gave one more confirmation of the impression I had long formed that the laymen of Tibet were by no means inimical, and that but for the opposition of the monks we might be on extremely friendly terms with them. (p. 228)

One of the problems with these monks for Younghusband is that, in a sense, they don't know Buddhism—or at least not the Buddhism codified by European scholars. Having done his Buddhism homework, Younghusband feels confident enough to differ with Tibetan monks about the meaning of their religion. When several monks tell him that they wish to keep the Indian army out of Lhasa in order to preserve their religion, Younghusband counters, "As the Buddhist religion nowhere preaches this seclusion, it was evident that what the monks wished to preserve was not their religion, but their priestly influence" (p. 166). And again, when negotiators tell him that the entrance of the Indian Army into Lhasa might threaten the Dalai Lama's life, Younghusband retorts, "I had studied their religion and [I told them that] I could hardly believe it was so weak that it would not stand our presence in Lhasa for a few weeks" (p. 258). Much that is wrong with the Tibetan clergy is especially attributed to the figure of the 13th Dalai Lama. Bogle had been extremely flattering of the Third Panchen Lama, a sentiment noted by Younghusband (p. 15), but the 13th Dalai Lama is portrayed as a coward, a despot, and a duper of innocent soldiers, who, Younghusband notes, believe his amulets can protect them from the bullets of the Indian soldiers:

> There was no possible reasoning with such people. They had such over-weening confidence in their Lama's powers. How *could* anyone dare to resist the orders of the Great Lama? Surely lightning would descend from heaven or the earth open up and destroy anyone who had such temerity! . . . [W]e might just as well have spoken to a stone wall. Not the very slightest effect was produced. After all, our numbers were not very overwhelming. The Tibetans had charms against our bullets, and the supernatural powers of the Great Lama in the background. . . . They had formed no plan of what they should do if we did advance contrary to the Great Lama's orders. But for that there was no need; the Lama would provide. Such were their ideas. (pp. 174–5, emphasis in original)

While some Victorians found a rational and atheistic creed in Buddhist texts and thrilled to the life of the Buddha presented by Sir Edwin Arnold in *The Light of Asia,* still others argued that Buddhism was nihilistic and degraded. For Younghusband, Tibetan Buddhism simply has not lived up to the promises found in the ancient texts.

Younghusband draws further support for his distrust of the Tibetan monastic system from Ekai Kawaguchi, a Japanese monk whose *Three Years in Tibet,* describing life in a Lhasan monastery, was published in English in 1909. Kawaguchi lived at Sera disguised as a Chinese monk until 1902, when he was suspected as a spy and fled the country. Kawaguchi had few kind words for Tibetan monks, whom he found lazy, sexually immoral, dirty, and lacking in spiritual development. In *India and Tibet,* Younghusband uses Kawaguchi's text to "bear out the casual impression we got during our stay in Lhasa:" "[Lamaism] has had a pacifying effect, it is true. . . . The numerous figures of the placid Buddha . . . have hypnotized the people to a sense of peace and rest" (p. 314). Noting that the Tibetans used to be warriors, Younghusband suggests that the calm they have since discovered is of the wrong type:

> [T]he peace that has been nurtured has been the quiescence of sloth and decadence. The Buddhist idea of repose and kindness all can appreciate. . . . Yet the idea may have its danger and be as likely to lead downward as upward. It may lull to rest and render useless passions and energies which ought to be given play to. And the evil of Lamaism is that it has fostered lazy repose and self-suppression at the expense of useful activity and self-realization. (pp. 314–5)

Using a colonial dichotomy that divides the active British from their passive subjects, Younghusband links Tibetans' passivity to their lack of a sense of service (p. 312) and their utter selfishness:

> The Tibetan's main idea, in fact, has been to save his own soul. He does not trouble about others so long as he can save himself. Indeed, he thinks it will require all his energies to do even that much, for at heart he is still full of his original religion of demonology. (p 313)

In his own life, Younghusband resists any such insistence that one must choose the pursuit of enlightenment over all other duties; after all, while he was in Tibet, he managed to lead an army, conduct negotiations, and still engage in a spiritual search. And while Younghusband criticizes these Buddhists for adhering to an "original religion of demonology," the man who had struck out on his own spiritual adventure might be accused of still harboring the old Victorian Christian values of service and work in the world. Indeed, the general would spend much of his adult life exploring ways to discover the right combination of "useful activity and self-realization" he found lacking in Tibetans—and it is that fateful union of duty and epiphany that Younghusband will find for himself on the Tibetan plateau. Younghusband cannot achieve this realization directly through Tibetan religion, though, as he sees it as oppressive and degraded. And before he can arrive at epiphany, he has important encounters with two exceptional lamas.

If Younghusband is heir to suspicions about the clergy from Britain's version of Tibetan Buddhism, he also inherits from the texts of Bogle, Turner, Manning, and Kipling the possibility of a significant relationship between lama and Anglo. As Younghusband himself argues, his work is the culmination of Bogle's. In that sense, Younghusband takes up a position vis-à-vis these lamas that carries the force of other such encounters, and he is struck by their good qualities as well as their faults. Younghusband admires the gentleness and kindness of both Ta Lama, the Abbot of Tashilhunpo, and Ganden Tripa ("Ti Rimpoche"), the Dalai Lama's regent, although he is unimpressed by their "intellectual capacity" (p. 310). He envies the amount of time the Ta Lama is allowed to devote to spiritual matters (p. 126). He describes this lama as "charming" despite his lack of worldly knowledge, evidenced by the lama's insistence that the world is not round but "flat, and not circular, but triangular, like the bone of a shoulder of mutton" (p. 128). Similarly, the Ganden Tripa is described as

> a benevolent, kindly old gentleman, who could not hurt a fly if he could have avoided it. No one could help liking him, but no one could say that he had the intellectual capacity we would meet in Brahmins in India, or the character and bearing one would expect in the leading men of the country. And his spiritual attainments, I gathered from a long conversation I had with him after the Treaty was signed, consisted mainly of a knowledge by rote of vast quantities of his holy books. (p. 310)

Younghusband's suggestion that "[n]o one could help liking him" echoes Bogle's estimation of the Teshoo Lama over a century earlier: "[He] is so universally beloved . . . not a man could find in his heart to speak ill of him."[19] And like Kipling's lama, Younghusband's lama has a propensity for rote quotation. A dignified, gentle Tibetan with spiritual gifts less impressive than his humanity—we have seen this lama before. If Turner took up Bogle's place in front of the Panchen Lama's reincarnation, and Kim was Bogle and Turner reincarnate to Kipling's Teshoo Lama *tulku*, Younghusband is Kim grown to maturity, and the Ganden Tripa is the elderly stand-in for Kipling's lama. If the resemblance is not already apparent, Younghusband goes on to assert that the Ganden Tripa "was full of kindliness, and . . . more nearly approached Kipling's Lama in 'Kim' than any other Tibetan I met" (p. 325). It is through this intertextual lama that Younghusband's epiphany is set in motion.

The epiphany appears in a chapter called "The Return." Returns—the "aggregation" phase of Victor Turner's tripartite model of ritual and pilgrimage—have figured prominently in the texts of Bogle and Turner, and Younghusband's text is no exception.[20] Younghusband's turning point is determined by the conclusion of the treaty, a treaty for which, we are told, he had to fight tooth and nail. Having entered Lhasa in August, Younghusband was under considerable pressure to complete the negotiations before the winter advanced and snow closed the mountain passes. As he writes:

> I had to set to work with all speed, but with the appearance of having the utmost leisure, to negotiate the treaty. Hurried as I was, I had yet to assume an air of perfect indifference whether the negotiations were concluded this year, next year, or the year after. And irritated as I might be, I had above all to exercise as much control as I could possibly bring to bear to keep down any feelings of hastiness or exasperation, which might ruin our chances of securing the eventual good-will of the people. (pp. 251–2)

When the epiphany comes, then, it comes in a flood of great relief for Younghusband—as well as for his readers. At last the tedious repetition of the minute particulars of the negotiations for the treaty (that would later be retracted) are fixed. At last the narrative can move on.

After the treaty is agreed upon in Lhasa, duly signed in the Potala palace, and stamped by the Ganden Tripa with the Dalai Lama's seal, Younghusband reports that he can finally feel at ease. He now wishes to view Lhasa's monasteries and temples, because "[r]eligion was the chief characteristic of the people," and lamas guide both the religious and political life of Tibet's citizens (p. 309). Such a combination of religion and politics was something Younghusband himself sought to unite, but the monasteries fail to impress Younghusband; he seems to expect all monks to be engaged in meditation and philosophical analysis, but he finds instead that the monasteries are largely populated by what he sees as the less savory variety of ignorant monks who seem "coarse and besotted" (p. 309). And while Perceval Landon, a London *Times* special correspondent, will structure his monumental book, *The Opening of Lhasa,* around his penetration of the Jokhang Temple and its "holiest of holies,"[21] Younghusband, like Manning before him, feels out of place there: "I was even shown round what might be called the high-altar [of Lhasa's central temple], in spite of my protestations that I might be intruding where I should not go" (p. 317). So it is not Lhasa's sacred structures that will excite him. Instead, it is the conclusion of the treaty that most precipitates his realization.

The Ganden Tripa has given the British officers a small statue of the Buddha. Younghusband reports:

> We were given to understand that the presentation by so high a Lama to those who were not Buddhists of an image of the Buddha himself was no ordinary compliment. And as the revered old Regent rose from his seat and put the present in my hand, he said with real impressiveness that he had none of the riches of the world, and could only offer me this simple image. Whenever he looked upon the image of Buddha he thought only of peace, and he hoped that whenever I looked on it I would think of Tibet. I felt like taking part in a religious ceremony as the kindly old man spoke those words; and I was glad that all political wranglings were over, and that now we could part as friends man with man. (pp. 325–6)

After the political dealings are over and Younghusband's duty is done, after thousands of Tibetans, Indians, and several Britons have been maimed and killed, Younghusband feels relief; he imagines participating in a religious ritual. Buddhists believe that consecrated Buddhist images are enlivened and actually contain a sacred presence. Younghusband, as something of a nature mystic with iconoclastic Protestant roots, does not involve the image in his ritual in the mountains, though it would later seem to become a personal symbol of what he accomplished in Tibet. (Seaver reports that it rested by his death bed and his daughter placed it on his coffin; French reports that it sat on his desk while Younghusband was writing *Within,* and French even uses a Buddha image to mark section breaks in his biography of Younghusband.[22]) But if a Tibetan Buddhist ritual is off-limits, Younghusband does have access to a kind of secularized spiritualism: he is a reader of Kipling, a lover of Wordsworth, Byron, and Whitman; he is heir to a discourse about the possibility of significant and transformative experience in the world, particularly in the mountains. All of these interpretive forms provide him with rhetorical models and allow him to make textual sense of his own experience. After leaving "Ti Rimpoche," Younghusband goes out into the mountains, looks at the sky and the city of Lhasa and experiences a sense of elation:

> The scenery was in sympathy with my feelings; the unclouded sky a heavenly blue; the mountains softly merging into violet; and, as I now looked towards that mysterious purply haze in which the sacred city [Lhasa] was once more wrapped, I no longer had any cause to dread the hatred it might

hide. And with all the warmth still on me of that impressive farewell message, and bathed in the insinuating influences of the dreamy autumn evening, I was insensibly infused with an almost intoxicating sense of elation and good-will. This exhilaration of the moment grew and grew till it thrilled through me with over-powering intensity. Never again could I think evil, or ever again be at enmity with any man. All nature and all humanity were bathed in a rosy glowing radiancy; and life for the future seemed naught but buoyancy and light.

Such experiences are only too rare, and they but too soon become blurred in the actualities of daily intercourse and practical existence. Yet it is these few fleeting moments which are reality. In these only we see real life. The rest is ephemeral, the insubstantial. And that single hour on leaving Lhasa was worth all the rest of a lifetime. (pp. 326–7)

Readers are invited to feel the emotion swelling up—"I was insensibly infused with an almost intoxicating sense of elation and goodwill"—and continue to grow—"This exhilaration of the moment grew and grew till it thrilled through me with over-powering intensity"—until it has to come out in the declaration of unity: "Never again could I think evil, or ever again be at enmity with any man. All nature and all humanity were bathed in a rosy glowing radiancy; and life for the future seemed naught but buoyancy and light." The antagonistic distance between self and other is, for the moment dissolved, and all creation is brought into unity. But in another sense, the epiphany here can also be seen as a textual phenomenon. It depends on a structure that is rooted in Christian tradition, emphasized in spiritual autobiography and conversion narratives, shifts to secular writing, is popularized in Victorian novels, and transfers from Kipling's novel to Younghusband's account.

Given Younghusband's interest in Buddhism and Asian religions more generally, we might wonder whether there is anything of Buddhist notions of enlightenment in Younghusband's realization. In some ways, the shape and significance of Younghusband's realization more closely resembles that of Kipling's lama than that of Kim. The Lama's realization gives him a bird's eye view of "all Hind" and a sense of the greater soul of which he is a part: "Yea, my Soul went free, and wheeling like an eagle, saw indeed that there was no Teshoo Lama nor any other soul. As a drop draws to water, so my Soul drew near to the Great Soul which is beyond all things."[23] Despite their similarities, this resemblance will not take us any closer to Buddhist nirvana, for, as we have seen, this realization—aborted out of love for Kim—has more in common with Vedantic notions of *moksha* than with Buddhist ideas of enlightenment. But could Younghusband be drawing on still other representations of nirvana? For many Victorians who read about

Buddhism, nirvana seemed to be more about annihilation and negation than liberation, and was thus not something any self-respecting person would want to participate in.[24] For example, in his book on Buddhism, Monier-Williams writes that the "true knowledge" discovered by the Buddha under the *bodhi* tree was only

> a mere partial one-sided truth—the outcome of a single line of thought, dwelt upon with morbid intensity, to the exclusion of every other line of thought which might have modified and balanced it. It was an ultra-pessimistic view of the miseries of life, and a determination to ignore all its counterbalancing joys. It was a doctrine that this present life is only one link in a chain of countless transmigrations—that existence of all kinds involves suffering, and that such suffering can only be got rid of by self-restraint and the extinction of desires, especially of the desire for continuity of personal existence.[25]

Not only does Monier-Williams read nirvana negatively, he offers no detailed or graphic representation of the Buddha's nirvana on which Younghusband might draw for his epiphany.

Waddell was less dismissive of nirvana, writing that it might be thought of as "the 'going out' of the three Fires of Desire" as well as a "sinless calm" that is reachable in this life.[26] But even in Waddell's book, the depiction of enlightenment is not given much space. Waddell includes a line drawing of the "Temptation of Sakya Muni" taken from an Ajanta fresco, under the quick mention of the Buddha's "struggle and final triumph." Below the drawing is a passage from Milton's *Paradise Regained,* Book IV, transposed to a Buddhist context: "Infernal ghosts and hellish furies round/Environ'd thee; some howl'd, some yell'd, some shriek'd,/ Some bent at thee their fiery darts, while thou/Sat'st unapalle'd in calm and sinless peace."[27]

Undoubtedly the most popular depiction of the Buddha's enlightenment in English appeared in Sir Edwin Arnold's *The Light of Asia,* a text that went to one hundred editions in Britain and the United States.[28] In Book Six, Arnold describes at length the several watches of the Buddha's vigil, his battles with personified emotions and desires, and the stages through which he passed to finally triumph over samsara and attain "nirvana—sinless, stirless, rest—/That change which never changes!" And, in Arnold's depiction, with the dawning of the sun, comes the dawn of awakening:

> Lo! The Dawn
> Sprang with Buddh's Victory! Lo! in the East
> Flamed the first fires of beauteous day, poured forth

> Through fleeting folds of Night's black drapery.
> High in the widening blue the herald-star
> Faded to paler silver as there shot
> Brighter and brighter bars of rosy gleam
> Across the grey. Far off the shadowy hills
> Saw the great Sun, before the world was 'ware,
> And donned their crowns of crimson; flower by flower
> Felt the warm breath of Morn and 'gan unfold
> Their tender lids.[29]

In Arnold's depiction of the Buddha's enlightenment, as in Younghusband's epiphany, the focus is on the sky—the changing sky becomes a metaphor for the internal state of the person, a trope common in Romantic poetry. So rather than Arnold's version of the Buddha's nirvana influencing Younghusband, it is more likely that similar Romantic imagery of the sky colors both Arnold's and Younghusband's work. Indeed, Younghusband's ejaculation here would seem to have things in common with the following passage from Wordsworth's "Tintern Abbey," which Younghusband included in his *Heart of a Continent:*

> I have felt
> A presence that disturbs me with the joy
> Of elevated thoughts: a sense sublime
> Of something far more deeply interfused,
> Whose dwelling is the light of the setting suns,
> And the round ocean, and the living air,
> And the blue sky, and in the mind of man:
> A motion and a spirit, that impels
> All thinking things, all objects of all thought,
> And rolls through all things.[30]

The oceanic feeling described here is echoed in Younghusband, its engulfing tendency, like that in Whitman's "Song of Myself," uniting all of nature and all of humankind in spirit.

Thus, Younghusband's epiphany is a kind of intertextual phenomenon that shapes his experience. And his account of this experience will have work to do. For the all-consuming tendency in Wordsworth and in Younghusband's epiphany share something with the drive of colonialism. With Younghusband's assertion that the things of the world are ultimately "insubstantial," he plays down the importance of his own participation in the British imperial project, whose practices are coming to face criticism at home and in India. The oceanic feeling he experiences turns out to be synonymous with a drive for imperial expansion. In the final pages of his book, Younghusband argues that "some inward compulsion from the very core of things" drives Britons to assert their authority in places like Tibet (p. 434). An "inner necessity . . . surging up from the inmost depths of our beings" (p. 435) compels Britons to deal with "weak and disorderly people" (p. 437). And because the British feel a natural impulse towards harmony, unity, and order, they cannot tolerate isolationist Tibet; they "find they have to intervene to establish order and set up regular relations—they are, in fact, driven to establish eventual harmony, even if it may be by the use of force at the moment" (p. 437).

Drawing on the structure of epiphany, Younghusband finds the justification for imperialism deep within himself; his spiritual moment is put to work on behalf of the British empire. While Bogle seems to have been all over the place, through epiphany Younghusband makes himself, his work, and imperialism cohere. Refashioning various textual precedents, Younghusband writes a place for a coherent self, and, in effect, his "inmost being" is colonized. Imperialist discourse clears out a space, a territory *within* Younghusband, as it were. Unlike Bogle before him and more like Kim, Younghusband, by finding a place in the narrative, finds a fit in the world. Travel becomes transformation. And the myth of epiphany in Tibet inherits a burdensome legacy.

Patrick French, however, has a different reading of Younghusband's epiphany. Arguing against some commentators' tendency to imagine that Tibet somehow made both Younghusband and his mission pacifist, French comments on the way that

> [t]his extraordinary manipulation of the facts is typical of the way that Younghusband's identity has been colonized by his various chroniclers. Either he was a *Boy's Own* swashbuckling imperialist, or he was a peaceful, luminous mystic; or alternatively he had a split personality.
>
> The reality, as I came to perceive it, was both more complex and more human. Younghusband's experiences in Tibet were a formative part of an extraordinary journey of personal discovery and development. His rare, quirky, almost child-like view of life enabled him to go through an enormous range of apparently contradictory experiences, and encompass them all. As Jan Morris wrote in *The Spectacle of Empire,* Younghusband "most nearly filled the part of Everyman" in the great imperial drama. He never stood still, never stopped changing.[31]

In this passage French strives to make Younghusband make sense. In arguing that Younghusband's rare "view of life" enabled him "to go through an enormous range of apparently contradictory experiences, and encompass them all," French enforces the notion of the coherent self and the colonialist dream of mastery; he does not allow that—in his life—Younghusband may not actually make sense. And while it may be that the entirety of Younghusband's *life* shows a certain adventurousness of spirit, within the *text* of *India and Tibet,* the various parts of Younghusband's activities, experiences, and values are made to come together. Despite its oceanic inklings and tendencies, this self is portioned off from others; it must retain a certain distance from Tibetan others in order to function. Unlike Bogle's text, which as I have argued, really moves, Younghusband's impulse in this text is to make sense, to collect, to retrench, and to define. Horizons, in other words, need to be found. (And in that way, they are irretrievably lost.)

As Seaver notes, once back in England, Younghusband would frequently be called upon to lecture, and he often chose his Tibetan experience as his topic. This portion from a 1938 speech elaborates Tibetan epiphany into a revelation of love:

> Elation grew to exultation, and exultation to an exaltation which thrilled through me with overpowering intensity. I was beside myself with unintelligible joy. The whole world was ablaze with the same ineffable bliss that was burning within me. I felt in touch with the flaming heart of the world. . . . I was boiling over with love for the whole world. I could embrace every single human being. And henceforth life for me was naught but buoyancy and light.[32]

In this way, the myth of Tibetan epiphany was further textualized and narrativized. The finding of horizons became *the* story to tell, retell, and refashion. For subsequent travelers to Tibet, for later writers of Tibetan travel, Younghusband leaves a paradigm, a structure, a dream of transformation. For even if Younghusband accomplished his spiritual epiphany at a particular moment in imperial history, the space described and inscribed in his description of the movement, once opened, would not be closed again. He "pioneered," if you will, a certain notion of transformation in Tibet; he argued for a certain correspondence between the world and the inner life of "man." He joined the idea of secular pilgrimage and mystical enlightenment to the act of physical travel in Tibet. He opened up a territory, set a horizon of expectation through which Tibet becomes the place to which Westerners might travel to attain self-realization. Instead of allowing things to shift and move then, this kind of epiphany proscribes movement. Epiphanic realization becomes a fixed structure and an expectation that is sought transhistorically, and is ahistorically used and refashioned by later travelers. Just as yaks, sky-burial, monks, and mountains become part of the

baggage handled by successive travel-writers on Tibet, inner transformations become part and parcel of later accounts of Tibet in English. That
Younghusband's realization so baldly serves the imperialist project, that his
notion of himself is integrally connected to imperial discourses, is part of
the legacy borne by subsequent readers and writers of accounts of travel to
Tibet in English. In this way, the horizons that we find, which often seem
so new, frequently reinscribe old paths.

One antidote to such repetitious circling, as I have argued, is suggested
by Bogle's manuscripts. His refusal to stand still, he resistance to getting
"fixed," offer if not a solution then a series of unanswered questions that
urge us to reflect, criticize, and extend ourselves. Instead of containing
movement, instead of holding fast to dreams, Bogle's texts suggest a kind of
wandering in which one's self is never fully recovered.

To say that, of course, is to tear down the old expectation only to offer a
new one, to postpone the dream of transformation, to place a horizon elsewhere. This is where we are. This is where I am left.

Postscript

In 1984, at the age of 22, I started out on a two-year jaunt in South Asia
that would take me to Tibetan communities in India, Nepal, and Tibet
proper; my first destination was the Tibetan refugee settlement at Mundgod, Karnataka State, India. Prime Minister Nehru had donated the land
to the Tibetan refugees in the 1960s; the refugees had since cleared the
jungle terrain, creating farms and small businesses, reestablishing two major
monasteries—Drepung and Ganden—and making a home for several
thousand Tibetans. I had no contact in the camp at Mundgod, so I went to
the nearby city of Hubli, where I saw a young Tibetan man selling sweaters
on the street there. I asked him if there was a hotel at Mundgod; he wrote
this down on a slip of paper: LC #1.

It took several buses and the kindness of several Tibetan strangers—easy
enough to pick out from the crowd—to get me to LC #1, which turned
out to be Lama Camp Number One, otherwise known as Gajang Dangtse
monastery. My arrival and request to stay there caused a flurry of activity:
bottles of orange soda were brought, someone dashed off to find an English
speaker who might interpret for me, another rushed to make up the room
in the basement of the monastery. Within an hour I was standing before the
abbot of Ganden, the Ganden Tripa, who showed me his photographs of a
visit to Wisconsin, my home state. He told me, through the interpreter,
Migyur: "We haven't got many things as in America. But what we have is
yours. Think of this as your home." Later, the English-speaking lay secre-

tary of the monastic college offered me some reading material. The book he gave me was *The Practice and Theory of Tibetan Buddhism* by Geshe Sopa and Jeffrey Hopkins. At the time, Geshe Sopa, an esteemed Sera lama, was teaching at the University of Wisconsin-Madison, where I had spent the summer studying Hindi. I took notes on the book and tried to follow its instructions on meditation while, outside my window, whooping and gesticulating monks engaged in energetic debate.

Travelers to refugee settlements in India require official permits, but I was able to sidestep this because the local inspector was Maharashtrian, and I was able to speak with him in his mother tongue, Marathi. He granted me three days' grace. One monk in particular, Ngodrup, was assigned to my care; every time my teacup was empty he filled it. He fed me the same meals given to the highest-ranking monks: noodles, strips of sautéed water buffalo, and *momo,* or steamed dumplings filled with meat. I dared not tell him that I had been vegetarian for five years; I was a guest, and, in any case, we could only communicate in broken Hindi. At Ngodrup's encouragement, I resolved to study Tibetan and learned my first Tibetan words while staying there: words for turquoise, coral, that's good, that's bad, and, naturally enough among all those monks, the words for the monastic colors of maroon and gold.

As Bogle writes of his time at Tashilhunpo, my days were "monastick in the greatest degree."[33] I listened to a whirlwind of chanting, attended to the young monks' singsong recitation of texts, watched the tea-bearing monks scamper up the steps of the recently built monastery. I toured the hospital and dairy, and dealt with modest and repeated requests for money from laymen and monks alike. A dozen young monks came to my window to have a look at me. Through the same window, I watched while Tenzin, a tall monk with a languorous grin, swept the courtyard in the hot southern sun; he wrapped the over-shawl of his robe about his head like a turban. When it came time to leave, Tenzin, Ngodrup and two other monks from the administrative staff of Gajang Dangtse waited with me for the bus, plying me again with orange soda and offering me a small carpet to take home. When the bus rattled up, Ngodrup pushed through the crowd of passengers to find me a seat. I had been crying since I packed up my things and walked away from my room in the monastery. For in some way, I felt a part of that place and it of me. The monks teased that I was crying like a bride who was leaving home for the first time; to be sure, I had not shed a tear when I left Wisconsin. Ngodrup threw a *khata* about my neck; Tenzin stood outside waving. The bus jolted forward, leaving the monks behind, Younghusband and Bogle ahead of me.

PART TWO

TIBET IN ENGLISH

CHAPTER 1

New Age Namtars:
Tibetan Autobiographies in English

*I*n the fall of 1995, I arranged a visit of Tibetan monks to Kenyon College, where I was teaching at the time. Like many such traveling groups, the monks of Drepung Loseling monastery offered American audiences sounds of their famous overtone chanting, glimpses of folk and religious dances, and a sample of Gelukpa forms of philosophical debate. Four monks stayed with my family for several nights. Their visit also happened to coincide with the playoff games for the World Series, and the Cleveland team my husband T. S. and I were cheering for was in the running. After the monks' performance of "Sacred Music, Sacred Dance" before an admiring crowd, the monks, T. S. and I settled in front of the TV for the game. None of the monks knew the rules of baseball, and they were eager to learn. Only one of them, Geshe Damdul, was fluent in English, so with him as translator and my little knowledge of Tibetan, T. S. and I set out to explain the baseball's intricacies. The monks were familiar with cricket and soccer, so many comparisons were made among those games. And they learned fast: what a "ball" is; why a foul tip is not a third strike; why you can run past first base after a hit but cannot overrun second or third. The quiet monk they called "Elvis" because of his grown-out sideburns sat with his legs tucked under him on the couch. It didn't take long before Geshe Damdul Namgyal was wearing a baseball glove and a Minnesota Twins cap, slapping his fist into the glove. And soon the monks identified the Latino pitcher Dennis Martinez as one of them: "He looks like a Tibetan!" When the game went past one A.M., T. S. and I retired, leaving Elvis and the geshe before the TV; they watched till the end and reported next morning that, in fact, "we" had won.

That afternoon, three of these same monks visited a class I was teaching on Western representations of Tibet. These recent exiles told stories in Tibetan, translated again in the quiet, kind voice of Geshe Damdul, of the hardships they faced in Chinese-occupied Tibet—no chance to learn Buddhism, no chance to be literate in Tibetan, no way to really choose one's own life—as well as of their recent escape from Tibet to India, and what it meant to them to be able to study at reestablished Tibetan monasteries in India, the places that sent them out into the wide world to raise money for a burgeoning monastic population.

At the time I felt proud and amused to have spent so much time with these monks and to have seen them in a number of settings. Having traveled among Tibetan communities since 1982, I was comfortable with many Tibetan mores and glad for a chance to return the hospitality I had been extended. And of course, something of the Tibetans' charisma rubbed off on me, raising my own prestige within the small college community. But looking back on it now, two things strike me about their visit. First was the ways in which the monks' public performances on the stage and in class fit certain models of Tibetan-ness: their concert showed them as religious, colorful, devout and even humorous beings; in the classroom the refugees seemed humble, devout, religious, and politically-besieged people. All of these self-presentations seemed to accord with popular Western representations of Tibetans, made both in the media and by a growing number of Western supporters of Tibetan self-determination. The stories that seem not to have been told in Western representations of Tibetans, however, were the ones that could account for the monks' interest in baseball and cricket as well as their ability to move between seemingly alien worlds—the modern crass world of American culture and the apparently ancient, religious world of Tibet—without contradiction.[1] For while some of my students were surprised that monks could show an interest in Walkmen and ping-pong, the forms of Tibetan culture I had glimpsed in my travels included not only idealized versions of Tibetans, but also versions of Tibetan-ness less easy to categorize: it included monks and nuns but also beer-drinking intellectuals, Tibetan members of the People's Liberation Army, over-worked mothers, leather jacket-wearing entrepreneurs, teenage disco dancers, photographers, and terrarium-makers, many of whom still identi-fied themselves as Buddhist and who moved freely among a variety of cultural positions.

Connected to this, another thing strikes me about their visit: my students' and my own desire to hear these Tibetans' stories, to have them tell us about their lives—even if we had to hear it in translation. The stories they offered did not include baseball, miles of American highways, their reactions to the starry-eyed gazes of college audiences. All of that was left out. Their narratives—while they were no doubt true in many senses—fulfilled multiple expectations of Tibetan-ness: their own sense of a Tibetan subject as humble, devotedly Buddhist, and nationalist, and our own view—shall I call it Western, American, Anglo?—that Tibetans should be religious, exotic, and politically oppressed. In a sense, this scene of life story telling mimics a larger process of Tibetan self-presentation to Westerners that has been going on for the past four decades.

Beginning in 1957 and increasingly since 1990, a number of Tibetans have produced self-presentations in the form of English-language autobiographies; these texts offer versions of Tibetan-ness to an eager portion of the English-reading populace.[2] How might we read these Tibetan autobiographies in English? Should we see them as participants in the Tibetan tradition of creating *rangnam*—full liberation, first-person narratives that tell the story of a Buddhist subject's achievement of enlightenment? Are they simply a kind of capitulation to Western desires, telling readers the stories they want to hear in a way they want to hear them? Or might they be something less easy to categorize?

As I see it, the making of Tibetan autobiography in English is an extension of the valued Tibetan tradition of creating *rangnam* and *namtar* (biography); it is also, to some extent, a reply to the myth of epiphany, a response to a Western tendency to idealize Tibetan culture and religion and all its apparent representatives: Westerners seem to think that all Tibetans are special people, so any Tibetan's life story is worth telling. For the stories told in these books are not the conventional Tibetan stories of how Buddhist exemplars came to be enlightened beings, as in the prevailing *rangnam* tradition; instead they often tell the tales of non-traditional Tibetan subjects—lay men and women, political prisoners, non-tulkus, and monks without degrees, for example. The making of Tibetan autobiography in English emerges from a tangled and complex set of circumstances, conventions, and expectations. In some ways, these autobiographies are created out of a deeply Tibetan impulse to create a life story; in some ways the making of Tibetan autobiography in English is a phenomenon of diaspora and is born out of the recent experience of Chinese colonialism in Tibet and the subsequent exile of over 100,000 Tibetans; the two impulses sometimes work in concert.

On the reception end, I refer throughout to "Western readers," but it is hard to pin down who exactly the readers of these texts are. In this study I am particularly interested in the reception of these stories by non-Tibetan audiences in the United States and the United Kingdom. In Part One, we learned something of Britain's interest in Tibet; Americans' particular fascination with Tibet was handed down from the myth of epiphany, nurtured in part by Cold War politics, and created in reaction to the perceived complexity and emptiness of modern life. Into this spiritual and cultural void have arisen Anglophone films on Tibet, the commodification of Tibetan artifacts, advertisements using Tibetan images, pro-Tibetan political action groups, public appearances of Tibetan monks, numerous books on Tibet, as well as Tibetan autobiographies in English. Because of the fascination with Tibet in the United States, diverse American and, to a lesser extent, British audiences have played important roles in the construction of Tibetan self-presentation.

The intertwined history of Anglophone representations of Tibet and Tibetan self-presentation invites me to imagine inventive ways of reading these texts. For while on the surface some Tibetan autobiographies in English present an "authentic Tibetan"[3] of simple, strong belief, untainted by Western influence—a Tibetan who many Westerners and Tibetans have come to define as distinctly Tibetan, it is possible to uncover other ways of reading such autobiographies and thus discover ways in which standard images of Tibetan-ness are challenged, if not transformed. Reading against the image of the idealized, authentic Tibetan, in my analyses of these texts I find contestatory versions of Tibetan-ness, versions which may or may not derive from traditional notions of what makes a Böpa, the Tibetan term frequently used nowadays to signify "Tibetan." For even in some autobiographies which seem not to challenge idealized Western notions of Tibetan-ness, it is possible to read against the grain to discover (or construct) other versions of Tibetan identity, resisting notions of selfhood, representations that do not just confirm popular assumptions but move beyond them to offer different notions of what Tibetans might be. As Ashis Nandy writes in a different context, "a living culture has an obligation to itself, not to its analysts"; if Tibetan self-presentations neither perfectly mirror Western desires nor seamlessly bespeak some construction of "traditional" Tibetan values, then perhaps we have come some distance in recognizing that contemporary Tibetans can be the agents of their own history and culture, instead of simply the objects of Western fantasy.[4]

In "Tibet in English," then, I explore the complex and refracted ways in which Tibetan autobiographers working in English encounter, struggle with, and resist the expectations placed on them by Western readers and publishers, even as they work out of, along side, and against indigenous Tibetan notions of life story telling, as in the *namtar* tradition. What they create is, I think, something "mixed," but it is not thereby degraded. Rather than simply exploring the influence of Western and American desires on Tibetan autobiographies, I am concerned with exploring the ongoing exchanges between the English-speaking Westerners and Tibetans,

exchanges in which both Tibetans and Westerners are actors and participants as well as desiring subjects. In order to represent a complex view of
these Tibetan autobiographical subjects, I proceed this way: in chapter 1, I
go on to highlight a number of theoretical and critical issues relevant to my
project. I consider the genres of Tibetan *rangnam* and *namtar,* their traditions
and assumptions, and what they mean for this study; I then consider issues
of authorship and readership by surveying the field of Tibetan autobiographies in English in a general way. What do Western readers want from these
texts? Why do Tibetan writers write them? What expectations do both
bring to the exchange? For just as the touring Tibetan monks at my college
responded to their audiences' expectations, produced images of themselves,
and played out Buddhist notions of patronage on American soil, Tibetan
autobiographies in English work within a complex situation that involves,
among other things, conflicting notions of authorship, the construction and
expectation of the authentic Tibetan, and the refurbishment of Tibetan
notions of patronage. Exploring these different and yet interconnected
issues not only highlights my orientation to these texts in a broad sense, it
allows me to lay out my tools for reading and to situate the study within
larger concerns about Tibetan production and Western reception of
Tibetan autobiographies in English.

After this general introduction, in chapters 2-8 I consider selected book-
length autobiographies.[5] Pairing comparable autobiographies, I explore issues
of authorship, genre, and self-presentation. Starting with autobiographies
by two of the Dalai Lama's siblings—Jetsun Pema's *Tibet: My Story* and
Thubten Jigme Norbu's *Tibet is My Country*—I pair autobiographies in
order to consider their different ways of representing what typifies Tibetan
identity. In subsequent sections I compare divergent accounts of a monastic
education; two versions of the Dalai Lama's autobiography; two accounts
by incarnate lamas or *tulkus,* the life stories of two aristocratic lay women;
the several personal accounts of two political prisoners; and, finally, the singular story told by an exile who chose to return to Tibet. Instead of offering an overarching narrative that binds all these stories together and
uncovers a unified, authentic, or even coherent Tibetan, I am interested in
interpreting the dynamic, multiple, and shifting ways that Tibetans represent themselves in autobiographies in English and the creative and resisting
ways readers might approach them in order to discover and construct other
versions of Tibetan-ness. Because I am mindful that the difference between
what is Western and what is Tibetan is not a matter of inherent, unchang-
ing essences, and because I am interested in how the very terms "Tibetan"
and "Western" are defined in ways that codify people's sense of themselves
and the world, I approach these texts as moving objects and myself as a

shifting reader. Taking up a kind of Bogle-ian reading—one that acknowledges movement, contradiction, changes of heart—I consider how these texts negotiate a diverse and complex set of expectations in their efforts to present something of a Tibetan life.

TIBETAN *RANGNAM* AND ENGLISH AUTOBIOGRAPHY

Before I consider the "hybrid" texts of Tibetan autobiographies in English, let me briefly and generally consider the two literary traditions from which they arise: the Tibetan *rangnam* and *namtar* traditions and the English autobiographical tradition.

The Tibetan biographical tradition of creating *namtars* or "full liberation" stories is an old one, expressed both in oral and written forms; *rangnam,* or autobiographical life story telling, is closely related to it. Taking the life of the Buddha as a kind of blueprint, Tibetan *rangnams* and *namtars* have been telling the story of a person's achievement of Buddhist enlightenment almost since the birth of Tibetan writing in the eighth century. Within the autobiographical tradition and its closely related biographical tradition, the *rangnam* form arose out of an historical, religious, and cultural context unique in the Buddhist world. As traditionally conceived, the life stories narrated in Tibetan follow a conventionalized script: as in the life story of the Buddha, the story of the (usually male) subject's (often mischievous) childhood is followed by the story of his renunciation, his encounter with religious teachers, his realization, and his subsequent call to teach others what he has discovered.[6] Following this general outline, Tibetan *namtars* and *rangnams* include the stories of such religious exemplars as bodhisattvas, "saints," purveyors of "crazy wisdom," and other enlightened beings. Told in all Tibetan cultural regions from Bhutan to Ladakh to Kham and now in exile, related in all classes of society, *rangnams* and *namtars* cover a lot of territory. From the story of the "cotton-clad" Milarepa to the antinomian Drukpa Kunley, from the first Panchen Lama to the tantric consort of Padmasambhava[7]—*namtars* and *rangnams* offer tales of the achievement of enlightenment "in one lifetime, in one body, even in these degenerate times."[8] Because Buddhist doctrine generally maintains that the attainment of such release depends upon the sincere efforts of a practitioner and not on the intervention of some divine being, *rangnams* and *namtars* offer stories to live by, models to be emulated. Once having heard or read the tale, the sincere practitioner is instructed and invited to take up the path to liberation with confidence and vigor.

Although other biographical and autobiographical traditions might offer similar inspiration and instruction (as in the hagiographies of Christian saints), the particular shape of the lives related in *namtars* and *rangnams* is uniquely Buddhist. Indeed, within the Buddhist world, Tibetan Buddhism's particular emphasis on tantric practice emerges as one of the key factors in the making of the *rangnam* genre. Unlike more gradualist Buddhist approaches to enlightenment, tantric practices offer to catapult both lay and monastic practitioners into enlightenment. It is through such practices that a human breaks through the usual chains of suffering and delusion; it is only because of such practices that he or she has a significant story to tell. Because of the specificity of the subjects and the tales represented in Tibetan life stories, the Tibetan tradition of autobiography has been distinctly different from that in English and has tended to focus primarily on religious exemplars. Even though, as Janet Gyatso writes, "the term does not always have such a lofty connotation—'namtar' can be used prosaically to describe any account of the events in a life, even a sinful or ignorant life—usually the label indicates the Buddhistic character of the narrative."[9] And although not all Tibetan *namtars* or *rangnams* expressly focus on spiritual matters—as Gyatso notes "Tibetan literature is full of conventional accounts of experiences and careers"—the Buddhist framework for *namtar* distinguishes it from English and European biographical and autobiographical genres.[10]

In comparison, as it evolved, the prevailing English autobiographical tradition came to cover a wider range of subjects and orientations. Although it is rooted in Protestant spiritual autobiographies, by the nineteenth century the scope of the autobiographical subject had expanded to include secular writers as well. By the twentieth century the genre in its literary and popular forms came to include all manner of beings, from football players to movie stars to artists and authors and perpetrators of lurid crimes. The degree to which these subjects emphasize their self-understanding and realization thus ranges widely, and certainly departs from the traditional construction of autobiographies in Tibetan.

There are other important differences between Tibetan and English autobiographical traditions: one of these centers on the very notion of the self represented in such stories. While the English-language tradition of autobiography developed around the notion of a soul or a self and tends to focus on personality, within the Tibetan tradition, such concentration on the "ego" or soul or self is understood as one of the chief causes of suffering—the very thing which the Buddhist path seeks to address. Tibetan *rangnams* then depend on very different premises than most English-language autobiographies; recognizing both a conventional notion of self—the "I" of everyday experience—and the ultimate emptiness of that self, Tibetan *rangnams* ultimately strive to represent "subjectivity without essence," as Gyatso puts it.[11] As in poststructural thought, Tibetan Buddhist autobiography begins from a kind of radical deconstruction of subjectivity—subjectivity with nothing permanent at the base of it.

While Buddhist authors tend to accept the ultimate emptiness of a personal self, the situation in the West has been quite different. The discovery and representation of the uniqueness of the individual self has been a central concern in Western autobiography. Rooted in a genre that worked out one soul's relationship to God, framed within a worldview that emphasizes the importance of individual and personal achievement, Western autobiography, as the theorist Georges Gusdorf writes, arises out of "certain metaphysical preconditions," and is generally produced by an historical figure who

> knows that the present differs from the past and that it will not be repeated in the future; he has become more aware of differences than of similarities; given the constant change, given the uncertainty of events and of men, he believes it a useful and valuable thing to fix his own image so that he can be certain it will not disappear like all things in this world.[12]

Readers have frequently used such texts to reflect on their own experience or to better understand an historical period, but in the broadest sense, they have accepted autobiographies as a narrative written by a "real person concerning his own existence," a story that both recounts the development of personality and places the hero's name in the historical record.[13]

My comments here only highlight general trends in the traditions of English and Tibetan autobiography and do not describe recent innovations in both traditions. But given these general outlines, where should we locate Tibetan autobiographies in English? Are they Tibetan, English, or some kind of monstrous (or gorgeous) hybrid? For not only are these texts written in a language other than Tibetan; many of them relate the life stories of subjects unusual to the *namtar* tradition. In addition to stories of religious exemplars like the Dalai Lama, the recent wave of Tibetan autobiographies in English include the autobiographies of two of the Dalai Lama's siblings; along with the life stories of esteemed lamas, we have the tales of several lesser monks, some of whom never even finished the monastic curriculum. And in addition to Buddhist renunciates who devote their lives to the dharma, we also have the stories of armed freedom fighters, English-educated intellectuals, aristocratic women, and secular exiles. Do the subjects represented in these texts participate in Western notions of selfhood or Tibetan ones? How would we know? And how should we read them? Palden Gyatso, for one, acknowledges the significance of the *namtar* tradition within Tibetan culture but suggests that his life story does not lead up to a tale of full liberation.[14] Should we accept disclaimers like this at face value, or read them as gestures that, because they enact conventional humility, actually demonstrate the exemplary status of the stories? Are these texts New Age *namtars* of exemplary Tibetans for Western readers? Or something new entirely?

TIBETAN WRITERS, NON-TIBETAN READERS

Because these texts are presented in English and are, for the most part, published in the United States and the United Kingdom, they hail particular audiences: English-speaking readers in those places.[15] Interested in informing readers of English in the West about Tibet's culture, religion, and recent history, writers of these texts frequently take care to explicate concepts and practices that may be unfamiliar to those readers: Jetsun Pema goes into a long explanation about the discovery of the 14th Dalai Lama, and Dawa Norbu discusses the funerary practices of lay Tibetans.[16] Other writers leave things out to accommodate these same readers: Jamyang Sakya and Julie Emery note that because their book "is written primarily for Western readers . . . we have not identified high-ranking lamas and those in the Tibetan nobility with their formal titles."[17] And when Thubten Jigme Norbu published his autobiography in 1960, he refused to speak at length about Tibetan Buddhism, perhaps out of fear that a brief survey of Tibetan Buddhism could only further distort its reputation after the success of Lobsang Rampa's books in the West.[18]

Despite these accommodations to their largely Western audience, however, it should be noted that Tibetan autobiographies in English are not read only by Westerners or by non-Tibetans. Many Tibetans do read English and some Tibetan autobiographers aim to address them; in *House of the Turquoise Roof,* Dorje Yudon Yuthok, for example, states that she writes in part for a younger generation of Tibetan women.[19] Because I am especially interested in the ongoing relationship between ethnic Tibetans and English-speaking Westerners (problematic as that term may be) in this study, I focus on that interaction and thus concentrate on a largely Western readership, all the while understanding that the division between what is Western and what is Tibetan is not always clear: after all, we live in a world in which Westerners can be Tibetan Buddhists and Tibetans can be Westernized and secular.

But if we focus on non-Tibetan Western, Anglophone readers, what do such readers want from these autobiographies? What do they get?

Of the 30 Tibetan autobiographies in English I have been able to identify—the number grows all the time—I see several common traits. Firstly, even though a range of people are represented in these life stories, every single autobiographical subject to date is or has been an exile. Secondly, and this seems to accord with the Tibetan *namtar* tradition, the majority of autobiographical subjects identify themselves as Buddhist. Thirdly, almost every Tibetan autobiographer is a Tibetan nationalist who believes in Tibet's right to self-determination, if not in full-fledged independence. Sometimes this nationalism is expressed through subjects' willingness to go to prison for their beliefs, sometimes through their willingness to fight for the resistance, and sometimes simply through the fact of their exile. Thus, the Tibetan-ness constructed in these texts is closely associated with exile, with Buddhism, and with nationalism.

If one way to think about what American and other Western readers want from Tibetan autobiographies in English is to think in general terms about what one can find there, another way to think about what Western readers want (and learn to want) from Tibetan autobiographies in English is to consider what is *not* in them, and to explore what this means for Western representations of Tibetan-ness. What is generally not in these texts are images of pro-Chinese Tibetans (there are many, after all), Tibetans in Tibet (who make up the majority of ethnic Tibetans), non-Buddhist Tibetans or almost anybody who violates the exile, Buddhist, nationalist norm.[20] The reason for these omissions, I think, is that, in one strategic definition of Tibetan-ness forwarded in the West and among Tibetan exiles, to lack one of these identities—exile, Buddhist, nationalist—is to risk being considered something less than fully Tibetan. While such a conception may contradict other local definitions of authenticity—after all, many Westerners and Tibetan exiles continue to valorize the seemingly "simple Tibetans of strong belief"[21] *within* Tibet—let us consider the stay-in-Tibet Tibetans and the lack of their representation in English language autobiographies.

There are no doubt practical and political reasons for the lack of anglophone autobiographies of Tibetans who remain within Tibet: few Tibetans in Tibet know English; few Western or English-speaking scholars and writers who would be capable of translating such *rangnams* have been allowed to study in Tibet; collaboration between English-speaking exiles or foreigners and domestic Tibetans may be politically dangerous for both parties. All of these difficulties may be reason enough for the lack of non-exilic autobiographies. But I think something else may be at work here: many who follow Tibetan issues in the West operate on the largely unspoken notion that because Tibetans in Tibet have been frequently deprived of what is understood as the fullness of their Buddhist tradition, and because they have not fled their oppressors, they represent a kind of tainted Tibetan-ness.[22] Similarly, the stay-in-Tibet Tibetan presents a political conundrum for many pro-Tibetan independence fighters: if Westerners and Tibetan exiles argue that conditions within Chinese-occupied Tibet are brutal and oppressive, the Tibetan who remains in Tibet seems to contradict or at least challenge their assertions about what Chinese-occupied Tibet is like. If the situation really were unlivable, then real Tibetans could not live there. Or to put it another way, to stay in Tibet means to compromise—or to be com-promised. Of course, this is not an argument articulated by those who are in favor of Tibetan independence; instead it is the unspoken part of the assertion—the logical corollary—to the notion that real Tibetan-ness now only thrives in exile. This has been the message of many Western pro-Tibetan groups: Tibetan culture in Tibet is under siege; only in exile does it have the freedom to live. And as Jetsun Pema notes in her autobiography, "In our own country, under the Chinese occupation, our culture or any-thing that identifies Tibet as a separate entity suffers systematic destruction and is on the verge of annihilation. Our culture is alive only in exile."[23] If Tibetan culture only exists in exile, then, following the same logic, the only "real" Tibetans live there too.

Likewise, the central role of Buddhism in defining Tibetan authenticity leaves out portions of the Tibetan population; historically there have been Tibetan Muslims, Christians, as well as Bonpos, and presently there are sec-ular Tibetans. Furthermore, the emphasis on Buddhism can lead to some complex Tibetan self-definitions. As one 20–something, Swiss-educated, German-speaking, white collar Tibetan man described it, "I think Tibetan identity means also—it's just necessary that you are also very much Bud-dhist. It seems to me. Our religion has always been an element—the dom-inating element in our culture for the Tibetan people."[24] For this exile, what matters in determining Tibetan authenticity—always a slippery task—is Buddhist identity. Because of this, this Swiss exile, who himself claims not to be Buddhist, spends much of his time in a youth group rais-ing money for Tibetans in India and Tibet who seem to embody a whole-hearted, unquestioning faith in the dharma. While his own life seems complex and culturally mixed, the life of the authentic Tibetan seems to him simple, almost unifocal: they have "simple, strong belief."[25]

But given all this concern with who and what makes a real Tibetan, we might well ask: where do such images of authenticity come from? As I see it, the image of the authentic Tibetan has been produced over the past sev-eral centuries through the interaction of Tibetan self-presentations with Western representations of Tibetans. This complex negotiation of images creates versions of Tibetan-ness that are neither "wholly" Western nor "purely" Tibetan. As Donald S. Lopez, Jr. describes this situation in *Prisoners of Shangri-La: Tibetan Buddhism and the West,* when Tibetans came into exile after 1959 they encountered images of themselves already in existence in the West:

> It was as if a double of Tibet had long haunted the West, and the Tibetans, coming out of Tibet, were now confronted with this double. In this sense the Tibetans stepped into a world in which they were already present, and since their belated arrival—often encouraged by the devotees of Tibet, missionaries of a different stripe—they have merged seamfully [*sic*] into a double that had long been standing. . . . If to see one's double is to see one's fate, then what has occurred since 1959 has been a sometimes fitful accommodation of this double; as though mimicking a phantom, the Tibetans' self-presentation, as in a science fiction film, sometimes merges with its evil twin and sometimes stands alone, while the observer is rarely able to tell them apart. As in the mirror scene in *Duck Soup,* it is only when one of the pair has turned away for an instant that the viewer knows that in fact there is no mirror between them, that they are two and not one; one is in disguise.[26]

The representation of the authentic Tibetan, whatever variant features it possesses, is a product of this mirroring and negotiation of images: it is the outcome of a complex negotiation of Western expectations of Tibetans and Tibetans' own personal and cultural ideals, though as Lopez warns, "the observer is rarely able to tell them apart."[27]

Because of this, we can see authentic Tibetans in a number of places: we can glimpse her in Scorsese's *Kundun,* beseeching the Dalai Lama to flee Tibet and the Chinese; we can see her in many Tibetans' comportment when the Dalai Lama takes the throne to give a religious teaching. An authentic Tibetan is devout; his faith is unquestioned and uncompromised: he participates in religious rituals, makes offerings, utters mantras—his face adorns another TV documentary, as he mutters "Om Mane Padme Hum." The authentic Tibetan can also be glimpsed among the monks who go on tour in the United States, sharing their sacred dance and music with college audiences. If one sifts through the layers of images, going back in time, another version of an authentic Tibetan appears in the smiling, simple, and virtually indistinguishable natives of Shangri-La in Frank Capra's *Lost Horizon.* The authentic Tibetan is also there among the Tibetan pilgrims who make their way from distant villages to see the holy places of Lhasa. He's also there among the amulet-wearing soldiers who fought against Younghusband's army—and in Kipling's Teshoo Lama. And in what is perhaps the first glimpse of the authentic Tibetan in English, Bogle described Tibetans who greeted the Panchen Lama with "a look of Veneration mixed with keen joy in their Countenances."[28] The image of Tibetan authenticity in the West, though often made to appear as a freestanding and completely indigenous presence, is a phantasm, a hybrid, a complex production of cultural exchange, one which will frequently guide the making and reception of Tibetan autobiography in English.

Given the parameters of authenticity suggested above, readers of Tibetan autobiographies in English will not get many stories about secular, white-collar Tibetans nor about Tibetans who seem otherwise compromised. The desire for an authentic Tibetan on the part of both exiled Tibetans and their Western admirers frequently precludes the representation of hybridity in Tibetan lives and identities. In most of the popular narratives of Tibetan lives these days—whether they take the form of autobiographies, biographies, or travel writing—evidence of "mixed" cultures and values is cause for disappointment and a sign of failure. Thus, for example, it is generally okay if a lama wears Clarks or Birkenstocks under his maroon robes and thus participates in a kind of surface mixing of styles. But it would not be okay if a Tibetan monk wanted to *buy* Gucci shoes, and photos of the Dalai Lama with Sharon Stone make many people cringe.[29] Because Tibet has been construed as an ancient, spiritual culture, Tibetan encounters with the "modern world" threaten old dichotomies, suggesting not Tibet's anachronism but its coevalness.[30] Thus, in his description of the Dalai Lama's use of an electric fan and a microphone during Buddhist teachings in Pasadena, Orville Schell seems to long for a time when the "ancient" and modern were not so mixed—when Tibet stayed in place: "We are in almost every sense a long way from the Potala."[31] Other kinds of mixings are similarly taboo; thus, for the most part, what the English reading public has been served (what they crave?) has been the old standard fare: Tibetans as Buddhist exemplars; Tibetans as a dignified people defending their traditional and unique culture and religion. What we generally do not get are the life stories of Tibetans who occupy posts within the Communist system; we don't get the life-stories of Dharamsala *restaurateurs*, or the Tibetan traders who sell their wares to tourists on the beaches of Goa, or the ones who run heroin between Europe and Nepal. The implicit suggestion is that, somehow, these people are not really Tibetans—at least, not the best example of Tibetan-ness. And even when there is a possibility of exploring hybridity or cultural interaction within the narratives of standard exiled, Buddhist, and nationalist Tibetans, that chance is usually suppressed. Thus, as I will discuss below, we are asked not to look too far into the cosmopolitan character of the life of Jetsun Pema, nor to ask too many questions about the adaptations many exiles have made in the West, whether these occur in the form of their daily life, their worldview, or their political perspectives.

The single example of an autobiography by a Tibetan who chose to return to Chinese-occupied Tibet, discussed in chapter 8, is the exception that proves the rule: Tibetan autobiographies in English are only about certain kinds of Tibetans. The inclusion of cover photographs of monks in maroon and gold robes, women in traditional jewelry, and laymen in fox-fur hats and *chubas* are all designed to indicate that we are in the realm of the Tibetans who have preserved their identity, keeping it free from the taint of the West.

If the logic of publication has anything to do with the logic of reader's desires, the next question is: Why do most Western readers of Tibetan auto-biography in English want authentic Tibetans? What do they hope to get from them? In the popular literature, Tibetan culture is often described as preserving something modern culture has lost: spirituality, a close relationship with nature, compassion for other living beings, a simple life. In order to communicate these things to Western readers, Tibetan autobiographers cannot seem to have been compromised too much by the West, or by what is equally abhorrent, Chinese Communism. If they are too westernized, their elixir will not cure. That Tibetans are sometimes linked to Native Americans in popular literature (Sandy Johnson writes that "both traditions were rooted in the same spiritual earth"[32]) suggests that Americans in particular elevate Tibetans out of a mixture of fear and guilt. Traveling troupes of costumed, dancing, singing, and chanting Tibetan monks have succeeded Buffalo Bill's Wild West Show, and Tibetan self-identifications as barbarians who have been civilized by Buddhism coincide nicely with the Western fantasy of the "noble savage."

And as in Hilton's and Capra's vision of Shangri-La, authentic Tibetans are supposed to preserve the best of human civilization while at the same time rejecting what is coarse, violent, and selfish. They might, like the Dalai Lama, be indulged an interest in watches or motor cars, or even be allowed to be fluent in English, but they must nonetheless maintain an overall air of traditional Tibetan, Buddhist, nationalist values. For this reason images of Tibetans that proclaim their spirituality and traditional values have more appeal than the few that offer a more complex view. Johnson's *The Book of Tibetan Elders,* with its images of Tibetans as "spacemen and cave dwellers,"[33] spiritual masters and oracles, does something different for readers than Vincanne Adams's more theoretically nuanced representations of Tibetans in Lhasa's karaoke bars.[34] Robert Thurman's image of Tibetans as "psychic cosmonauts" is less troubling to many readers than Donald Lopez's vision of Tibetans as seamful doubles of Western fantasy.[35] In the popular view, Tibetans promise because of their very otherness, because of their presence—their seeming ability to live more spiritually connected, more conscious, more meaningful lives. And this presence promises to transform Western selves.

A QUESTION OF PRESENCE

The title "Dalai Lama" is seldom used in Tibetan; instead, when speaking about the 14th Dalai Lama in Tibetan, one refers to Gyalwa Rinpoche, Yeshe Norbu, or speaks about the travels of Kundun, addressing the sacred personage himself as Kundun-La, "honorable presence." For Tibetan Buddhists, the Dalai Lama is the presence of (a form of) enlightenment on earth, an incarnation of the bodhisattva *Chenrezig* (Skt. *Avalokiteshvara),* the dynamic and recurring emanation of the union of wisdom and compassion, the realization of the Buddha-nature that in most of us is only or mostly nascent. So beneficent is the presence of the Dalai Lama that devotees will touch their hands and rub their prayer *malas* over the place where he has sat; so necessary is his presence in the world to our well-being that one common Tibetan Buddhist ritual involves requesting the Dalai Lama and other such reincarnate lamas to live long amongst us. And in a sense, presence is what Tibetan autobiographies in English proffer. For some readers, these texts do not just offer the story of a real Tibetan as told by that Tibetan. They offer the presence of that Tibetan, the emanation of that Tibetan in a (Western) reader's life, and it is through such presence that the reader is educated or even transformed.

Even though some strands of Western literary theory deconstructed the cult of the author some time ago, many Western readers approach autobiographies with the general expectation that the text presents something of the life of a real person, that is, that they present a presence and not simply a sign or a representation. What readers have come to expect from autobiography, in part, includes the understanding that the "I" of the enunciation (the speaker) and the "I" of the utterance (the spoken, the protagonist) refer to the same person, that both speaker and protagonist can be identified with the author whose signature graces the title page of the book, and that the name of the author itself refers to a "real person" in the world. As Philipe Lejeune argues:

> The entire existence of the person we call the *author* is summed up by this name [on the flyleaf]: the only mark in the text of an unquestionable world-beyond-the-text, referring to a real person, which requires that we thus

attribute to him, in the final analysis, the responsibility for the production of the whole written text. In many cases the presence of the author in the text is reduced to this single name.[36]

The confusion of narrator/protagonist, author, and person in the world seems particularly marked in the case of Tibetan autobiographies in English. In Tibetan autobiographies in English, as in other English-language autobiographies, the identity of narrator, narrated, and author is signaled not only by the signature of the narrator/narrated's name on the cover and title page, but also by the frequent inclusion of the subject's portrait on the cover. So Lobsang Gyatso in his maroon robes grins at us from the cover of his book; similarly, the Dalai Lama graces the cover of his two autobiographies. All but one of the Tibetans interviewed in Vyvyan Cayley's *Children of Exile* warrants a photograph. The clothbound edition of Palden Gyatso's life story not only boasts photos of the author/ narrator/protagonist inside, the entire volume is clothed in monastic red and gold, colors the imprisoned monk was long forbidden to wear. All of these images and inclusions combine to suggest: what we have here is the real thing. That readers frequently confuse the representation of a life with people in the world is suggested by readers' comments on Amazon.com's website; there readers often give the highest 5–star rating to Tibetan autobiographies that (at least in my opinion) are tediously written or poorly edited. To criticize the book would seem like criticizing the person "in the world."[37]

As Western literary theory suggests, however, autobiographies are never simply presentations of a life full-blooded and breathing. They are always re-presentations, made things, fictions of a sort. And in the case of many Tibetan autobiographies, they are not even writings that come from the pen of the author listed on the title page and pictured on the cover. Instead, many of these autobiographies in English were first *oral* texts, as it were, texts produced through interviews that were then recorded, collected, transcribed, translated, arranged, and edited by someone else, always a fluent English speaker, of course, and usually an *Inji* (Westerner) and not a Tibetan at all. And frequently the ghostwriter is not even given a byline. Instead, most accounts of Tibetan lives in English have insisted on the "auto" part of the autobiography and played down the role of the editor or ghostwriter, as in the autobiographies of Jetsun Pema, Thubten Jigme Norbu, and the Dalai Lama.[38] (Pay no attention to that man behind the curtain.) In the case of the ghostwritten text, the problem of the dream of presence becomes even more acute.

When a book is ghostwritten, the signature on the title page refers not to the person who engaged in the writing of book (in mechanical and editorial terms), but rather to the interviewed subject—to a voice connected to but different from the words on the page. Palden Gyatso may very well be the personage identified with the "I" in *The Autobiography of a Tibetan Monk,* but he can only be construed as the writer of the book by a kind of sleight of hand: this self-proclaimed autobiography is actually a polyvocal text, one in which another has played a very active role as transcriber, translator, and editor, as is mentioned briefly in Tsering Shakya's preface to that book. The case is the same with Yuthok's *House of the Turquoise Roof,* Jetsun Pema's *Tibet: My Story* and others. The purported author of the book is the interviewed subject, a speaker in a microphone, but not the person who arranged the words on the page. If mention of the editor or ghostwriter appears at all, it is in the preface or forward; more rarely, the name of this writer is noted after that of the protagonist on the title page.[39]

Exceptions withstanding, in most cases, the mediation of a ghostwriter is played down for several reasons. The first has to do with the Western cult of the author. As Lejeune writes, what Western readers demand from autobiography is "the personal form of a discourse assumed by a real person, responsible for his writing as he is for his life. We consume the full-fledged 'subject,' which we want to believe is true." For this reason, in almost all ghostwritten autobiographies "the mediation of the 'ghostwriter' will either be hidden, or if it is admitted, it will be blurred or changed."[40] Most Western readers of Tibetan autobiographies in English, then, come to them with certain values and habits of reading: they do not want equivocation, ambiguity, or people who are really only texts. Secondly, given that most of the personages represented in these autobiographies have Tibetan as a first language and do not speak English or do so less than fluently, there has to be an intermediary if Anglophone readers are to get the story at all. But I believe that there are still other reasons for playing down the involvement of ghostwriters, and they have to do with readers' desires.

The desire to tap into the dream of presence is strong—if not irresistible—in the case of Tibetan subjects because of what it allows readers to feel. The first person narration of the autobiography allows the reader the sense of entering into a kind of dialogue with a Tibetan other: the "I" of the narrative calls for a "you," a position to be taken up by the reader. Because Westerners long saw Tibet as a "forbidden land" and considered Tibetans mysterious and isolated others, the fantasy of having a Tibetan right in one's home, one's hands, one's head is too much to resist. And once "contact" with the Tibetan has been made, the myth of epiphany— detached now from the *place* of Tibet—can circulate more freely; reading the life of a Tibetan—contact with that Tibetan—becomes something that can transform readers, making them into a new "you."

Evidence of such transformations can be found in readers' comments on the Amazon.com website. While they cannot offer an exhaustive or scientific view of "what readers want" from Tibetan autobiographies, such readers' comments—both signed and anonymous—offer a sample of how some people respond to these texts.[41] The comments of one reader suggests the ways in which the dream of presence factors into the process of reading, when he/she writes, "As I read *Freedom in Exhile* [*sic*] I had to keep reminding myself that it was a book and not a letter from His Holiness to myself."[42] The book seems to offer the "real thing"—and something special to Western readers. Other readers' comments on this site make claims for the potential of Tibetan autobiographies to transform readers. As one reader from California writes, "I started reading the book *[Freedom in Exile: The Autobiography of the Dalai Lama]* out of interest and finished the book a wiser person."[43] Or as another reader from Taipei writes of Palden Gyatso's story, this book "must be a compulsory read for anyone trying to be a better person . . . ;"[44] and yet another writes, "You'll be a better person for reading this book."[45] While it is useful to have an autobiography to access, for some readers the very existence of Tibetans in the world can bolster Western lives. As one reader comments:

> It's not the Dalai Lama that [*sic*] is great. It is the Tibetan people. Everytime [*sic*] one of those bodhisattvas dies, it affects us all. From an Einsteinian viewpoint, everything is connected. And when one of these guys dies, it affects us all. . . . [E]verytime [*sic*] one of those ET's [?] in Tibet are tortured, jailed, or killed, we lose something of ourselves.[46]

While the argument is framed in a scientific/Buddhist/environmentalist notion of interconnection, the underlying notion at work here is that Tibetans are the "good" and even "enlightened" people who by their very existence—an existence discoverable through representations of them— ennoble the lives of all the rest of us poor souls.

If travel to Tibet once promised epiphany to Western travelers, now in the situation of exile and diaspora, reading Tibetans' life stories is enough to transform readers. But what do Tibetans get out of the exchange? Some readers' comments on Amazon.com suggest that in exchange for personal growth, Tibetans get support. As one reader from Texas comments, "I can't imagine reading this book and not being moved to support Tibetan [*sic*] independence."[47] That Tibetan autobiographers encourage readers to take up such political commitments is suggested in a number of texts. As Heinrich Harrer notes, Thubten Jigme Norbu was only persuaded to tell his story when Harrer told him that "with such a book he could help his country and his people."⁴⁸ Similarly, Jetsun Pema notes that she writes because "I know that many men and women still believe in truth and justice, and still stand up for these principles."⁴⁹ The plea for support is never as direct as, "Please send money. Please write your congressman," but the sense is that these stories must be told, and that aroused readers will be called to act upon their inspiration.

REFUGEES AND PATRONS

One of the first times that lay Tibetan men and women told their tales for a Western audience occurred just after thousands of Tibetans fled Tibet in 1959. After days, weeks, and sometimes months of grueling travel over the Himalayas, Tibetan refugees worked their way to safe haven in India. And when they landed in India many of them were asked to recount the atrocities they had witnessed in Tibet. The Dalai Lama's brother, Gyalo Thondup, organized the interviews; one of the interviewers sent to the camps in Assam was Tashi Tsering, who noted the experience in own autobiography:

> [Gyalo] wanted the world to know how the Tibetans had suffered at the hands of the Chinese and said he needed me to help him collect the narratives of the refugees so we could tell their story to the world. I was to interview as many people as I could and write down what I learned. . . . I tried to get as many eyewitness accounts of the uprising and flight as possible, taking careful notes in Tibetan. But it turned out to be more difficult than I expected. Most of the people I spoke to were illiterate and did not have an orderly or logical way of controlling and expressing their thought. They had simply been a part of the general panic that gripped the country, and their stories were of the sufferings they had incurred on the journey through the mountains, not at the hands of the Chinese. I had a hard time getting concrete evidence of Chinese atrocities.⁵⁰

According to Tsering, because the refugees were unused to speaking of themselves and their lives in this way—because, in effect, they lacked appropriate narrative models—their stories had to be fashioned for them. And because what little they said did not strongly support the theme of Chinese oppression, their stories had to be recast by those with a stronger sense of what the world needed to know. Eventually these narratives became part of the evidence for the International Commission of Jurists which in 1960 condemned Chinese occupation of Tibet on charges of illegality and violations of human rights. While little of real political value came out of the Commission's report or from subsequent efforts to get the United Nations to intervene in Tibet, the sense that the life stories of ordinary Tibetans mattered was born on the Tibet-Indian border. It was through their stories that "the world" would come to know of the situation in Tibet. And in this way, the Tibetan urge to tell one's story in English can also be seen as emerging from a new twist on an old Tibetan and Buddhist notion, that of patronage.

In *Tibetan Nationalism*, P. Christiaan Klieger argues that structures of patronage—structures rooted in early Buddhism and reshaped throughout Tibetan history—have significantly organized several key relationships—those between Tibetan monk and layman, between Tibetans and Mongols, and between Tibetans and Manchus:

> The *mchod-yon [chö-yon]* (T. "priest/patron") dyad is a state-level expression of a more general patron/client relationship (*sbyin-bdag) [jinda]* whereby a lay patron is responsible for the material needs of his religious preceptor. This is a very old idea in Indian religious systems (Skt. *shramana/danapati* "mendicant/gift-giver") from which much of Tibetan culture is derived. The cleric, who has normally renounced the world, receives the material necessities of life, whereby the donor receives religious instruction or merely intangible merit for these contributions.[51]

With roots in early Buddhism, the patron/client relationship shaped exchanges between Godan Khan and the Sakya lamas in the 13th century, and defined the proper spheres of influence for the Dalai Lamas and their Mongolian and Manchu protectors from the sixteenth to the twentieth centuries. With the Tibetan diaspora, as Lopez also notes, "Tibetans in exile, led by the Dalai Lama, have . . . been forced to turn to new patrons—in Europe, the Americas, Australia, Japan, and Taiwan—for whom they perform the role of priest by giving religious instructions and initiations and from whom in return they receive financial contributions and political support for the cause of Tibetan independence."[52] While in Lopez's construction, the "priest" in the relationship continues to be a religious teacher of some credential, Klieger suggests that the patron/client dyad structures relationships between even lay Tibetans and Westerners. In this new arrangement, "all patriotic Tibetans" have assumed the role of the client, or the religious assembly, for Western patrons, donors, and supporters. Instead of being "tainted" by this exchange with Westerners, however, Klieger argues that "[s]uch role behavior has tended to keep exiles 'Tibetan' primarily because it is ideologically compatible to historical forms."[53] In this reinterpretation of patronage in diaspora, to be worthy of support is another way of being authentic; to receive support is to have one's Tibetan-ness affirmed.

In the early days of Tibetan exile, patronage from the West came in a variety of forms. Some organizations gave medical and educational support; Switzerland offered asylum to Tibetan orphans and refugees; and the United States gave Tibetan resistance fighters training, supplies, and ammunition through the C.I.A.[54] The recent burst of publication in Tibetan autobiographies in English can be seen as another attempt to gain support from the "outside" world. Both a response and an incitement to a newly enlarged and enlivened international community of Tibet supporters, many of these books offer a Tibetan-ness that can only survive, it would seem, through continued Western sponsorship.

The exchange that defines patronage can also be analyzed within the terms of "I" and "you" that shaped my discussion above. The "I" of the narrative is the authentic Tibetan; the "you" is the patron. And as we have seen, Tibetan patronage depends upon particular notions of what kind of subject the client of "I" should be: he or she must be a worthy field of merit. In the context of present day patronage, the Tibetan "I" in the equation must be an authentic one; only then will the "you"—the patron, the supporter—be assured of a place. To challenge the position of the "I" is to threaten the entire exchange; thus, when the ideal of the authentic Tibetan is challenged by Western critics or by Tibetans themselves, the whole apparatus that exchanges desires, images, funds, and asylum threatens to crumble. (Indeed, I have heard the opinion voiced that the image of the authentic Tibetan—even if distorted—is nonetheless essential in the fight for Tibetan independence.) Because so much depends on this exchange, anyone who dares to suggest that Tibetans are in fact human beings with foibles like other people, that Tibetans can still be Tibetan and wear blue jeans or work in Swiss banks, or that Tibetans (consciously and unconsciously) manipulate Westerners' ideas of them to gain support is vulnerable to accusations of "traitor," "turncoat," "pro-Chinese."[55]

In order for the system of patronage to work, Western readers must not only identify the "I" of the narration with a real Tibetan out in the world, they must take up the role of "you" to that "I." They must feel that they have been spoken to. But this is not the only position available to them. In other moments of reading, readers can slip from the position of "you" or object to take up the position as subject—the "I" of the narrative. In this act of identification through reading, the reader imagines him or herself as, or takes the place of the (idealized, threatened, courageous) Tibetan. Such a slip between reader and narrator is made possible by the mobility of the term "I," a term that only refers to something within a particular context:

"I" only acquires meaning when someone speaks it, and, theoretically, anyone can speak it. In the process of reading, then, readers can fill the "I" of the narrative with their own subjectivity, and thus identify (precariously and vicariously) with the narrator and protagonist of the story. While it may seem far-fetched that anyone would mistake oneself for someone else, this on-again, off-again process of identification is analogous to the "suturing" that occurs in the viewing of a film, and is suggested by the comments of one Amazon.com customer-reviewer who writes, "The reader is not merely reading an account by account of the events in the Lama's life, but actually reliving and absorbing them."[56] In a sense, events in the life of the Dalai Lama become part of this reader's own life story: she relives them, absorbing them into her own subjectivity.

An analogous process of identification is suggested by an example from Tibetan Buddhist ritual. In some practices of tantric visualization, the meditating subject is invited to abandon common sense notions of selfhood and visualize him or herself as—to identify with—an enlightened being or deity. The goal of such a practice is nothing less than transformation; the aim is for the meditator to emerge from the ritual, not as a deluded creature caught in the web of samsara, but as an enlightened Buddha, a being that is, of course, in and of itself empty. In a sense, as Janet Gyatso argues in her discussion of the practice, the ritual process involved in such a *sadhana* reveals to practitioners that "identity and experience as expressed in body, speech, and mind can be created and controlled if there is an understanding of how they are constructed."[57]

While tantric visualization is quite different from reading, such a practice suggests something about the possibilities involved in identification. Certainly, in many cases, such an act of identification—whether it occurs in reading or in visualization—can be seen as a kind of ideological coercion—a fixing of subjectivity, whether that subjectivity is understood as transformed through the Western myth of Tibetan epiphany or the Buddhist myth of enlightenment: "I become the other/another." In my analysis so far I have tended to suggest that readers' dreams of transformation through identification with Tibetan others are problematic—that identification with either the "you" or "I" of discourse is limiting, even coercive or delusional. But, as I see it, reading does not involve only coercion or delusion. The elasticity of subjectivity that is demonstrated in readers' abilities to identify with subjects other than themselves (or in Buddhist practitioners' tantric visualizations) is not unlike the movements made by George Bogle that I so value. Reading subjects seldom take up stable and unified positions; instead, they weave in and out of identifications and dis-identifications, finding themselves here, then there, then somewhere else again. As I see it, reading involves movements among a number of positions: at one moment, readers might identify with the narrator; at other moments they can take up a place as listener—as "you" to the narrator's "I." At still other times, readers read *through* and *against* the whole process. To be sure, the belief that readers can be transformed through reading can be understood as unwitting capitulation to ideologies that work on readers transparently and coercively, suturing them into available discourses. But because the various identifications and movements involved in reading entail a kind of *loosening* of identity, these shifting identifications can alert one to the very constructedness of identity and thus undermine prevailing ideologies. Reading in that case becomes a kind of resistance of notions of essential selfhood.

The kinds of reading I practice on Tibetan autobiographies in English in the pages that follow work to recognize the multiple and contradicting ways that I, as a reading subject, respond to and interpret these texts. For although I am a reader who is familiar with both Western and Buddhist theories of subjectivity—a true believer in the notion that selves are constructed, ultimately illusory, and effects of language—when it comes to reading autobiography, habits of identification and presence still come into play. As Lejeune writes in "The Autobiographical Pact (Bis)" when he is accused of falling into the very cult of the author he would critique:

> It's better to get on with the confessions: yes, I have been fooled. I believe that we can promise to tell the truth; I believe in the transparency of language, and in the existence of a complete subject who expresses himself through it; I believe that my proper name guarantees my autonomy and my singularity . . . ; I believe that when I say "I," it is I who am speaking: I believe in the Holy Ghost of the first person. And who doesn't believe in it? But of course it also happens that I believe the contrary, or at least claim to believe it.[58]

In my readings of Tibetan autobiographers I want to keep this play and contradictoriness alive. (Have you done it too? Have you taken up your place? Have you identified the "I" of my story with some person in the world?) My aim in taking up such shifting positions, however, is not to simply display my flexibility. Instead, I want to assert the importance of reading against dominant ways of constructing Tibetans and Tibetan-ness.

As I have noted, in the manichean arena of Tibetan-Western relations, anything less than full submission to the myth of the good, pure, authentic Tibetan is often interpreted as betrayal to "the cause." So let me clarify: I do not doubt that Tibetans have suffered immensely under Chinese occupation. I have seen the signs of it in Tibet; I have been pulled aside by Tibetans there who, when they learn I speak a little Tibetan, are eager to tell me about their years in prison, to ask me about the health of the Dalai Lama, to find out if he might ever return. It is precisely because Tibetans have made such self-presentations to me—in Tibet, in exile—that I am interested in the whole phenomenon of Tibetan self-presentation. Let me try to be clear: to examine such representations is not to doubt that torture and imprisonment and oppression have occurred. Indeed, I have participated in various political actions in support of Tibetan self-determination. But I am concerned about the terms through which such actions are often carried out. As I see it, Tibetans need not be angels in order to be entitled to human rights; as Lopez writes, "The ravages wrought by China's policies in Tibet, resulting not only in the destruction of monasteries, temples, texts, and works of art, but in the deaths of hundreds of thousands of Tibetans, would seem enough to sustain the clear contrast with life in Tibet prior to the invasion" and thus also to support Tibetan aspirations for self-determination.[59] In my reading of Tibetan autobiographies I seek out other ways of reading Tibetan-ness—alternatives to the myth of the authentic Tibetan. Because the desire for a traditional, Buddhist Tibetan coupled with the manichean tendencies to dichotomize the good Tibetan and the (evil Communist) Chinese is a dominant one, my task will not be easy.[60] Because the mixed, the liminal—the neither-here-nor-there— threaten cherished categories and a well-established structure in Tibetan-Western relations, anyone who attempts to explore alternative definitions of Tibetan-ness—hybridic forms of Tibetan identity—faces a lot of resistance—cultural, historical, ideological—all of which are often deeply and personally felt. But although my goal here is not to develop a coherent activist program, disbanding the myth of the authentic Tibetan may be the only way to salvage an effective pro-Tibetan politics. In any case, only by working against the old stories, reading against the entrenched notions of Tibetan-ness, can something else happen: a different story can be told, one in which ethnic Tibetans are allowed to play roles other than that of authentic Tibetan, one in which they are allowed to take up other tasks than the bearing of Western desires.

CHAPTER 2

Siblings of the Dalai Lama:
Jetsun Pema and Thubten Jigme Norbu

TIBET: WHAT STORY? WHOSE STORY?

The autobiography of Jetsun Pema, one of the Dalai Lama's sisters, offers the story of what readers might recognize as that of an authentic Tibetan. A Buddhist, a nationalist, and an exile, Pema possesses all the proper attributes, and the broad outlines of her story follow what seems to be a script in these exiles' tales: the story of her childhood, an account of exile, some relation of her adult life, an expression of her devotion to the Dalai Lama. And, in a gesture that invokes the system of patronage, at the start of her *Tibet: My Story, An Autobiography,* Pema declares her reasons for writing:

> We need the support of other peoples of the world. With the aim of a better understanding of the tragedy which has been plaguing my country, I felt that I could use my own 56–year-long life to tell the story of the suffering of an entire generation of Tibetans. In this way, my account would not be limited to the life of a single Tibetan citizen but would be the story of a whole nation.[1]

With this identification of "her story" with Tibet's story, the title of the book gains significance. The colon in the title of the book—*Tibet: My Story, An Autobiography*—is to be read as an equal sign: Pema's story is Tibet's story; Tibet's story is her story. Presumably, these stories share a common happy past, a tumultuous period brought on by the Chinese occupation and the exile of the Dalai Lama, followed by a valiant attempt to hold on to religion and culture against considerable odds. Reading this way, I can see the connections between her story and Tibet's story, though it is more difficult for me to recognize in the specifics of Jetsun Pema's life much that is common with the lives of "an entire generation of Tibetans." Indeed, in order to make that equation, Pema must emphasize only certain aspects of her life: birth in Tibet, exile, strong faith. For the details of her life would seem to distance her from most Tibetans. As a younger sister of the Dalai Lama, Jetsun Pema was born in a fine house in Lhasa, educated, and sent at age nine to Darjeeling to attend a convent school run by Irish nuns, where she became fluent in English and learned her catechism. After the exile of her divine brother, Pema was sent to be educated in Switzerland, where she learned French; she then returned to India to eventually take up the administration of the Tibetan Children's Village in Dharamsala. There, Pema's life has been intricately bound up with that of her world-famous brother, whose biography, in some places in her book, is given more attention than the specifics of her own life.

In its details, then, her story is hardly that of an "entire generation." How many other Tibetans would be able to dictate their autobiography in French? How many can count on the Dalai Lama for personal advice and counsel? And if her life is not really typical (whose life would be?), there are also ways in which it does not fit the profile of the authentic Tibetan, the kind of Tibetan Western readers have come to know and love. For example, while Pema is always careful to emphasize her Buddhist values—especially when discussing her life in the convent school—she also admits that she is not fully literate in the Tibetan language, and writes her "mother tongue" only haltingly.[2] And while she refers several times to her insistence on wearing the traditional floor-length *chuba* early in her stay in Europe, there is a photograph of her with a Costa Rican friend in Venice, in which she dons a fashionable shift that hits just below the knee. When Pema suggests that her life is representative of other Tibetans of her generation, these details are not the ones on which she would have readers focus. Indeed, when these aspects of Pema's unique and cosmopolitan life are placed next to the figure of the authentic Tibetan, it is precisely these details of contact with and influence by the West that suggest that—at least within stereotypical notions about Tibetan-ness—Pema fails to measure up.

But what if one took her word for it? What if, instead of playing down the elements of interaction and contact in order to locate a kind of pure Tibetan, one emphasized them? In that case, one could come up with a very different version of Tibet's story—one that focuses on exile and travel, multiculturalism and transculturation, bi- and tri-lingualism. Although the figure of the authentic Tibetan encourages readers to understand that despite (and not because) all Pema's contact with the West and Westerners, she is staunchly Tibetan, I read her text differently. Reading against the tendency to suppress the hybrid in favor of the timelessly authentic aspects of Tibetan identity, I see her travels and her contacts with non-Tibetans as *constructive* of Tibetan identity; in this way, a different picture of Tibetan-ness and of the autobiographical subject can emerge. Perhaps, after all, hers *is* the story of Tibet.

Because the very image of the authentic Tibetan depends upon an essentialized, monolithic view of Tibetan culture, one that is fixed to the place of Tibet, it may be useful to rethink the notion of culture generally. James Clifford, for one, has proposed that it may be more fruitful to conceive of cultures not as homogenous unities fixed to places but as sites traversed—sites of traveling-in-dwelling, sites of dwelling-in-traveling.[3] Such a model seems particularly appropriate for the Tibetan diaspora as it emphasizes the ways in which "real" Tibetan culture need not be located only in Tibet but is instead something that lacks strict borders, that moves, that comes out of a process of human construction. Indeed, such a rethinking even suggests that Tibetan identity itself is made through travel.

In his work on Tibetan pilgrimage, Matthew Kapstein notes its importance for historical constructions of Tibetan identity. Arguing that scholars who analyze "the religious dimensions of Tibetan cultural and national identity" should place greater emphasis on religious symbols than on state institutions, Kapstein makes a case for the centrality of pilgrimage in creating "the cultural unity of Tibetans" in "old Tibet":

> Pilgrimage, among other things, promoted trade in both goods and information. It brought persons from far distant parts of the Tibetan world into direct contact with one another and thus militated to some extent against divisive regionalist tendencies. By ordering the cycles of pilgrimage according to calendrical cycles, by establishing the locations visited and the routes traversed, and by promoting specific religious teachings, historical narratives, and symbolic interpretations of the landscape and the events taking place within it, the Tibetan religious world constructed for its inhabitants a common order of time, space, and knowledge.[4]

Kapstein's emphasis on pilgrimage here suggests the important ways that movement and interaction have been constitutive of Tibetan and Buddhist identities. As Jamyang Sakya notes, there is a Tibetan saying about Lhasa as a pilgrimage site: "One who does not get to Lhasa has only half a human life."[5]

In her work on Tibetan autobiography, Janet Gyatso offers a way of looking at Tibetan culture that takes in still other forms of travel. Arguing that despite the feudalistic (*mi-ser*) system that operated in much of pre-1959 Tibet, Gyatso notes that individuals "countenanced a significant amount of personal independence," all of which is evidenced by different varieties of travel: the mobility of individual workers within the feudal system, the movements of nomads, the travel of traders, the wandering of *yogins,* as well as the journeys undertaken by pilgrims.[6] If we add to this list more recent forms of Tibetan travel—the movements of exiles, dancing and singing monks on tour, the ever-traveling Dalai Lama—then a vision of Tibetan culture as constructed through movement, as at least partially produced by travel, contact, and exchange, begins to emerge.

Though Pema has herself traveled extensively, the understanding of Tibetan culture as constructed through travel remains latent in her text; because of the weight of monolithic and fetishized notions of Tibetan culture, the view of Tibetan culture as a more dynamic construct can only be discovered by reading against the forward thrust of the story. For instead of making something of the many accommodations, translations, and transculturations that make up her story, instead of allowing that the many travels she has undertaken are somehow representative of the ways in which Tibetan identity itself has been constructed through travel, Pema (and her editors, translator, and publishers) suppress the creativity of travel in favor of a celebration of the uniqueness of Tibetan culture, a uniqueness that can be preserved like a holy relic or an elegant Buddha image: "We have a unique, ancient culture and heritage which is useful in the lives of our people and has the potential to make a contribution to other peoples of the world. We, therefore, consider that it is our duty and our top priority to ensure the preservation of this culture."[7] Of course, to take Pema to task for not being versed in cultural studies is not exactly fair. Nonetheless, if one reads playfully, the title of her book—*Tibet: My Story*—might allow one to recognize that the author's many travels are indeed a small version of the forms of travel—nomadism, pilgrimage, trade, exile—that help to create "Tibet."

And there is something else at work here too. Just as her brother, the Dalai Lama, is called upon to be an exemplar, to fulfill the role of leader in the diaspora, to be a representative of the enlightened, Pema too is hailed in similar ways, called on to be a Tibetan, called on to speak her story, to serve. Although she has devoted much of her adult life to orphaned and impoverished Tibetan refugee children as administrator of the Tibetan Children's Village in Dharamsala, the accounts of her earlier life suggest that she was groomed for a different purpose: cordial social gatherings, the niceties of aristocratic society, perhaps even for teaching. Instead of following out this path, however, when she returned from her European travels, Pema seems also to have been called on to return to "Tibetan-ness," or at least to its conventional forms. To see her now—fine *chuba*, lovely face, gentle smile—one feels oneself to be in the presence of that endearing authentic Tibetan, but the life she has led departs from the old script. Indeed, the mismatch between the form of the autobiography and its details may be what contributes to its rather halting style; Pema is made to fit a model that does not fully contain her.

Such an effect may well be the result of Pema's efforts to respond to versions of Tibetan-ness she encountered in the West. In the reciprocal nature of patronage, without the notion of the purity of Tibetan culture, the whole premise of the *jinda* (patron-priest) relationship is threatened; without support, Tibetan-ness is threatened. Pema's extensive discussion of the activities of Tibetan Children's Village, her inclusion of the life story of a recent child exile, her mention of the many generous supporters the Tibetan exiles have received from all around the world, all seem designed to incite the spirit of charity. The book closes with a plea to outsiders to support the Tibetan cause:

> I decided to write this book so that the tragedy of the Tibetan people and the difficulties they face may be better known. May all those who, like us, value freedom and justice be aware of the developments of our recent tragic history and give us their support before Tibet is lost and Tibetan culture becomes a museum piece.[8]

In order to be a worthy recipient of outside support, Pema must play down her Western ways—must play down the notion that Tibetans are "tainted" by contact with other cultures. If *Tibet: My Story* is a new age *rangnam,* it is one designed to inspire the Western reader to give generously and thereby maintain the hope of a unique Tibetan culture.

Sanitized visions of Tibetans which attempt to preserve their fine Tibetan-ness—whether they are made by Tibetans or Westerners—arise out of particular habits of thinking about culture, about Tibetan identity, and about how to deal with cultural difference. Some of these habits derive from Western understandings of cultures as coherent and timeless "wholes"; some derive from conservative Tibetan notions about Buddhism and how it must be protected. Such views of culture tend to see interaction and "mixing" as evidence of degradation. This view of culture is also at work in a 1998 essay, "Virtual Tibet: Where the Mountains Rise from the Sea of Our Yearning" by the American journalist Orville Schell. Situating his analysis of the making of the film *Seven Years in Tibet* within a larger project of examining "the West's long-standing fascination with Tibet," Schell nonetheless presents Tibet as a kind of holy relic that must be protected from foreign contamination; the occasion is his visit to the site in Argentina where the film was shot.[9] (Coincidentally, Jetsun Pema herself appears in this film, playing the part of *Yum Chenmo*—the Dalai Lama's and her own mother; in *Kundun,* Pema's daughter plays the same role.) Despite his attempts to demystify the Western fascination with Tibet, Schell operates from a view of culture that is not unlike the one that organizes Pema's account: the best Tibetan culture is the pure one; cultural "mixing" is a problem. The Tibetan-style graphics that accompany Schell's piece tell part of the story and show a mixedness of cultures: a seated Buddha figure in sunglasses has his face powdered under a boom-mike; a wrathful deity defiantly empties a bottle of Evian on the ground; a noble Orientalized figure in brocade holds a clapper board. This mixedness is presented as evidence of a kind of unholy violation, an attitude that is further articulated by Schell's essay.

Schell declares that he is interested in the "strange cultural collisions" taking place in Argentina whereby white-skinned Americans avail themselves of the latest in exotic chic and Tibetan monks discuss soccer in Spanish (p. 42). Of his journey to the film set, Schell writes, "What I encountered was a fabulous world where old Tibet came to life before my eyes, and the past and the present, Hollywood and the Himalayas, ancient wisdom and the superstar *Kultur,* all collided in a jarring spectacle awash in cognitive dissonance" (p. 40). While it is no doubt true that cultures once divided by space are now in contact with each other, things only appear dissonant and jarring if one converts the geographical fact into an ontological one. If one maintains the old dichotomies of East and West, undeveloped and developed, spiritual and material, then clearly, the very presence of Tibetans—let alone simulations of them—in the "modern world" will violate ingrained sensibilities. If one holds on to a fetishized notion of culture, one is bound to be disoriented by what seems an unholy mixing of identities and images.

While presenting himself as someone who is sympathetic to some Tibetans' desires to be understood as modern people eager to break out of Western fantasies of them, Schell can only go so far. When one of the Tibetans he interviews offers an implicit critique of homogenized notions of culture—"'Lama chic' Westerners don't go for young Tibetans like us with long hair and jeans. . . . If someone doesn't have a robe and a shaven head, they don't think we're a real Tibetan" (p. 46)—Schell seems sympathetic. But Schell can only grant these Tibetans their Tibetan-ness in spite of their exile, in spite of their distance from Tibet, and in spite of their ability to reflect on Western images of who and what they should be. As he writes:

Still, as remote as they are from the actual place, after listening to them talk about their views on all the Tibetan movies being made, on being Tibetan, and especially about the West's fascination with it all, I get the sense *that in some indelible cultural way, they are still very much Tibetan.* What is equally evident is that they feel even more disoriented than I do. (p. 45, emphasis added)

These Tibetans' distance from the place of Tibet is a problem for Schell, but the argument that they are Tibetan "in some indelible cultural way" allows Schell to assert a kind of essential cultural authenticity. For what would an "indelible cultural way" consist of? If something is "indelible," it is incapable of being removed, permanent. But if it is "cultural," it is something transmitted, something learned. The circumlocution here manages to both invoke the image of the authentic Tibet and to present yet another cultural curiosity for perusal: the "real" Tibetan in exile.

In Schell's account the presence of Tibetans and the simulacrum of old Tibet in an industrialized, technologized world is jarring—they don't seem to belong together. Interestingly, this is a view not unlike one expressed by the hero of James Hilton's 1933 novel, *Lost Horizon.* Imagining Shangri-La as a place where a "separate culture might flourish . . . without contamination from the outside world," Conway suggests that Shangri-La has managed to avoid the impact of technology and modernization:

I use the word [contamination] in reference to dance bands, cinemas, electric signs, and so on. Your plumbing is quite rightly as modern as you can get it, the only certain boon, to my mind, that the East can take from the West. I often think that the Romans were fortunate; their civilization reached as far as hot baths without touching the fatal knowledge of machinery.[10]

Conway's hope for a place that preserves only the "best" of the modern West and leaves out the "contaminating" is echoed in Schell's essay. To mix cultures is to spoil them.

But the antidote to such "mixing," I would argue, is not to make Tibetans and Westerners line up in terms of the old dichotomous categories and thus assuage a sense of "dissonance," but rather to change the categories in order to recognize that cultures, people, and goods do not stand still. The dream of coherent, unified cultures, separate from each other is just that: a dream. If it were not for the coming together of what we now call Indian, Chinese, Tibetan, Nepali, and Mongolian actors, there would be no Mt. Kailash, there would be no Dalai Lama, there would be no Tibetan Buddhism. We need to shift conventional ways of thinking about Tibetans and Tibetan-ness so that we can accept the phenomenon of actor-monks speaking Spanish or Tibetan boys playing with Game Boys as part of a worldview that recognizes the fact of exile, the facts of cultural exchange, contact, globalization; critique starts from there. And in this way, too, we might be able to see that despite Pema's efforts to represent her typical Tibetan-ness through references to Buddhism, Tibetan nationalism, and her desire to preserve Tibetan culture in exile, her representativeness may actually reside more in her travels.

While I can only get at such a conclusion by reading against the main emphasis of Pema's autobiography, the autobiography of her eldest brother, Thubten Jigme Norbu, more openly accounts for his travels, suggesting their importance for his understanding of who he is in the world.

THE FIRST EXILE

Norbu was arguably the first Tibetan exile. Incarnation of the Tagtser Rinpoche, former abbot of Kumbum monastery and brother of the 14th Dalai Lama, Norbu became convinced early on of the oppressive nature of the Chinese occupation of Tibet and fled his home in 1950, making his way to the United States. His autobiography, *Tibet is My Country,* appeared in 1960; published in both English and German, this volume was written with the assistance of Heinrich Harrer, whose story is told in both the book and the film *Seven Years in Tibet.* But, to complicate Norbu's self-presentation, not long before his autobiography was published, another life story of a Tibetan appeared—in this case the story of T. Lobsang Rampa. *The Third Eye,* first published in 1956, tells the story of the education of a Tibetan monk, the surgical opening of his third wisdom eye, his flight inside a giant kite, and the growing spiritual powers that allow him to astrally project himself; it also, in a way, tells a story of travel. This book created a sensation when it was published, selling thousands of copies. But the author of this book was not a Tibetan at all, as it turns out, but the Englishman Cyril Henry Hoskin. Hoskin himself would come to tell elaborate stories of travel to account for his authorship; eventually his books on Tibet would sell more than those of any other author.[11] Thus when Harrer published Norbu's account, it was imperative to claim its authenticity against that of Rampa's works, which Harrer will not even deign to name:

> During the past few years in particular a wretchedly irresponsible pseudo-literature about Tibet has spread, once more causing a great deal of regrettable confusion. Just because it is so widespread we are unable to smile contemptuously and dismiss it as summarily as it deserves. The Tibetan

monk, [*sic*] makes do with two eyes just like any other person, and when he wants to fly in the air he uses an aeroplane for the purpose. That is the sober truth, and in consequence those who prefer fairy tales will probably be disappointed by what Norbu has to say, although it represents the first authentic autobiography of a Tibetan which has ever appeared in the outside world. Because of the unusual circumstances of his life Norbu has been privileged to see things that only a small group of specially chosen people ever see or know anything about. Even so, monks flying through the air without the aid of human inventions, third eyes, and so on, were not amongst them.[12]

Harrer's condemnation of Rampa is harsh, perhaps deservedly so. And what seems particularly irksome to him is that this impostor wrote under the name of a Tibetan; indeed, even after his exposure, Hoskin claimed to *be* a Tibetan, arguing that, in fact, he had given his body to a Tibetan lama who had, in effect, lost his own.[13] That the authors of both *The Third Eye* and *Tibet is my Country* believe themselves to be the Tibetan whose adventures they recount is not dealt with by Harrer's preface; instead, Harrer must dismiss Rampa in order to make way for "the first authentic autobiography of a Tibetan which has ever appeared in the outside world." That both books can be said to have been "ghostwritten"—one by the Tibetan spirit who occupied Hoskin's English body, the other by an Austrian who worked with a Tibetan—must also be glossed over. All efforts go towards identifying the man whose photo appears on the cover of *Tibet is my Country* with Thubten Jigme Norbu, with the "I" of the narrative, with the brother of the Dalai Lama, and with the friend of Heinrich Harrer. That Thubten Jigme Norbu is nonetheless a figure who *moves* is evident in his text. In effect, Norbu's autobiography tells a tale of travel that centers around the longing for home.

As a trained monk, this attachment to home seems somewhat incongruous. When monks enter the monastery, they give up their homes, changing their names, attire, and behavior to mark their new status. While many initially experience homesickness, the Buddhist monastic emphasis on renunciation and detachment from such mundane matters helps eradicate these feelings. Thus, in the autobiographical accounts of the Gelukpa monks Lobsang Gyatso and Geshe Rabten (discussed below), both mark a moment in their lives in which the vicissitudes of life at home are understood as only productive of suffering. Lobsang Gyatso reads that "One's native place is the prison of the demon Mara and one's parents are the snare that he uses to get one inside"; his teacher tells him to be wary of such attachments, noting that his family's concerns have the potential to "slowly build up to cause you to leave the spiritual life and go home, like a snare around the neck of a person being led off to jail."[14] Similarly, when Geshe Rabten returns to his home in Kham after beginning his studies at Sera, he sees

> that everything was in good order; yet I also soon discovered that the life there was not for me. When last at home, I had been only a boy, and my way of thinking was then completely different. I had loved playing around and felt that that way of life was well worthwhile. Now I viewed with different eyes the ways of behaviour, the kinds of conversation and the general lifestyle of the householders. I saw absolutely nothing there of true benefit; was struck by the difficulties and hardships they experienced, and perceived how they thus clung to mistaken ideas which to them meant a great deal. This all struck me as very strange.[15]

Tibetan *rangnams* typically narrate the subject's commitment to renounce worldly life, whose vicissitudes are often epitomized in the householder's existence. But Thubten Jigme Norbu's story offers a different take on the meaning of home.

After narrating events in his pleasant and often mischievous childhood, he tells about the confusion and heartbreak that attend him when he leaves home to take up his place in the Geluk hierarchy. As an incarnation of Tagtser Rinpoche, he is left by his parents at Shartsong monastery when he is of school age; there, he longs to be home, a longing that persists into his adult years, leading him, against the usual protocol, to follow his family to Lhasa when his younger brother is discovered as the newest incarnation of the Dalai Lama. Although he later returns to Kumbum monastery in Amdo in eastern Tibet, his experience of the Communists' oppressive dealings with Tibetans and Buddhism soon lead him to the decision to abandon Tibet altogether. But even after deciding to secretly flee Tibet, he is disturbed at the notion of losing his home yet again:

> I knew that I should in all probability never again set foot on Tibetan soil, that I should never again return to my home. . . . I was fleeing from arbitrary violence and seeking freedom. I had personally experienced the frustration of a free man when he is cast in chains, and I know that I could not live without liberty. Others gave me a helping hand and smoothed my path. But I never before quite realised that the price was to be my own country, and now I suffered all the tortures of exile. I would never have believed it so difficult to say farewell forever to my country. The idea of going abroad, where I should have to live with strangers and speak their tongue, seemed intolerable to me.[16]

The decision to leave Tibet seems to come after Norbu abandons the abbotship at Kumbum and flees to Lhasa; he is only allowed to leave because the Chinese believe that Tagtser Rinpoche will either persuade the young Dalai Lama to give into the Chinese or that Tagtser will kill him. But what Norbu fails to narrate here is the fact that when he fled Tibet he also abandoned his monk's vows. One can learn this important detail from the Dalai Lama's *Freedom in Exile,* but Norbu notes only that when he flees Tibet, "I exchanged my monastic robes for travelling clothes and set out on the journey which was ultimately to take me to freedom—but also to exile."[17] Because the Dalai Lama also dons laymen's clothes in order to disguise himself during various journeys, it is not clear from Norbu's autobiography that this moment of "disrobing" signifies a larger change in personal identity and public presentation. For Norbu, it would seem, exile transforms in a number of ways: it signals the abandonment of his homeland, a farewell to his monastic career, as well as his construction of himself as a kind of ambassador for Tibet. As the Dalai Lama notes, by this time Norbu was convinced of the necessity "to secure foreign support and to resist the Chinese by force of arms." Convinced also that in these extreme circumstances killing would not violate Buddhist principles, the Dalai Lama relates that Norbu decided to "renounce his monastic vows [and] disrobe" in order go abroad as an emissary for Tibet."[18] That Norbu's travels would involve meetings with representatives of the C.I.A., who wished to support the Tibetan resistance against Chinese Communists, is also left unaccounted for in his autobiography.[19]

We can only learn these details about Norbu by reading outside his autobiography—or around in it. For Norbu's abandonment of the monastic robes is mentioned obliquely in the postscript to the 1986 edition when Norbu announces that "I met my future wife in 1959 in Darjeeling, while visiting my brother Gyalo Thondup."[20] After Norbu and Kunyang, sister of the Sakya Tri-pa, meet again in Seattle in 1960, they are married. Perhaps because the ghostwriter or the publisher sensed that the seeming authenticity of Tibet's first real autobiographer would be threatened by the admission that even good lamas become laymen, that particular story, however veiled, is reserved for the 1986 addition.

In this postscript we also learn in a rush of dates and places the journey that Norbu's life has undergone since 1960—from the United States to Japan, all over Europe, Russia, India, Mongolia, and even to Tibet—and the number of occupations he has taken up—teacher of Tibetan language, museum curator, assistant to the Tibet Office in New York, professor, lecturer, and spokesman for the Tibetan cause. In Norbu's autobiography, the auto-ethnographer who emerges is not an informant who stayed home. The figure represented is both a fervent Buddhist and an outspoken political freedom fighter, a loving father and a lapsed monk, a man who is nostalgic both for old Tibet and the old neighborhood around Lexington Avenue, an native informant who, as Clifford suggests is frequently the case, has his own "interesting histories of travel."[21]

Thus when Norbu learns of the Lhasa Uprising, he is neither sequestered in the Norbulingka nor roused from his studies in the monastery, as Geshe Rabten was; instead, he is making soup in his New York City apartment when he gets the news on the wireless. As an exile who had left his natal home at a tender age, and as sibling of two other incarnations in turbulent times, Norbu and his family—like Bogle and his siblings at a different historical moment—are dispersed across the globe, with Gyalo Thondup first in India then in Hong Kong, Pema in Switzerland then in India, the Dalai Lama in India (and now with frequent stops all over the globe). Indeed, in a situation that seems expressive of modernist and postmodernist ironies, members of this family feel they can only be useful to their homeland when they are outside it. Thus when the male siblings of the family do come together for the first time, it is not in Tibet but in India. Norbu notes that there in 1956, "for the first time in our lives we five brothers were assembled round the same table."[22] And when during the same journey, Norbu unites with the rest of his family in a hotel room in Calcutta, they transform with tea and reminiscences "the rather dull and typical hotel room" into something that resembles "our old kitchen in Tengtser."[23] Such makeshift home-making marks the situation of exile in a striking way.

Clifford has suggested that the hotel is a modernist space par excellence, a site traversed by tourists, travelers, and exiles, "a place of transit, not of residence."[24] All through Norbu's account he passes through such sites of transience and mixed cultural identities. The monastic quarters where monks from various parts of Tibet meet with representatives from the People's Liberation Army, the New York apartment where he first hears the news of the Lhasa Uprising, the Calcutta hotel room where his family gathers, the U.S. airport lounge in which Norbu is greeted by an American scholar speaking Amdo dialect,[25] the rented house in Bloomington, Indiana where neighbor kids learn to call the mother of the Dalai Lama, *Mo-La* (Grandma)—all these are places of dwelling in travel, travel in dwelling for an exile who nonetheless declares that "Tibet is my Country." Norbu's consistent pro-Dalai Lama and staunchly pro-independent Tibet stance is taken within a life that has moved repeatedly, violently, and in that way, as Harrer declares (though he probably does not intend it in the way I read it), this life story "is a very typical reflection of the fate of the Tibetan people in our day. . . ."[26] In Norbu's life story, travel and exile become not a way of abandoning or losing the place of Tibet but a way of grasping it.

Despite these many travels, however, Norbu maintains a kind of unity of focus; if there is anything like a still point in Norbu's narrative, it is his steadfast allegiance to the idea of Tibet as it is manifested in the figure of the Dalai Lama. But even then, the focus is marked by movement. One of the more poignant images in the book expressing Norbu's orientation towards the Dalai Lama is told in a traveling tale. The scene appears in a chapter titled "To and Fro in the World;" Norbu has not seen the Dalai Lama in six years—not since 1950 when the elder brother fled the country without telling his family of his plans. When Norbu learns in 1956 that the Dalai Lama has been invited to come from Tibet to India to attend celebrations of the Buddha Jayanti, Norbu travels from New York to India to meet with various members of his family and in the hope that he might see his esteemed brother. Gyalo Thondub and Norbu organize a small traveling party to meet the approaching Dalai Lama, and wait out rumors and bad weather in a bungalow on the Indian frontier until

[a]t last, late one evening, we heard the bells of a large caravan coming down from the pass, and despite the heavy fall of snow we hurried up to meet it. Before long advanced scouts loomed up out of the mist and informed us joyfully that the Dalai Lama was not far behind. We pressed on, passing pack animals and soldiers of the bodyguard on specially picked horses, and before long we met the larger group of the Dalai Lama's immediate retinue. The Dalai Lama ordered the others to halt and he rode foreward to greet us. We prostrated ourselves three times before him and then handed our katas to the High Chamberlain, who had dismounted. He then placed katas round our necks in return. Smilingly, the Dalai Lama watched the little ceremony, welcomed us with a few friendly words, and then gave the signal for the caravan to go forward again.[27]

The recent exile rushes forward to meet the traveler and soon-to-be exile; the travelers are brothers, but their meeting is also shaped by the conventional relationship between the Dalai Lama and his devotees. What positions do they take up in this travel tale? Who are they when they meet? What happens when these two rushing streams coincide? The Dalai Lama smiles. The meeting stands still for only a moment. The caravan moves forward.

The notion of a Tibetan as someone who speaks only Tibetan, is fixed to the place of Tibet, and who has not (or should not) adapt to the modern world puts pressure on the autobiography of Pema and on that of her brother, Norbu. By reading against the grain of Pema's story and by selecting details of travel from Norbu's autobiography I have offered a different way of understanding Tibetan-ness, one which puts travel in the center and allows for the construction of shifting identities. Despite Norbu's attachment to Tibet, in this autobiography we are in the presence of a figure who moves, whose very transformations and shifts, silences and assertions, teach readers about the nature of impermanence, about modern practices of travel and self-presentation, about the chimeric nature of the self. For rather than speaking from a unified place (whether it is the place of Tibet or the culturally-sanctioned position of monk) Norbu is a "hybrid" subject: a Gelukpa who marries a Sakyapa, a Tibetan who resides in Indiana, a *tulku* with C.I.A. ties, and an auto-ethnographer who has lived both inside and outside the culture on whose behalf he speaks. Because of this, his work sheds light on the ways in which Tibetan culture is not a static thing, a jewel in a showcase, but an evolving, moving, dynamic phenomenon. And in that way, if we read *for* travel, a sense of Tibetan culture and identity emerges— one that resists being fetishized and fixed by those who limit Tibetan culture to a few exemplary and "authentic" representatives.

Postscript

Forty years after their meeting on the Tibetan-Indian border, Norbu and the Dalai Lama would meet again, this time in Bloomington, Indiana. The day after the Dalai Lama's large public talk at Indiana University, he offered a ritual for "aspirational *bodhicitta*" as part of the ceremony for laying the cornerstone of the Tsong Kha Sanctuary, near the site of a new *stupa* and the Tibetan Cultural Center that Norbu heads. Seventy-four-year-old Tagtser Rinpoche, dressed in a *chuba,* read a speech he had written for the Dalai Lama in Tibetan. It was a kind of introduction for the Dalai Lama, I suppose, but it was also an extended plea that the Dalai Lama not compromise with the Chinese, that he insist on independence, that he remain with us for a long time. Norbu was broken: the recitation was a long pleading, at times a kind of sobbing. Seeing their teacher so distraught, some of Norbu's students were visibly shaken; others Injis were moved by what was to most of them an incomprehensible though obviously emotional speech; some Tibetans were crying softly. When the Dalai Lama offered the short teaching, the mood was fervent, and European-Americans lined up with Tibetan exiles to recite an English translation from Shantideva's *Guide to the Bodhisattva's Way of Life.* The last lines of the text read:

May I be a protector for those without one,
A guide for all travellers on the way;
May I be a bridge, a boat and a ship
For all those who wish to cross the water.

The "I" of the passage asks to be something other than a small self, the little ego. The "I" asks to be the thing that transports, that moves others, taking them to a place they can only imagine. After the teaching, Tibetans went to the Dalai Lama's throne and rubbed their prayer beads on it, thereby taking on some of his holiness. The air was charged as the supplicants lined up to watch the Dalai Lama depart. Could we too be this kind of traveler, one who was not fixed to things or ideas, but one whose aspiration was a kind of transporting compassion? The Dalai Lama passed by, Norbu in his train.

CHAPTER 3

Monks' Tales:
Geshe Rabten and Lobsang Gyatso

SEARCHING FOR TRUTH

*I*n the popular imagination, the figure of the Tibetan monk most frequently signifies "Tibetan." It is the monk who often concerns Bogle, Turner, Waddell, and Kipling, the monk who bears much of valued Buddhist knowledge. It is the monk Western audiences have encountered in the dancing, chanting, and sand-*mandala*-making troupes of Tibetans who travel the United States. And even though the percentage of males who became monks in Tibet before 1959 was around 10 percent and is significantly smaller now, monks and former monks make up almost half of the list of Tibetan autobiographies in English. Two prominent examples are Geshe Rabten's *The Life and Teaching of Geshe Rabten: A Tibetan Lama's Search for Truth* and Lobsang Gyatso's *Memoirs of a Tibetan Lama.* Both texts relate the childhood and education of monks within the Gelukpa monastic system. Both demonstrate adherence to Tibetan biographical and autobiographical conventions. Both subjects find personal significance in the life of Milarepa, the eleventh-century ascetic and cultural hero. Both tell the tales of exiled lamas who collected a number of Western adherents. And both are produced with the prodding and assistance of white, English-speaking disciples. But they are quite different stories. While Lobsang Gyatso goes on for some 300 pages, Geshe Rabten stops at 119. While Lobsang Gyatso is prepared to "tell all" about life in the monastery[1]—its glory and its pettiness—Geshe Rabten's story is uncritical of the monastic system. And while Lobsang Gyatso's story, through his editor and student Gareth Sparham, seems to play with Western expectations about Tibetans, as I will argue below, Geshe Rabten's story, in a sense, seems to have been instrumental in creating some of those expectations. Published in 1980, it offers a vision of an orderly and emancipatory educational system, a picture of a coherent and peaceful Tibetan life, and a version of Buddhism that is at least somewhat compatible with logic and common sense. And while the long preface and epilogue in Lobsang Gyatso's book emphasizes the participation of Sparham, Rabten's translator and editor, B. Alan Wallace, seems eager to play down his role in the process of representing the *geshe*.

As it appears in this book, Geshe Rabten's story is an untroubled story. Indeed, so deeply engaged is the monk in his studies that in 1959 he does not notice the Chinese presence in Lhasa. As he notes:

> [T]he discipline of the Lharam class was so strict that we had no thoughts for anything other than our studies and practice. So the mere presence of the Chinese did not affect us. . . . One morning after a day of normal debating, I woke up at two or three o'clock to the sound of artillery fire. I looked out of my window towards Lhasa, and saw the city and surrounding area lit up like daytime with brilliant white flares.[2]

It is with some surprise that he watches bombs fall on the Dalai Lama's summer palace, the Norbulingka, in March of that year. But such political events in the "outside world" are side issues in the larger narrative. For Geshe Rabten tells a success story: he followed the monastic education and found the right path. And he offers an incitement: take up the Buddhist path and you too can be set free.

The production of such stories is not surprising, perhaps, given that the ghostwriter is himself a monk in training under Geshe Rabten's tutelage. (B. Alan Wallace includes his monk's name, "Gelong [novice] Jhampa Kelsang," after his English name on the title page.)[3] Having committed himself to a "foreign" religious system, Wallace may have some stake in proving its efficacy. And from all accounts Geshe Rabten was indeed a scholarly lama, an able teacher, a highly realized being. But, perhaps especially in comparison to Lobsang Gyatso's complex story, Geshe Rabten's narrative feels packaged, in a sense: too neat. The effort of the editor and autobiographical subject seems bent on keeping the story "Tibetan" and "Buddhist," keeping it pure. In what follows I read against that purity, working with the loose threads in the narrative to suggest how other stories are entangled with it.

Although the text seems designed to contain the problematics of its cross-cultural and inter-cultural nature, one signal of the mixedness of the text—one sign that the diverse interests and expectations that have been brought to it cannot fully be contained—is suggested in the foreword written by the Dalai Lama.[4] He writes in totality:

> Apart from the inspiration that the 'Life of Geshé Rabten' is bound to create, it will also show many of the Western readers that the study and practice of the dharma is a slow process, needing much patience and firm determination.
>
> The biography of Geshé Rabten will give the readers a glimpse of how monks in Tibet studied and trained. It is probably the first book on the life of a 'Geshé' published in the West and should therefore make it interesting as well as informative.[5]

The Dalai Lama explicitly notes that the book is designed for a Western audience, and, at the same time, implicitly links it to other Tibetan *namtars* in that it is meant to inspire. In arguing that the road to enlightenment is a slow path, the Dalai Lama emphasizes the scholastic aspects of Gelukpa monasticism rather than its more colorful tantric practices. Moreover, in generic terms, the Dalai Lama refers to the book as a biography rather than an autobiography. In this English publication, however, and within the conventions of English language autobiography, Geshe Rabten is listed as author. The book, offered as "A Tibetan lama's search for Truth," is caught between two different cultures of life story production and reception; unlike Lobsang Gyatso's text, however, which seems to play with these divergent conventions, Rabten's story seems to deny that gap. The translation of the tale from Tibet to the West, it would seem, is supposed to be seamless.

Another problem that the editor Wallace seems eager to avoid revolves around his role as interlocutor/ghostwriter. The narrative is structured around the short questions of a "disciple" and the longer answers of the *geshe*. For example:

> Disciple: When did you receive the full monastic ordination?
> Geshe: When I was in the Beginning Treatises class, I received the vows of a fully ordained monk from Phurchog Jhampa Rinpoché, who had previously given me the novice ordination. (p. 54)

Despite the fact that such an interview format calls attention to the role of the interlocutor and could undermine the emphasis on presence so prevalent in Tibetan autobiographies in English, readers are not invited to identify this "disciple" with the ghostwriter of the book, the one who translated, selected, and arranged this narrative; instead, the story is presented as a kind of transcript, a simple presentation of what was actually said. Readers are encouraged to take the *geshe's* words as *his* words, as if they were listening in on a conversation. Consider the opening lines:

Disciple: To begin with, perhaps you could speak of your childhood.
Geshé: I was born in a fairly well-off family in a village about fifty miles south west of Dhargyé Monastery. . . . (p. 3)

The conversational tone suggests that the text was not really altered at all. The disciple's reluctance to edit his lama's words (or to give the appearance that he did so) suggests that what we are getting here is the real thing—the very presence of the lama in the text. Wallace's editorial comments do little to alter that perception; we learn little about the production of the book, or about how data was recorded, transcribed, edited, or translated. Wallace notes in the preface only that he met Geshe Rabten while the latter was in retreat above Dharamsala, and the Englishman "asked to hear of his life, especially as to how he became a Geshe. After some hesitation, he kindly agreed, and the following is an account of what he said."[6] What readers have then is not the transcribed, translated, edited words of the *geshe,* but his voice—the next best thing to the lama himself.

The story this lama tells follows the formula for Tibetan *rangnam:* childhood, renunciation, meeting with teachers, acquiring disciples, attaining spiritual development. Of course, according to the rules of modesty, Geshe Rabten does not make many direct claims about his attainments, but we learn of the rigorous Geluk curriculum, his successful attainment of the *geshe* degree, the practices he undertakes, the retreats he engages in. Perhaps this is what makes the story so neat: there is very little conflict in it, whereas conflict is rife in stories such as Milarepa's. Similarly, there is little narrative development in this tale. If, as Lejeune says, Western autobiographies range from the self-reflective exploration of one's internal life to a kind of curriculum vitae, with Geshe Rabten's story we verge towards the c.v.[7] We are given a sense of a person who is fully in possession of himself and his recollections; he himself is an exemplar of the monastic curriculum he describes. And the Tibetan system, this text suggests, has much to offer the West.

As I have noted in Part One, this positive valuation of Tibetan Buddhism marks a change in perspective from Europe's views of Tibet a century earlier. Shifting from the nineteenth-century perception that Tibet possessed the most degraded of Buddhist traditions, by the 1970s and '80s many Western scholars came to see Tibetan Buddhism as a tradition that had preserved the integrity and purity of Buddhism in its translation of Sanskrit texts. The work of Western scholars of Tibet thus became the preservation of this ancient tradition. While some set about saving Tibetan Buddhism, others looked to Tibetan Buddhism as something that could save the West. When, for example, Wallace asks Geshe Rabten to compare the Tibetan monastic education with a European university education, he replies:

> It differs in terms of the fields of study, the goals of the training, and the manner of putting the studies into practice. Then, of course, in the monastery only the Buddhadharma [doctrine of the Buddha] is studied. The more one trains the mind in this teaching, the more it is relieved of its problems. And because the field of training is the Dharma, the mind experiences greater and greater happiness, regardless of physical hardships. In Western universities, both the subjects and the goals of study are concerned with this life alone. Thus, one's mental problems do not lessen as one studies. Nor does such an education yield increasing happiness and satisfaction, even if one's health is good. In fact, we can see from our own experience that mental happiness often declines during that kind of course. (p. 13)

Anyone who has suffered as a college student or a teacher in the West may recognize some truth to Rabten's statement, but it is really too reductive: the Western system produces misery, the Tibetan monastic system produces happiness. If we follow Rabten's comparison, one logical conclusion is that if Western education produces suffering, the Tibetan system can cure it.

Claims like these appear elsewhere in Western representations of Tibet: Tibetans are bodhisattvas that can save us, Tibet offers a zone of peace[8] that can preserve all that is good in the world. Geshe Rabten emphasizes Tibetan Buddhism's ability to cure the West in other parts of the text as well. When Wallace asks Rabten, "What do you feel attracts [foreigners] to you, and to your style of teaching?," as part of his answer, Rabten likens these foreigners to patients who are ill:

> For a patient to be inspired to take medical treatment, he must be convinced that his disorder and his causes may be dispelled. . . . Being convinced that his illness may be cured, a patient must then follow the advice given by his physician. Likewise, once we see the possibility of the final cessation of suffering and its source, we need to follow the reality of this path by putting the Dharma into practice. (pp. 114–5)

The theme of Buddhism as a curative reappears later in the book, where some of the *geshe's* teachings for Westerners are included:

> [I]t is extremely important for a patient to take medicine that will cure his ailment. The reason is that the patient dislikes the illness and wants to be free of it. But having the desire alone is not effective. Thus, taking medicine as a

method to prevent illness and to cure disorders is obviously very important. (p. 123)

The metaphor of Buddhism as medicine is a common one within the tradition, but Rabten's application of this trope to the situation of Westerners is worth noting. Those who have lived in modern Europe or America will not be unfamiliar with the notion that the West is sick: Western critics have diversely located the dis-ease of the West in its loss of faith, materialism, wars, racism, imperialism, sexism, rampant development, pollution, dualistic thought, et cetera. Indeed, the notion that the West had developed more and more elaborate ways to annihilate and degrade itself is one of the values that propels Hilton's *Lost Horizon*. By invoking the trope of Buddhism as medicine for Westerners, Rabten offers Tibetan Buddhism as a panacea, and thus brings into play existing Western fantasies about Tibet.

As is suggested in our discussion of the patron–priest relationship, in order to be effective, the elixir of Tibetan Buddhism must be of the purest quality. It must not be mixed with other cultures and religious traditions, and its physicians must have no doubts about its efficacy. Though Geshe Rabten's autobiography is informative about the rigors of Geluk training and enumerates the scholarly skills necessary to rise within the Tibetan hierarchy, and though it emphasizes the importance of commitment and diligence to the development of a religious (Buddhist) life, it offers readers a sanitized image of Tibetan Buddhist traditions. In arguing this I do not intend to cast aspersions on Rabten's moral character; it is the cultural and tropological character of his book that I am concerned with. Despite the tendency to polarize the Western and the Tibetan in Rabten's account, Rabten's words "arrive" in a context in which Tibet and the West are not mutually exclusive terms—in which "the West" and "Tibet" can be understood as created through interaction, misunderstanding, exchange.

Such a view of culture is unavailable in Rabten's text. Rabten's degradation of the West arises from a particular conservative discourse within the Tibetan monastic hierarchy, particularly in the Gelukpa sects around Lhasa. It is this conservatism that Lobsang Gyatso critiques, as I will discuss below; it was this attitude towards the "outside" world that Waddell and Younghusband made much of: contact with "outsiders" is threatening to the purity of Tibetan Buddhism. That the Tibetan term for Buddhist is *nangpa*—insider—and everyone else is *chipa*—outsider—supports such a view of things. To those dedicated to the protection of the dharma, modernization—even when the 13th and 14th Dalai Lamas propose it—can be seen as threatening Buddhism. From this point of view, keeping Tibetan Buddhism pristine is the duty of the monasteries, for lay men and women cannot do it, bound as they are to the wheel of samsara. The same notion of Tibetan monastics as pure and worthy helped to maintain Tibet's patron-priest arrangement with the Mongolians and Manchus, just as it supports Western sponsorship of Tibetans.

In this way the notion that Tibet can cure the West taps into cultural constructs from both sides. What emerges in the interchange is an old dream of transformation, one alchemically realized by the touch of Tibet. The old divisions remain in place; horizons lost can be found.

LAMA *POST MORTEM*

At first glance, Lobsang Gyatso's *Memoirs of a Tibetan Lama* seems to occupy the same territory as Rabten's book: the story of the education of a Tibetan monk and the shape his life took in the Gelukpa monastic system. And like Rabten's book, Lobsang Gyatso's is also offered as a *namtar.* The editor, Gareth Sparham writes, "*Memoirs of a Tibetan Lama,* published here for the first time, is a Tibetan *namthar*—a life story as Buddhist teaching." As he continues, Sparham suggests why this book follows a trajectory different from that of Geshe Rabten's story; Sparham notes that it is "written in the candid style of a tell-all autobiography by the famous Tibetan Buddhist teacher Lobsang Gyatso (1928–1997)."[9] With this "tell-all" character, the book offers unabashed revelations of the monk's faults and opinions—a story about the development of his personality, a personality that is practically Bogle-ian in its movements. At one moment Lobsang Gyatso thumbs his nose at the Tibetan Buddhist hierarchy; in the next, he lives within it. In its broad outlines the narrative seems to follow *rangnam* conventions; in its details it shows us a Western-style "personality." In some points it withholds idealized images of Tibetans; at other moments, these images appear in rehabilitated form. Lobsang Gyatso's memoirs offer a tale that is delightfully mixed, readable in a number of ways, working against, with, and for several sets of conventions.

And, in a strange way, the autobiography possesses a completeness elusive to most such stories. As James Olney writes, "no autobiography as conceived in a traditional, common-sense way can possess [narrative] wholeness because by definition the end of the story [i.e. the subject's death] cannot be told."[10] But Lobsang Gyatso's memoirs do the impossible: they tell the end of a life, the story of his violent death. One cannot get far into the book before one realizes that Lobsang Gyatso was killed in 1997. That this story can be recorded is only possible, of course, because of the involvement of an intermediary, in this case, Sparham, a Canadian disciple of Lobsang Gyatso, who recorded, transcribed, translated (along with two other of Gen-La's disciples), and edited the elder monk's reminiscences over a two and a half year period (p. 9). Although Lobsang Gyatso's name is listed as the author of the book, only a ghostwriter could record the horrible and moving details of the protagonist's murder, allegedly by supporters of the Tibetan deity Dorje Shugden.

Because Dorje Shugden is important to Lobsang Gyatso's life and death, I will briefly outline the nature of the debate over him. Worship of Dorje Shugden began during the lifetime of the Fifth Dalai Lama (1617–1682). Dorje Shugden is considered by many to be a protective deity for the Gelukpa tradition; others feel, however, that he is an evil spirit, a reincarnation of an angry rival of the Fifth Dalai Lama whose worship breeds Gelukpa sectarianism. Since 1976, the Dalai Lama has counseled Tibetan Buddhists to give up Shugden worship on the grounds that it breeds sectarianism and is harmful both to Tibet and to himself personally. Because a number of lamas, monks, and lay people were initiated into the worship of this deity by their gurus (especially the highly revered Yongzin Trichang Rinpoche), many feel torn between devotion to their guru and to the Dalai Lama. In some cases, the conflict has led to opposition of the Dalai Lama, who was himself initiated in the worship of Dorje Shugden. (He later returned this initiation to his teacher.) Conflict over the status of Dorje Shugden has led to accusations that the Dalai Lama represses religious freedom; these are often made by the followers of Kelsang Gyatso, who now heads the New Kadampa school in Ulverston, England. But even lamas with a close relationship with the Dalai Lama have entered the fray, including Geshe Rabten's disciple, Gonsar Rinpoche. Lobsang Gyatso, on the other hand, strongly supported the Dalai Lama's position against worship of Dorje Shugden. Many believe that he was murdered by supporters of Dorje Shugden, though no charges have been made; the Indian police believe his murderers have fled into Tibet.[11]

The reader's foreknowledge of Lobsang Gyatso's murder affects the way we look at the smiling face on the cover of the book and colors the reading of his life story; as Sparham notes, "inevitably the life of Lobsang Gyatso will be seen through the lens of his death" (p. 7). And even though the monk's bloody end is mentioned on the first page of the introduction, at the beginning of the afterword, and on the back of the book, when the details of the murder are narrated, they come as a shock. "They stabbed him through the eye, cut his throat, and unkindest of all, stabbed him though his heart" (p. 319). With that stabbing, reading the autobiography as a construction of a life—as I often tend to do—seems a better thing than accepting it as a part of the real. As Sparham suggests, "It would be better if this were the ending to a story book, not a description of the end of the life of the outspoken Tibetan monk who recorded these memoirs" (pp. 319–320). In this way, however, Lobsang Gyatso's murder invites us to imagine the eruption of the real into a text and thwarts the study of auto-biography as a kind of fiction, at least for the moment. To read the text as a mere story seems to dishonor Lobsang Gyatso's memory. Indeed, the first time I read the passage describing his murder, I felt like I was wounded.

But, of course, I was not cut. And the book is not a life, but a story of a life—that is what I know at other moments. My own shifts in reading Lob-sang Gyatso's book—from listener and witness to self-critic and textual analyst—suggest both the attractions and contradictions of reading: without those shifts, readers would stay fixed in place, and the idea of getting even a glimmer of another's life would remain dishearteningly distant.

So how does this story work? What happens in the narration of this life and its bloody end? And if it cannot give us the "truth" about events, what kind of story does it tell, and what does this story suggest about the fault lines in Tibetan identity, religion, and culture? As I see it, the "success" of Lobsang Gyatso's narrative depends on its continual movement among, adherence to, and undercutting of expectations: at one point, he sticks closely to *rangnam* conventions; at others, he criticizes the Tibetan Buddhist hierarchy. In one section he presents himself as a figure closely in line with the authentic Tibetan; in others he challenges Western stereotypes and ideals about Tibet, monks, and Buddhism. In effect, Lobsang Gyatso resists telling only one kind of story; the book negotiates the expectations of two different imagined audiences, inviting both idealizing readers and conserv-ative Tibetan Buddhists to rethink their positions.

In the opening lines of the text, Lobsang Gyatso both deflects the myth of Shangri-La and denies that his story is anything like a *rangnam,* a story of full liberation:

> My name is Lobsang Gyatso and there is nothing particularly special in my life. What you have with me, I'm afraid, is just an ordinary fellow spinning around in the world of life and death. . . . There are things in my life which are worth recording, no doubt, even which need to be said, but with me everything that has happened is confined to this ordinary world.[12]

Such a declaration discourages Western readers looking for Tibetan saints from expecting too much from this monk; his denial that the book is a *rang-nam* also paradoxically exemplifies the autobiographical subject's humility, a requirement in the *rangnam* tradition.[13] For despite (and through) this dis-play of humility, the book is largely structured by the conventions of the

Tibetan "outer" biography as described by Janet Gyatso: "an early renunciation of worldly life (often preceded by a mischievous childhood), followed by the protagonist's meeting with teachers, taking vows, entering a retreat, acquiring students, teaching, and finally, assuming institutional positions."[14]

We first see Lobsang Gyatso in his home village in Kham as a mischievous and lazy child, who on one occasion abandons the flock of sheep and goats he was supposed to watch in order to gorge himself on pork, a meat that in Tibetan custom is considered especially dirty:

> If truth be told, I was a naughty fellow and was known for it. Often when people met me they would say, "You are the young fellow who spent the whole day pigging out on pork instead of following your flock, aren't you?" Then they would give me a slap on the back and go off chuckling. (p. 19)

The boy was also notorious for his drinking: "I would drink so much [distilled spirit] that by nighttime I was quite tipsy and I would lie there in the evening drunk" (p. 28). Compared to the exploits of Milarepa, for example, who in his youth was greedy, vengeful, and murderous, such behavior might seem fairly harmless. But even gluttony and drunkenness are obstacles in the Tibetan Buddhist context, as Lobsang Gyatso suggests when his acquaintances chide him. Announcing his intention to become a monk, they tell him: "'You like beer and liquor too much to become a monk,' they said. 'How would a fellow like you, who everybody knows is naughty, who is so proud of himself, and who has such a liking for liquor ever be able to be a monk?'" (p. 28). Despite his mischief (or because of it, according to *rangnam* conventions), the young boy has a desire for renunciation:

> [W]hen I was very little another young fellow and I decided to leave home to become monks. This was even before I had started to look after the flock, so we could not have been more than five or six. We had wandered up a kilometer or two towards the monastery when a monk coming down met us and asked where we were going. "We are going to become monks," we said. "Ah yes, but becoming a monk is very hard and you have a long way to go. Aren't you too young?" he asked. (p. 27)

Eventually the boys return home, but the urge to join the monastery persists even in the midst of his worldly antics. He joins the local monastery, where his afflictions of selfishness and attachment persist, and he gets into numerous fights. He relates a story in which he gives a boy "a real thrashing. That was me, the monk, in those days, not a pretty sight, I'm afraid." But despite Lobsang Gyatso's claim that his behavior is "the sign of a horrible person (p. 30)," there is nonetheless a kind of delight in the telling of these stories, a delight that revels in the workings of samsara and the world.

If the relation of these exploits positions Lobsang Gyatso as the mischievous child and sinful young man of the conventional *rangnam,* they also serve to undercut some of the loftiness Westerners sometimes attribute to Tibetan monks. Lobsang Gyatso is not an incarnate lama whose divinity is confirmed by his own precocious actions and by high-ranking outsiders; he is, instead, a run-of-the-mill monk, one who chooses monastic life, a life that is not always equivalent to a spiritual life. The monastic life Lobsang Gyatso shows us, both in his home monastery and later on at Drepung, near Lhasa, is one that is as full of pride, anger, and violence as the world outside its doors. Not only does the young monk hang out in a gang with other monks and fight; he seems attracted to violence. As he writes, "In those early days as a young monk, I was still a pretty bad character, a delinquent really, naughty at the best of times. . . . Nobody would let me get my hands on a gun because they knew I was too volatile." When he is finally lent a gun, he uses it to contemplate breaking one of the five basic vows of a Buddhist. "One day I saw a big bird sitting up in the branches of a tree and took it into my head to kill it" (p. 32). This is not the kind Buddhist who abhors violence we have come to expect: recall Bogle's Payma, who would not shoot birds for sport, or Kipling's lama, who would not hurt a snake; think of the non-violence of the Dalai Lama. And not only is the young Lobsang Gyatso not gentle, he is not scholarly or meditative. Indeed, when he plans to go to one of the big Lhasa monasteries for the requisite three years, his guru says, "This boy is a born delinquent, it's true." But as in the case of Milarepa, a story to which Lobsang Gyatso refers several times, even the most violent and sinful person can find liberation with the proper effort. As his guru continues, despite Lobsang Gyatso's faults, "he has the spark of something in his heart, and I think there is still a chance that he may turn into something to bring credit to us all" (p. 43).

So far, then, the story follows the typical pattern for *rangnam.* But by using this pattern, Lobsang Gyatso manages to undercut several stereotypes about Tibetan monks: they live in a realm cut off from the mundane world and always maintain a saintly demeanor. When Lobsang Gyatso is placed at Drepung monastery ("I was an idiot when I first arrived, totally at a loss" [p. 58]), his version of the place undercuts some ideals about Tibetan monasteries, developed in part from Hilton's and Capra's Shangri-La: they are egalitarian, full of quiescent and meditative figures, and somehow free from the trivialities of the "outside" world. ("[N]othing but Priests; nothing from morning to night but the Chanting of Prayers &c.," Bogle wrote.[15]) Drepung seems less a place of quiet contemplation than a rigidly hierarchical institution filled with bureaucracy, and backbiting. Instead of contemplating *shunyata* (emptiness, Tibetan: *tongpa nyi)* as Geshe Rabten does in his account of his life at Sera monastery, the novice Lobsang Gyatso thinks mostly of food and home (p. 74).

As a newcomer to Drepung, Lobsang Gyatso knows neither monastic nor social etiquette. But in an interesting way, his inability to fit into the monastic scene is precisely what makes him a better practitioner. Recalling that back in his home village, he "was one of the worst monks, egotistical and arrogant," Lobsang Gyatso notes:

> From these early experiences in Drepung, however, I became very deferential and retiring, quite the opposite of my earlier self. Back at home everybody had said I would never be able to last at Drepung because of my arrogance, that I would come up against the discipline and get into trouble. But now here I was, after just a few weeks, totally deflated and deferential. (pp. 65–6)

It is precisely because the monastery is *not* utopia—it is full of fighting, knife-carrying, lazy, petty, stupid, and prideful monks—that its deprivations and pettiness have the desired effect of inciting his renunciation. It is exactly because the monastery is not Shangri-La that it can do its work.

As I have noted, Lobsang Gyatso's account of his hardships and difficulties echoes the trials of one of Tibet's most famous yogis, Milarepa, whose *namtar* is widely known by Tibetan Buddhists. When Lobsang Gyatso has to carry a load of butter on his back for several miles and the leather strap he uses cuts into his skin, his penance is reminiscent of Milarepa's penance with Marpa, in which he must carry stones up a hill on his raw and oozing back. (Such seemingly brutal duties may also undercut ideals about the gentle nature of monastic life.) Rather than rebelling against this trial, however, Lobsang Gyatso takes up Milarepa's story as an example, one his teacher uses to encourage him to continue to shun the traps of domestic life even as it shapes his own life story. "Look how [Milarepa] struggled, living just on the first leaves of the nettle bush and making such an effort that in a single lifetime he reached the stage [*sic*] of enlightenment itself" (p. 96). Encouraged to understand his own struggles in light of Buddhist exemplars, Lobsang Gyatso listens carefully to other *namtars* as well:

> My study guru told me the stories of the holy beings and how poor they had been, how much they had to struggle—how Sonam Dragpa, the famous teacher of Loseling, had not even proper clothes to wear when he studied,

how Jamyang Shepa, the famous teacher of Gomang, had to eat the dry left-over offering cakes, and how Trehor Chupon Rinpoche had nothing but a cracked earthen pot to cook in, and how he lived on soup. Of course, he also told me again and again how Milarepa had lived in cave [*sic*] eating nothing but nettles which had made his skin turn green, but how by such hard work, he achieved the state of enlightenment in one life. These stories made me feel that living as a poor person was the correct way to be, and the stories gave me a great inspiration, the capacity to go on. (p. 101)

The *namtars* do the work they are supposed to do, instructing and inspiring the monk. Through these orally-transmitted texts, Lobsang Gyatso finds a way to interpret his own experience; indeed, the texts he encounters inevitably shape his understanding of the trajectory a life can take. And, because the narrative form of the *namtar* is culturally and religiously sanctioned by Tibetan Buddhism, it is one available to the Buddhist Sparham as well. *Namtar* conventions offer Lobsang Gyatso and Sparham both a means for selecting the events that will be narrated and a way to interpret them. Using these stories hermeneutically, Lobsang Gyatso can understand his hardship as a kind of penance he pays for the bad merit he accrued earlier in his life.

One of Milarepa's practices that Lobsang Gyatso imitates is meditation in a cave. Such a practice is not unusual for Tibetan monks and nuns, and many *namtars* and *rangnams* offer stories about practitioners' significant experiences while engaged in such meditation. But because the figure Lobsang Gyatso has presented is one who is frequently egotistical, strug-gling, and mischievous, the story of his meditation in the hills above Lhasa (I can't help but recall that Younghusband "meditated" there too) marks a shift in his personality. Because readers have been taken through a narration of his all-too-human struggles to find a place for himself in the monastery, Lobsang Gyatso's account of his experience there might be seen as a quaint participation in English autobiographical conventions. But there is some-thing different about the nature of Lobsang Gyatso's discovery: he does not find himself; he finds, in Buddhist fashion, that "self" is one of the roots of suffering, that egotism is the very thing that will keep him from realization, and that compassion for others is the only antidote.

Sitting in my cave I watched my breath going in and out. As it came in I imagined all the problems of others coming in and landing on my selfishness, which sank down into the vast accommodating earth leaving me patient and capable. Sometimes I imagined my selfishness in the form of an owl or a dangerous snake and imagined chasing it away. (p. 118)

When such contrition and self-reflection are related after tales of his earlier mischief, they gain a kind of poignancy. His realizations do not just seem like the crossing of academic hurdles that take one through the monastic curriculum (as is the case in Geshe Rabten's autobiography); instead, such practices (as they are told in Lobsang Gyatso's story) are contextualized by a human life.

Perhaps my receptiveness to this passage in Lobsang Gyatso's tale simply derives from habits of reading Western-style autobiography. Interestingly, though, in that example and many others, Lobsang Gyatso's autobiography can be read as participating in two traditions simultaneously: it shows both his renunciation (in the *rangnam* tradition) and the intensely personal way that renunciation reshapes his personality (in the English-language one). While much of his tale does not challenge the typical *rangnam* conventions, the emphasis placed on the different parts of Lobsang Gyatso's life suggests something about the *uniqueness* of his preoccupations and concerns—the formula is always filled in with what comes off as the distinctive personality of Lobsang Gyatso. Thus, although we learn something about his struggles to study (which is conventional), scholars working in Western institutions might begin to see Lobsang Gyatso as a figure not unlike themselves: he wants to get a degree so he can study but gets caught up in the bureaucracy and finds himself in administration. The final chapters of the collaborated section show Lobsang Gyatso taking up one administrative position after another, first as house guru, then as grainkeeper, and finally as a teacher-in-exile of lay children; he shows himself as crafty, cantankerous, and proud, something of an underdog in an institution built around hierarchy and status. Not only does such a story complicate the popular image of a monk engaged in meditation and spiritual development, it offers a figure who rises and struggles within an entrenched institution. By representing the Tibetan monastic system as flawed and hierarchical, Lobsang Gyatso emerges as a kind of hero who can both recognize and resist its inequities.

Such a critical eye towards the religious hierarchy makes his story stand out among Tibetan autobiographies in English. And even if the book includes the requisite tale of his journey into exile, Lobsang Gyatso's unswerving criticism of the hypocrisy and greed he sees among Tibetan monks and *tulkus* on this trip make his story unique. Others who relate their desire to follow the Dalai Lama into exile tell a tale of hardship, fear, and struggle along the road to India within a narrative of unwavering faith in the Tibetan Buddhist system; while the Buddhist framework is in Lobsang Gyatso's book too, it goes farther. In a chapter called "Last Pilgrimage and Exile," Lobsang Gyatso describes gun-toting monks, a *rinpoche* who wears his reliquary box on a gun belt (Lobsang Gyatso refuses to seek his blessing), and bitter monks who are ready to renounce their guru to the Communists (pp. 274–276). He also points out his own failings, describing his temptation to steal food on the way, as well as his frustration with a despairing young *tulku* in his care, whom he at one point threatens to abandon (p. 279, 289).

By pointing out the imperfections of the Tibetan Buddhist hierarchy, a system which institutionalizes the recognition of enlightened beings, Lobsang Gyatso emerges as a very human being—as a kind of whistle-blower within the Tibetan system. But he does not, thereby, emerge as the typical authentic Tibetan of "simple, strong belief" in such passages; he asks too many questions, has too many doubts. And when he arrives in India, doubt and sorrow seem to get the better of him. Incited to stop wearing the heavy woolen monks' robes in the warmer climate, his removal of the visible sign of his identity throws him into a depression. "I entered a downward spiral of negative thoughts, seeing no hope, and it affected me badly" (p. 291). It is only in relation to Buddhism and monasticism that he knows who he is; removed from the habits of monastic life, he, like other exiled monks, finds himself at a loss. Lobsang Gyatso narrates a story from this period in which he is shocked out of his depression by the sight of another monk studying a scripture, a book he has carried with him into exile. Lobsang Gyatso borrows the book, the *Lamrim Chenmo* by Tsongkhapa, and, in a common Tibetan Buddhist practice, opens it randomly for a divination. He reads: "There is no place, wherever you may go—the results of your earlier actions will follow you." And he finds another passage, which states that there is no farther distance than that between your thoughts and the dharma (p. 292). In a manner that is reminiscent of Kipling's "textual encounter" with Besant's novel,[16] Lobsang Gyatso finds his inspiration in this book: "It is amazing, if the time is right, how a single line of a spiritual book can have the force to motivate a practice for an eternity" (p. 293). Instead of being an always already enlightened being, this scene shows Lobsang Gyatso as a man who struggles in his spiritual life in a way that is more accessible to some lay readers than the tales told of near-mythical *tulkus* and renunciates.

In an interesting fashion, Lobsang Gyatso's epiphany of reading seems to fix his faith. We never see him doubt again. Thus, when he relates that he, along with other newly-exiled monks, longed to see the Dalai Lama when he passed through a railway station some distance from Mussoorie, he takes on a role like that of the Tibetan of "simple, strong belief." Ignorant of the ways of public transportation, these monks walk several days across alien Indian farmland to get a glimpse of the Dalai Lama. Because Lobsang Gyatso has largely withheld the image of himself as an authentic, devout

Tibetan up to that point, when the story does offer something that approaches that image, the figure seems somehow more true, more real, more possible. One has the sense that, yes, perhaps such beautiful and apparent simplicity can be won, but it is not discovered without a struggle.

Neither does it preclude criticism of the structures that support and promote Buddhist institutions and practices. For despite his "strong belief" in Buddhism, Lobsang Gyatso can still be highly critical of Tibetan cultural and religious systems. While both Tibetans and Westerners have attempted to portray old Tibet as a kind of vast refuge for diverse flora and fauna—the Dalai Lama writes, "It is no exaggeration to say that the Tibet I grew up in was a wildlife paradise"[17]—Lobsang Gyatso remarks that "there was a carelessness even then [when he was a child] about the trees and forests—even back then our people were at fault in the way we went up and indiscriminately cut any trees we wanted without any thought for their place in the environment" (p. 19). Similarly, while some critics can only see Chinese evil in the takeover of Tibet, Lobsang Gyatso freely criticizes the old Lhasa government for their handling of the Chinese Communist encroachment on Tibet: "[E]ven though the whole world was adapting to meet the challenges of modernity, the officials of the Tibetan government were stuck in old ways and did not change at all" (p. 230). Indeed, Lobsang Gyatso will even go so far as to argue, "Too much belief in Buddhism and an inflated notion of their own country . . . explains how [the central government] came to have such silly ideas" as to believe that the Chinese would not invade Tibet (p. 248).

Such arguments make Lobsang Gyatso seem a man of common sense, a man who is iconoclastic in his unwavering faith. But it would be wrong to see Lobsang Gyatso as a kind of Buddhist rationalist. Western-influenced versions of Buddhism—from the Sri Lankan Protestant Buddhism described by Gananath Obeyesekere and Richard Gombrich,[18] to the American and European reinventions of the tradition, to the Dalai Lama's own proclamations to Western audiences—sometimes suggest that Buddhism is fully compatible with science and reason. Such an attitude is particularly emphasized in the Dalai Lama's recent best-sellers, *Ethics for a New Millennium* and *The Art of Happiness;* one not need be a Buddhist to benefit from Buddhist teachings. Similarly, Walpola Rahula in his rationalist *What the Buddha Taught* writes: "[I]n Buddhism emphasis is laid on 'seeing,' knowing, understanding, and not on faith, or belief."[19] But it would be wrong to mistake Lobsang Gyatso's sometime irreverent and commonsensical expressions as consistent with Western rationalism. Indeed, many of his descriptions include details that are frequently suppressed in recent popular

Western versions of Tibetan Buddhism that want to emphasize its (Western) psychologism and rationality.

For example, Lobsang Gyatso frequently uses divination to determine a decision; he has faith in oracles, and believes in the reality of gods and demons and protectors. Thus, it would be particularly misguided to think that Lobsang Gyatso opposed the worship of Dorje Shugden on the grounds that this figure was not "real." In the case of Dorje Shugden, Lobsang Gyatso's argument is that he is an evil spirit, one unworthy of devotion, one that can encourage dissent among various schools of Tibetan Buddhism. The distinction between the common sense view and the more theological one is muted in Sparham's discussion; we are told only that Lobsang Gyatso wrote a book in the 1970s "in which he criticized the Dalai Lama's teacher Trichang Rinpoche for his propagation of the Shugden cult" (p. 321). Among Tibetan Buddhists, the debate over Dorje Shugden is not centered on whether or not deities and spirits are symbols of states of mind, as some rational-minded folk might imagine, but what kind of being this particular figure is, how seriously one should take one's vows to one's teacher, and whether worship of Shugden fosters a sectarianism that is dangerous to the coherence of the Tibetan community. By skirting some of the details of the Shugden debate, Sparham allows Lobsang Gyatso to appear as a kind of rational and ecumenical figure who is moved to act out of his utter faith in the Dalai Lama.

For Lobsang Gyatso's allegiance is, finally, to His Holiness. When, against Lobsang Gyatso's wishes, the Dalai Lama asks him to teach monks in exile, he must agree. Lobsang Gyatso is inspired by the Dalai Lama's argument that though such teachers may be personally postponing the study of Buddhism, they are nonetheless helping to preserve "the doctrine of the enlightened ones" for Tibet and Tibetans: "That talk by His Holiness filled me with inspiration and removed all my doubts. . . Whatever I might say, think, or do would be in line with his vision" (p. 306). The autobiography proper ends on that note of commitment and a declaration that his work as a teacher "has always been work that caused a happiness ever present within" (p. 306). Knowing that Lobsang Gyatso would die for this faith and commitment heightens the pathos of these declarations.

Because Lobsang Gyatso's part in the narration only takes him up to the early 1960s, Sparham's description in the afterword of the monk's subsequent achievement comes as something of a surprise. For although Lobsang Gyatso never earned the *geshe* degree (often compared to a Ph.D. for Gelukpa monks) and he is not an incarnation, he traveled internationally to teach the dharma. He is even called a "lama" by the Dalai Lama himself.

The Dalai Lama has argued that "a lama (as one's religious teacher) need not be an incarnation and that an incarnation is not necessarily a lama."[20] A lama should be an esteemed teacher, worthy of merit. To call Lobsang Gyatso a lama, then, is a high compliment indeed. It is also part of a number of tensions that animate the book: Lobsang Gyatso is called a "lama" by the most famous lama of all, and yet he claims to be an entirely worldly man. He plays with the Tibetan conventions of *rangnam* and utilizes conventions from the autobiography in English to present himself as a complete person. He debunks idealistic images of Tibetans but still lives up to the image of the authentic Tibetan. His image smiles at us from the cover, he declares his happiness at the end of the book, and yet we know he was brutally murdered.

The story Sparham tells of this murder is chilling and unflinching:

> They came in the evening just before dark and stabbed him. They stabbed him through the eye, cut his throat, and unkindest of all, stabbed him through his heart. . . . It was a terrible wound, into the kindness of a person, the place where Gen-la finally lived, a wound to make sure there was no retreat from which to return, and it sucked the mind, like a vortex, back down the path it had traveled. . . . [I]n the seconds before he was murdered he grabbed a bag off one of his killers and grasped it so tightly to himself that they could not pry it loose. It is one of the main pieces of evidence in the case against the murderers . . . (pp. 319–321).

Sparham's manner of relating the murder comes close to representing the simple "facts" of the murder. Indeed, the initial lack of figure in the language and the momentary suspension of interpretation gives power to the emplotment that comes next. For Sparham reads the murder as an expression of the debate over the status of Dorje Shugden, a debate that, as Lopez has argued, exposes the fault lines in competing identities within the Tibetan community as well as a gap in Tibetan Buddhism's representation to the West. The debate over Shugden helps to point out the distance between the Dalai Lama's (and other Tibetan monks') sometime rationalistic interpretations of Buddhism to the West and the deeply "religious" and sectarian values and structures that animate and produce a multivalent and complex set of traditions.[21] It is in the gap between rationalism and religion, and between resistance and debunking, that Lobsang Gyatso's autobiography does its work.

In my readings of the two monks' tales, I have tried to complicate the image of the Tibetan monk in the West. In my reading of Geshe Rabten, I aim not to undermine him as a teacher but to outline the discourses within which his text operates and which it perpetuates. In my interpretation of Lobsang Gyatso I have emphasized its mixed character, highlighting the way it fulfills and resists a diverse set of cultural and generic expectations. Just as Ritu Sarin and Tenzin Sonam in their documentary, "The Reincarnation of Khensur Rinpoche,"[22] offer images of monks doing such things as wiping a child's snotty nose, playing karom, operating both an abacus and a handheld calculator as well as chanting, making divinations and offerings, Lobsang Gyatso's text inserts a measure of the mundane into the monastic. Although Geshe Rabten offers Buddhism as a cure for Western ills, I see Lobsang Gyatso's text as a kind of antidote to Western representations of monks who fly and levitate, on the one hand, and monks who, like Kipling's lama, cannot manage a simple thing like buying a train ticket. Beyond that, the very fact of Lobsang Gyatso's murder and the larger Dorje Shugden controversy that frames it—no matter which side one takes—gives the lie to the notion that violence has never been committed in the name of Buddhism. As the life of Milarepa shows—a life that both Rabten and Lobsang Gyatso admire—a life that includes raining down murderous hailstorms on the enemies of Buddhism at the command of his guru, Marpa—violence has been no stranger to the Tibetan Buddhist tradition.

CHAPTER 4

The Double Life of the Dalai Lama

uddhism posits the cycle of samsara, a chain of living, dying, and rebirth, to which all sentient beings are subject due to their *karma.* For Buddhists, this chain of rebirth, impermanence, and suffering is a problem, the solution to which is enlightenment. While, for Tibetan Buddhism, most people in the world are simply victims of rebirth and are lucky to find themselves in a human body at all, there are other kinds of beings who actually choose to manifest themselves in human form—a choice they undertake out of their compassion for other beings. These beings are incarnate lamas or *tulkus,* whose rebirth is strictly voluntary.

The concept of *tulku,* distinct to the Tibetan Buddhist tradition, has been adopted by all sects of Tibetan Buddhism since the fourteenth century. The Dalai Lama is arguably the most famous *tulku,* whose institutionalization began in 1578, when Sonam Gyatso (1543–1588), a Gelukpa monk, was dubbed "Dalai Lama" by the Mongolian overlord Altan Khan.[1] (Sonam Gyatso was actually the third Dalai Lama; the first two were named retrospectively.) The current Dalai Lama, Tenzin Gyatso, is thus the fourteenth in a line of reappearing lamas, who since the innovations of the "Great Fifth" Dalai Lama (1617–1682) in the seventeenth century, have assumed preeminent religious and temporal powers within the Tibetan hierarchy. Each Dalai Lama is understood as a manifestation or emanation of the bodhisattva of compassion, Chenrezig, who is himself seen as the patron deity of Tibet, and—in some myths—the progenitor of the Tibetan race.

Despite some Western tendencies to assume that the Dalai Lama ruled over all of Tibet and that he is in some sense an absolute monarch—the "god-king" of Tibet—the extent and the magnitude of Dalai Lama's powers have varied over the decades. Given the situation of Tibetan exile, however, the current Dalai Lama, the center of the Gelukpa monastic system of which both Lobsang Gyatso and Geshe Rabten are part, has become the single most important figure around which Tibetan identity circulates. As one Tibetan exile in Switzerland told me in 1996:

> Every time [the Dalai Lama] gives a speech, he always says, it doesn't matter where you live; it's the same. You should be best where you are; you should do the best. He makes you stronger. . . . [W]e lost a country, but we are lucky to have a person like this.[2]

Within Tibet, the Dalai Lama remains a salient symbol, so much so that the Chinese government has sometimes made possession of his image illegal. Travelers in Tibet are frequently accosted for "Dalai Lama photo," and his image has become a kind of currency. When three Tibetan-exile delegations were allowed to travel to Tibet in 1979 and 1980, they were frequently overwhelmed by the emotions expressed by Tibetans there for the Dalai Lama, so that a delegate such as Lobsang Samten, brother of the Dalai Lama, was practically deified. One participant in the third fact-finding mission described the Dalai Lama's continuing significance for a pan-Tibetan identity in this way:

> [W]herever we went, in Amdo or in Kham or in Central Tibet, lots of younger generation—children of maybe 6, 7, 8, 9, 10, maybe 15 years old, lots of them—they come to us asking for Dalai Lama's photo. Sometimes they even cannot say Dalai Lama, they don't know "Dalai Lama," they have to say "*tushi*." *Tushi* means like Mao, *tushi* means the head. . . . And they say, "I would like to have a photo of our *tushi*"—it's Dalai Lama. It's very funny. . . . And sometimes we found [out], in the course of so many incidents like this, . . . that some of them were being sent by their parents, because the parents do not dare to show their faces, so they send children. But some of them, the children themselves they come to us, and they stay for hours. If we don't give them, they stay for hours, until we give them something—some Dalai Lama photo or some blessings or some red thread around—they don't go. And that was very surprising because there was very little chance that they can be trained in this way. Like elderly people when they come to us, we understand, then it's like of course. . . .[3]

The delegate's telling of this story inscribes a fervent faith in the Dalai Lama among Tibetans within Tibet that seems to defy the constraints of their circumstances. When delegates give Dalai Lama photos to Tibetans in Tibet, they reaffirm their common identity.

While not all Tibetans focus on the Dalai Lama in this way, in the West the Dalai Lama has become the symbol of Tibet par excellence. Nobel Peace Prize winner, indefatigable traveler, best-selling author, the Dalai Lama has become a household name—one of the three most widely known human beings in the world, alongside the Pope and Michael Jordan.

That the Dalai Lama as sacred center has not stood still, however, is suggested by the existence of his two autobiographies. While most other figures have to be content with telling their life stories once and once only, the most famous Tibetan of them all, the most celebrated incarnating lama in the whole hierarchy, tells his life story twice.

The Dalai Lama's first autobiography was published in 1962, a few short years after he fled into exile in India. At that time, few would have predicted that after forty years he would still not have returned to his homeland. According to the Dalai Lama in his introduction to the 1997 reprinting of the book, *My Land and My People* was designed to document "my early life in Tibet, the events that led to the Tibetan uprising of 1959, and my flight into exile."[4] That over 100,000 Tibetan refugees would go on to recreate monasteries, establish schools, develop industries, and spread out over the world could hardly be recorded in that book. That the Dalai Lama himself would become an internationally known figure could not then be foreseen. Thus, in 1990, it seemed necessary to offer another version of his life, *Freedom in Exile: The Autobiography of the Dalai Lama.* As the Dalai Lama writes in his introduction to the second book, he has two main reasons for offering the story of his life: "Firstly, an increasing number of people have shown an interest in learning something about the Dalai Lama. Secondly, there are a number of historical events about which I wish to set the record straight."[5]

The Dalai Lama only briefly mentions his first autobiography in his second (p. 169). Rather than the second being the continuation of the first, the two books stand as equally definitive. When the first autobiography appeared in 1962, it was simply titled *My Land and My People.* When the second autobiography, *Freedom in Exile,* appeared in 1990, it bore the subtitle *The Autobiography of the Dalai Lama.* The use of the definitive article "the" here suggests that this new story supercedes the earlier version. As if to counter such a suggestion, when *My Land and My People* was reissued in 1997 (presumably to coincide with the appearance of Martin Scorsese's film, *Kundun),* it was given the following subtitle: *The Original Autobiography of His Holiness the Dalai Lama of Tibet.* This subtitle, by emphasizing the originality of this particular autobiography, claims a kind of authenticity unavailable to the second story: after all, it was there first. In a sense, the titles of both autobiographies each suggest that it is the "real" autobiography—one by being *the* autobiography, singular, the other by being "original." It is as if, as sometimes happens in the Tibetan tradition, an enlightened being decides to manifest itself in the form of two different *tulkus:* both are authentic, both are real.

A photo of the Dalai Lama graces the covers of both recent paperback editions of these autobiographies. And, on both, the Dalai Lama is listed as author. As is common to most Tibetan autobiographies in English, the role of a ghostwriter or editor is played down. Although the Dalai Lama is by no means fluent in English, his 1962 autobiography, *My Land and My People,* is presented as his own work, with no mention of assistance.[6] In *Freedom in Exile,* the Dalai Lama notes, "I decided to tell my story directly in English," but he does go on to note that he has "limited resources" and a fallible memory; he thus offers his "thanks to the concerned officers of the Tibetan Government in Exile and to Mr. Alexander Norman, for their assistance in these areas" (pp. xiii–xiv). The role Norman played in the manuscript is not detailed there, but as Daniel Goleman reports elsewhere, Norman apparently approached the Dalai Lama in the 1980s with the suggestion that "it was time for a more complete account [than that in *My Land and My People*]. They worked together on the book. Mr. Norman taped the Dalai Lama for several hours at a time and prepared a manuscript from the tapes, which they later rewrote together."[7] As seems to be the protocol in the ghostwritten text in English, the notion that the Dalai Lama got help with his own life story is suppressed. This would seem especially important in the case of an incarnate lama, for if a realized being cannot tell his own story, who could? As Lejeune notes in another context, "the illustrious, or exemplary, person must be a full and complete subject. . . . [A]s soon as he discloses his life in a book, the hero must be in control of the writing, or at least what represents it symbolically, the *signature.*"[8] Readers steeped both in Western myths of authorship and dreams of Tibetan presence look for the fullness of subjectivity in the self-presentations of Tibetans—rather than its emptiness, as a Buddhist interpretation would have it. Like the lama who offers the blessing of his touch to supplicants, the Tibetan autobiography in English must seem to relay a power by coming directly from the hands of its author.

If within the genre of English-language autobiography and memoir, it is conventional to sign the name of the subject on the ghostwritten text, within the Tibetan tradition, it is a different story. In her discussion of Tibetan *namtar,* Janet Gyatso notes that while readers of Tibetan *rangnam* expect that the stories may be edited by the subject's disciples (whose names are mentioned in the colophon), "Tibetan life stories that are actually composed by someone else, even if written in the first person, are not called rangnam."[9] In some ways, then, the Tibetan demand for identification of author, narrator, and protagonist seems even greater than in English-language autobiography. Nonetheless, very different understandings of presence and its role in reaching readers seem to be at work here. In the Tibetan tradition, the secondhand account is as efficacious as the first: both biographies and autobiographies can teach and inspire readers. Like a protection cord or *sungdu* blessed by a lama and brought from a teaching for one who could not attend, a second- or third-hand telling does not fail to convey a boon. In the English-language tradition, on the other hand, a certain pride of place is given to the autobiographical text. This is not to say that the biography is a belittled genre, but that, in the English tradition, the insistence on the presence of the author/autobiographical subject is suggested by the suppression of the role of the ghostwriter—even if it is widely known that the autobiographical subject is not fluent in English, as in the case of the Dalai Lama. The dream of selfhood, the desire for the fullness of subjectivity, marks English language autobiographies while Tibetan Buddhist *rangnams*—if they are to exemplify Buddhist values—have to acknowledge that selfhood is an illusion that perpetuates suffering.

Despite the appearance that the Dalai Lama's two English autobiographies convey the fullness of a personality, in his case the existence of two seemingly complete and independent autobiographies thwarts the Western dream of a unified selfhood. While conforming to conventions by which autobiographies make sense of a life—use of the first person "I," present reflections on previous actions—the very existence of two stories undermines the notion of a coherent self, and, in accord with Buddhist values, exemplifies the possibility of "subjectivity without essence."[10] Thus, rather than offering the presence of a unified person or self, these texts can be seen as demonstrating the practice of skillful means—the notion that the dharma can be rhetorically adjusted to reach different audiences in different times and places. The existence of two original, singular autobiographies offers an inkling of a different kind of presence, a presence fully in accord with Buddhist values, a presence not of person or personality (which from a Buddhist perspective are ultimately unreal and insubstantial) but a manifestation of the dharma's ultimate reality, the presence on earth of an aspect of enlightenment. Kundun.

Or that is one way to look at it. For how can I entirely divorce my very Western desires for presence from a Buddhist sensibility that denies that kind of presence and offers a different one? I can only go on, moving like the religious person described by Clifford Geertz, a figure who does not stay fixed in one perspective, be it religious, aesthetic, scientific, or commonsensical.[11] At one moment, I know that the Dalai Lama is a man like any other man, with faults and contradictions and strange opinions. From another perspective, too, I know that he is nothing less than a manifestation of enlightenment on earth.

But if the Dalai Lama, as a manifestation of an enlightened being, is a traditional subject within the Tibetan genre of *namtar,* how does he present himself to his readers? And what kinds of inspiration and instruction does he offer? As Janet Gyatso notes, Tibetan autobiographers are faced with the rhetorical problem of representing themselves as both exemplary and humble. In effect, they must display their accomplishments without seeming to do so. Although some Tibetan autobiographers in English seem to participate in the Tibetan tradition of *rangnam* in that they relate the exploits of subjects Tibetan Buddhists would consider realized beings, the didactic purposes of telling their life stories have to shift within the context of the genre of English-language autobiography. Some Westerners may indeed fantasize about Tibetans in general as enlightened beings, but it would be impolitic for Tibetans to claim such things about themselves. Thus, although Tibetan Buddhists recognize the Dalai Lama as a bodhisattva, his own claim to divinity must be subdued, if not squelched in the Western context. In his utterances before Western audiences and English readers the Dalai Lama proclaims such things as, "I am a simple Buddhist monk," and even, "You probably came here expecting something from me. I have nothing to give you." Such humble declarations counter Western descriptions of him as a god-king and a living Buddha; they also have the advantage of elevating him thereby. The tension between the grandiose claims others make about him and his own self-descriptions makes him seem all the more modest and simple, and more in line with popular Western assumptions about what a Buddhist monk should be.

In his own autobiographies the Dalai Lama mixes an earthy sense of humor, frank descriptions of his faults, brief discussions of the meaning of Buddhism, as well as such things as his Five-Point Peace Plan. Thus we learn in *Freedom in Exile* that shortly after his birth—a birth that caused his ill father to suddenly recover—the newborn made a mess on his sister (pp. 7–8) and that, as a young child, he insisted on sitting at the head of the table (p. 9). Recollections such as these gesture towards the conventional presentation of mischief in childhood in *rangnam;* they are also juxtaposed with more complex statements, as when the Dalai Lama addresses his own relation to divinity. As he notes, "I am held to be the reincarnation of each of the previous thirteen Dalai Lamas of Tibet. . . . I am believed also to be a manifestation of Chenrezig, in fact the seventy-fourth in a lineage that can be traced back to a brahmin boy who lived in the time of Buddha Sakyamuni." By placing these claims to divinity in the passive, the Dalai Lama puts the burden of defining sacrality on others, and puts his own view of the matter more ambivalently: "I am often asked whether I truly believe this. The answer is not simple to give. But as a fifty-six year old, when I consider my experiences during this present life, and given my Buddhist beliefs, I have no difficulty accepting that I am spiritually connected both to the thirteen previous Dalai Lamas, to Chenrezig and to the Buddha himself" (p. 11).

Aside from these few enigmatic statements about "spiritual connection," in his autobiographies the Dalai Lama appears as a very down-to-earth man. His representations of Buddhism emphasize its practicality and focus on meditation, a practice that can take a variety of forms in Tibetan Buddhism but is also familiar in the West as a kind of relaxation technique. Indeed, there is little of the mysterious or mystical in his account. If the Tibetan *rangnam* form traditionally has outer and inner aspects in which the outer autobiography tells the story of events in the world and the inner conveys something of the subject's spiritual development, both Dalai Lama autobiographies dwell almost exclusively on outer events. The two autobiographies tell roughly the same story of his birth and discovery, his move to Lhasa, his education, his ascension to power at age 16, his dealings with the Chinese, and his exile in 1959 at the age of 24. *Freedom in Exile* picks up where *My Land and My People* leaves off and goes on to discuss the early years in India, the fate of the refugees, the importance of Western and Indian patronage for the preservation of Tibetan culture and religion, the results of the fact-finding missions to Tibet, and the agonistic relationship between the Tibetan government-in-exile and the Chinese government. In all of these discussions, the Dalai Lama comes across as a very reasonable person, one who wants only what is best for his people, a man who does not think that he is all that great but who has instead had greatness thrust upon him.

Indeed, as in many of his public appearances in the West, in *Freedom in Exile* the Dalai Lama frequently comes across as a person who is far too innocent and kind for the hostile world in which he finds himself. His Five-Point Peace Plan, presented before Congress in 1987 and outlined in the book, distinguishes him as political figure with admirable if impractical goals. In this plan, he proposes that Tibet be made a Zone of *Ahimsa* (Non-violence), that it become a place where human rights are respected, that the population transfer of Han Chinese into Tibet be brought to a halt, and that negotiations on Tibet's status be earnestly undertaken. In all, the plan envisions that "the Tibetan plateau" (and not, presumably, just the Tibetan Autonomous Region defined by the Chinese) become a peaceful site populated entirely by Tibetans. In a sense, the Dalai Lama's plan to make Tibet a Zone of Ahimsa seems patently sensible if practically out of reach; in effect, with such a proposal, the Dalai Lama comes off as a sane—if nationalistic—man in an insane world.

The Dalai Lama's "sanity" here, of course, depends on Westerners' prior acquaintance with a place like the one he describes. When he calls for the demilitarization of the Tibetan plateau, the prohibition of nuclear weapons and other armaments, the transformation of Tibet into "the world's largest natural park or biosphere," and the promotion of human rights' organizations, among other things, the Dalai Lama echoes the Western fantasy of Tibet as a place that never had a standing army, and whose people always acted out of Buddhist principles. In effect, with this proposal the Dalai Lama reclaims Shangri-La—a place that preserves all that is best in the world—and makes it fully Tibetan.

If such a vision of Tibet seems to mark his transcendent if impractical vision, another measure of the Dalai Lama's down-to-earthness appears in the chapter "Of 'Magic and Mystery,'" whose title echoes the account of a French writer, Alexandra David-Neel's *Magic and Mystery in Tibet*.[12] Noting that "[m]any Westerners want to know whether the books on Tibet by people like Lobsang Rampa and some others, in which they speak about occult practices, are true. They also ask me whether Shambala . . . really exists" (p. 209). In this chapter the Dalai Lama works to rationalize many of the things that have made Tibet famous. Proclaiming that he is "a strong believer in the value of modern science," the Dalai Lama explains his willingness to let Western scientists investigate the effects of meditation on its practitioners, and expresses his wish to have the phenomenon of oracles investigated by "some sort of scientific inquiry" (p. 211). He describes the practice of *tulku* selection as "more logical than it may first appear" (p. 215), and is careful to undermine the notion that he himself possesses any extraordinary powers: "I should say here that I have no powers of clairvoyance" (p. 217). Careful to mark his own ordinariness, the Dalai Lama bemoans the fact that his duties have prevented him from taking the lengthy retreats necessary for real attainment: ". . . I consider myself to be very much in the primary grade of spiritual development" (p. 208). Even so, the possibility that there may indeed be some truth to the rumor of the marvelous in Tibet is left open when, at the close of the chapter, the Dalai Lama argues that just because science cannot account for some things does not mean they do not exist: "Through mental training, we have developed techniques to do things which science cannot yet adequately explain. This, then, is the basis of the supposed 'magic and mystery' of Tibetan Buddhism" (p. 220).

The figure that appears in *Freedom in Exile* is one who seems to have found a happy fit between his religious life and the rational, material world. As Lopez has argued, however, representations in the West of the Dalai Lama as a rational man and Buddhism as a kind of modern, universalist doctrine have led to confusion when the less "rational" and more religious aspects of Tibetan Buddhism and his own role in it have been exposed for popular consideration, as in the debate over the worship of Dorje Shugden.[13] How could such a rational man believe in evil spirits and oracular announcements, let alone legislate how others should conceive of them? How can a champion of Gandhi's ahimsa condone India's detonation of a nuclear bomb? What do we make of a religion than can identify Steven Seagal as an incarnation and accept Richard Gere and Adam Yauch as patron saints? What do we make of an incarnation of a bodhisattva who will let Apple use his image to sell computers?

No doubt we will do what we have always done—debunk and remythify him, find our best selves in his image and lose them again.

My reading of the Dalai Lama is designed neither to reinscribe him as "holier than thou" nor to rationalize away his power. For even if the Dalai Lama operates as a symbol for many Tibetans and Westerners, symbols are very powerful things: they construct lives and selves; they shape our experience of the world and each other. But I do want to inject a bit of skepticism in the recent fascination for the Dalai Lama in the West, to encourage a bit of self-reflection. Difficult as it is to recognize the dynamics of representation, the Dalai Lama's self-presentations in English operate in a world in which he is already deified and lampooned, a world in which images of lamas have long animated our imagination. One need only recall Bogle's representation of his relationship to the Third Panchen Lama, Turner's adorations before the infant Panchen Lama, and the distrust of lamas that Waddell and Younghusband solidified in their writings in order to see that the current Dalai Lama is a late-comer in the Western representations. To expand on a standard Tibetan Buddhist teaching, investigate your teacher, the representations made of him, and your own desires closely before you bow down.

CHAPTER 5

Reincarnate Lamas:
Chögyam Trungpa and Chagdud Tulku

EMANATION, BODY

*A*s we have seen, a *tulku* is the bodily emanation of an enlightened being who is able to choose the manner, time, and place of his reappearance on earth. Unlike in Hindu systems of reincarnation, however, it is not a soul or atman that moves from body to body, and unlike most other forms of Buddhism which argue that no *thing* is transferred from life to life, in the Tibetan system, it is consciousness that transfers from life to life. This matter of multiple lives presents a curious rhetorical situation for someone recounting his or her life. If he or she is an incarnation, where should the narration begin? How many lives should be recounted?

The tendency in several *tulku*-autobiographies in English is to treat this multiplicity of lives as a matter of course. Thus, in both Chögyam Trungpa's *Born in Tibet* and Chagdud Tulku's *Lord of the Dance,* the narrating subjects (both from the Kagyu school) not only describe their present births but also go briefly into the biographies of their predecessors, particularly their immediate predecessor. Chagdud Tulku begins his book with a scene in which his previous incarnation offers a reliquary box to the woman who would bear his successor and explicitly states the karmic connection between them; later he notes that his predecessor was "famous as a wild *siddha* who drank prodigious amounts of *arak* and on occasion bent heavy iron swords into folds. Chagdud Tanpai Gyaltsan, like the incarnations of Chagdud before him, had an extraordinary realization of the essential insubstantiality and mutability of the phenomenal world."[1] In his autobiography, *Born in Tibet,* Trungpa devotes an entire chapter to his predecessor, the Tenth Trungpa Tulku, focusing especially on his ability to direct his own spiritual development, regardless of the wishes and designs of monastic authorities. Indeed, the story of the Tenth Trungpa Tulku—who became something of "a second Milarepa"[2]—helps his successor settle a question in his own mind; the narration of his life acquires a moral—with resonances of yet another story—that gives him a precedent for forging his own spiritual path. If the stories of such exemplary figures as the Buddha, Padmasambhava, Milarepa, Tsongkhapa, Gesar of Ling, and many others offer Tibetan Buddhists models that both instruct and inspire, *tulkus* have a special relationship to the life stories of their predecessors, stories that cannot only help shape their lives but stories that in some sense tell their lives, construct them, create them.

But just as Milarepa had to deal with questions of what to eat and where to live while he undertook his spiritual practices, *tulkus* too, as Ken Wilber writes, "must deal with very human issues in establishing the continuity of their spiritual path from one life to another."[3] Although considered emanations of enlightened beings, *tulkus* have to be educated and trained, and they must deal with the difficulties of corporeality. The most lurid examples of the problems of uniting the enlightened mind with a human body are suggested by allegations of sexual harassment on the part of lamas as well as by accusations that supposedly celibate monks have had sexual relationships with their students.[4] Trungpa's own manner of dealing with sexuality once he came to the United States has made him famous, if not notorious. In the case of his published autobiography, released before he moved to Colorado and founded the Naropa center in Boulder, the very real human issues Trungpa considers are how to save his own life and the lives entrusted to him; his autobiography switches midway from being an account of his education within the Karma Kagyu monastic system to a tale of high adventure as Trungpa leads a throng of refugees on a harrowing journey from Kham to exile in India. For although he is "born in Tibet," much of the book is concerned with his struggle to get out of the place, an effort that requires much of him spiritually and physically.

In what may be the most detailed and exciting description of a Tibetan journey into exile, the emphasis in Trungpa's account is often on worldly events—on the limits of human bodies and minds when they are faced with difficult terrain and lack of food. One description in particular expresses the very physical nature of the journey. The party finds itself at the edge of a precipice; from here a ladder made of pine trunks descends to the middle of a river. From there still more pine ladders cross "a series of rocks to the farther bank."

The porter looked very cheerful and said 'It's only a ladder; just follow me.' I was still roped to the two porters. When I got on the ladder I saw how immensely long it was; we seemed to be so high up that a man at the bottom looked like a mere dwarf. It was made of single pines lashed together from end to end, with notches cut in the wood for footholds. When I climbed down the first few notches I could see the swirling green waters of the river underneath; a few more steps, and I felt I was poised in space over an expanse of water. There was a cold wind coming up from a large cave under the rock into which the river was pouring; worst of all, the ladder shook in a terrifying way with the weight of the many porters who were trying to help me. (p. 199)

The detailed physical description echoes tales of adventure rather than of piety. The book shifts from being a kind of traditional *rangnam* into a page-turner of sorts, a tale more reminiscent of the Everest adventure story told by Jon Krakauer in *Into Thin Air* than the life of Milarepa. And in some ways such a shift in genre seems perfectly fitting for this exile's tale: it marks a shift in being. If the first part of the book shows a *tulku* undertaking a number of Buddhist practices and relationships to important teachers—a being who continually apprehends the emptiness of the self—the second part of the book displays a subject who is a kind of courageous actor in the world, a figure more in line with a self-apprehending traveler.

But if Westerners' ability to interpret such physical adventures is shaped by discourses of adventure, romanticism, fitness, and others, Trungpa's grounding in Tibetan Buddhist thought leads him to reckon the whole trip as a "pilgrimage" to the sacred land of India, a trip that is ultimately a lesson in impermanence. Forced to the limits of their physical endurance, these travelers use Buddhist theodicy to understand their trials:

Our journey to India must be thought of as a pilgrimage; something that in the past few Tibetans have been able to make. Whether or not India has changed, the spiritual blessing imparted to that country by the presence of the Buddha remain: the places where he lived, freed himself from the bondage of *Samsar,* taught, and died have an eternal value.

In this way, Tibetan exile is rendered not as a result of political and military circumstance but as a way for the travelers to grow spiritually:

It is fortunate for us that our way is hard and that we are struggling against greater difficulties than the pilgrims of the past, for by this means we shall learn and profit the more from our journey. We should not be thinking only about the enemies threatening us from without.

For this Buddhist traveler, to fall into the trap of the self-affirming adventurer is to profane the journey. As he argues:

> Each moment we should be aware of ourselves and of the forces of destruction that threaten each man from within. If we fail in this, we are indeed putting the spiritual object of our journey in jeopardy; each step along the way should be holy and precious to us. (p. 208)

Thus, travel—and going into exile specifically—become an opportunity to confront egotism and the very roots of suffering.

Just as Trungpa's participation in a lineage that leads back to the Kagyu masters Marpa, Milarepa, and Gampopa offers him a way to understand himself (p. 9), his thorough education in Buddhist thought gives him a way to interpret his exile. After walking for months over treacherous country, the travelers stumble across the border to India and within a few days are flying from the Himalayan foothills to the plains below:

> This, our first flight, was a strange new experience, skimming over cloud covered mountains, seeing far below us the small villages and footpaths leading up to them; only by the moving shadow of the plane on the ground could we gauge how fast we were travelling.
>
> We thought about the teaching of impermanence; this was a complete severance of all that had been Tibet and we were travelling by mechanized transport. As the moments passed, the mountain range was left behind, and the view changed to the misty space of the Indian plains stretching out in front of us. (p. 248)

As in the lama's account of his epiphany in Kipling's *Kim,* the traveler is lifted out of the details of travel and is able to recognize, from a distance, Tibet, India, and the workings of impermanence. The experience of exile thus becomes a way to affirm Buddhist teachings; pulled out of the comforts of his homeland, Trungpa recognizes exile as a kind of spiritual opportunity, a way to escape what he would later call spiritual materialism—the traps of the self that would solidify its identity around the comfortable and familiar.[5] Seen from a vantage point forty years after that exile, and from a perspective that takes into account Trungpa's exile to England and Colorado and something of his life and death there, that moving moment, tracked by a shadow, shifts too; we can see him at an early time, heading into the unknown West, the West that would do so much to and with him.

MARVELOUS MAN

Early European accounts of Tibet mentioned many marvelous things: people who ate the dead carcasses of their deceased parents, men who fashioned drinking bowls out of human skulls, shaggy oxen. But perhaps the weirdest thing encountered by Christian missionaries in the Middle Ages were priests that looked like Christians, with shaved heads, miters, and rosaries, who lived "chaste lives" in large cloisters. Searching for the marvelous, these travelers from Christendom were surprised to encounter an image of themselves, one which they could not reconcile with the images of barbarity and sinfulness they saw elsewhere among the Tibetans. When George Bogle traveled to Tibet in the eighteenth century, he was not content with these travelers' reports. Instead, much of Bogle's account seems designed to make Tibetans seem down-to-earth rather than marvelous, highly civilized rather than barbarous. While European writers spent much of the nineteenth and early twentieth centuries rebuilding the image of Tibet as exotic and strange, Western scholars in the latter half of twentieth century have worked to banish intimations of the marvelous and barbarous from the image of Tibet in order to let in other versions of the place.

In the case of Tibetan self-presentation, Tibetan autobiographers and biographers in English have had to deal with a particularly galling precedent in T. Lobsang Rampa, as we have seen in the case of Thubten Jigme Norbu's story. Thus when the anthropologist David Snellgrove sets out in 1967 to offer the biographies of *Four Lamas of Dolpo,* he writes that the lives he presents "may not seem at first quite as exciting and extraordinary as that notorious autobiography of the bogus Tibetan lama, Lobsang Rampa. But on his terms I have no wish to compete."[6]

In many ways, though, the tales told by Rampa of monks who fly in giant kites, see auras, astrally project, and hole themselves up in caves for years on end are not less fabulous than those told within the Tibetan *namtar* tradition. Even the life story of the Buddha has this miraculous character; among other things, he is conceived when his mother dreams that a white elephant enters her body, he walks and talks upon birth, and he manages the considerable feat of forging the path to enlightenment. Before his own conversion to the Buddhist path, Milarepa dabbled in magic; when he dies an enlightened man, female divinities (*dakinis*) assemble, rainbows fill the sky, and he sings a song from the cremation cell. David Germano's recent work on the contemporary *terton* ("treasure-finder") Khenpo Jikphun dares to relate the Nyingma master's many miraculous acts, ranging from his spontaneous recollection of detailed tantric teachings to his location of *terma*—"treasures" such as images, treasure chests, and texts—all over the Tibetan landscape. Germano even relates one story in which Jik-phun, in the midst of an outdoor teaching, catches a mysterious green marble globe that falls from the sky.[7]

In a similar way, the English-language autobiography of Chagdud Tulku, *Lord of the Dance,* is replete with stories that push the limits of secular credulity. With its tales of portentous dreams and accounts of practices that test the bounds of the empirical world, the book recalls the marvelous as it is related in *namtars* of Milarepa and other adepts, the yarns of Lobsang Rampa, and Marco Polo's account from Gengis Khan's court. Polo writes:

> During the three months of every year that the Lord resides at that place, if it should happen to be bad weather, there are certain crafty enchanters and astrologers in his train, who are such adepts in necromancy and the dia-bolic arts, that they are able to prevent any cloud or storm from passing over the spot on which the Emperor's Palace stands. The sorcerers who do this are called TEBET and KESIMUR, which are the names of two nations of Idolaters.[8]

While Polo is clearly astonished by such activity and is quick to attribute it to the influence of the devil, Chagdud Tulku offers a similar account of his influence on the weather in a matter-of-fact way. "I was in the full flush of my retreat accomplishments and didn't hesitate to demonstrate them. For example, if it suddenly began to rain or snow, I would blow into the air and the rain or snow would stop by the power of my accumulations of mantra" (p. 62). Versed in the famous *tunmo* practice, as an adolescent Chagdud Tulku is able to dry wet sheets in the dead of winter—all with the yogic warmth of his body. He frequently reads his dreams to foretell the future, and he once prays so fervently that a statue of Milarepa "seemed to come alive, to look at me and smile" (p. 61). Indeed, the other marvel that Polo attributes to the Tibetans monks at Genghis Khan's court—moving cups without touching them[9]—does not seem distant from the kinds of accom-plishments narrated by Chagdud, as when he "witnesses" events in far-off places (p. 216) or, in an elaborate acknowledgement of his access to the consciousness of his predecessor, dumps hot coals on his own head (p. 73). Thus, while many recent debunkers of the Shangri-La myth (myself included) struggle to show that Tibet was never a magical and mysterious land and that even the highest lama is but a simple Buddhist monk, Chag-dud Tulku's account reinvokes the idea of Tibet as a place of marvels, a place that is far different from the world we take as real.

The question is, though, is this the *conventional* marvelous—the mar-velous we have come to expect of Tibet—or something different? For it is also possible to read Chagdud's book as offering a perspective utterly at odds with Westernized secular, "common sense" or Christian views of the world. While the Dalai Lama's autobiographies seem to be translated tales—stories made palatable for the widest possible Western audience—Chagdud makes few concessions of that sort. At times, reading Chagdud's book, one gets the sense not simply that he *believes* different things from people in other cultures; one is reminded that to live out a religious tradition is to inhabit a fully meaningful world. In that way, the book is an antidote to the Western contention that Tibetan Buddhism offers something good for all of us, and we can pick up bits and pieces that will enhance our lives. As a counterpoint to a piecemeal, eclectic, or New Age approach to religion, Chagdud Tulku's autobiography reminds readers that a belief in a monotheistic God (or lack thereof) cannot just be exchanged for an acceptance of Buddha nature: with Chagdud's autobiography one is encouraged to recognize that the seemingly strange phenomena that inhabit and enliven his story arise because he inhabits a complete system of religious and cultural symbols, which have tremendous explanatory and referential power for his particular religious community. Chagdud Tulku gives particular significance to things—he *sees* particular things—because he is a *nangpa*—an "insider"—what Tibetans call a Buddhist; he sees other things because he is a *ngagpa*—a tantric master. And with his story we are in unabashed realm of Geertz's "really real,"[10] which for Chagdud Tulku is a tantric Buddhist system of symbols and meanings that function to construct a world and reconfirm its facticity at every turn.

The wealth of the symbolic system available to Chagdud Tulku is expressed in both the variety and the specificity of the symbols with which he can interpret events. For example, when he asks Tulku Ado to divine whether he should undertake a pilgrimage to Lhasa, the elder lama invokes the stories of exemplary adepts in his divination: "Don't go. Nyagla Padma Duddul achieved rainbow body. He didn't go on pilgrimage; he meditated. Milarepa also achieved enlightenment by meditating, not by pilgrimage" (p. 103). So there's one answer: divination is a culturally valued practice, and offers one way to deal with Chagdud's question. But he still wants to go to Lhasa, and he has still other resources. Soon after, he has a dream in which the dharma protector Ekadzati appears to him and urges him to "Go to the center" where he can escape from the "devouring tiger from the east" while there is still time (p. 104). Dreams are given special significance within the Tibetan Buddhist tradition, and those of a highly realized incarnation like Chagdud Tulku, whose dreams have been shown to clarify the reality of complex situations, are not to be dismissed. Given the rich resources of his particular Tibetan Buddhist symbol system, Chagdud Tulku has access to a meaningful alternative to the answer given by Ado Tulku, an alternative that is also religiously and culturally sanctioned, and thus does not bring him into conflict personally, interpersonally, or religiously.

The danger, however, in representing these religious symbols in the context of an English-language text or in summarizing his use of them (as I have just done) is that they become open to other interpretations. In the example above, Chagdud's choice to follow his dream can seem mere expediency. And when, for example, Chagdud's fingers brush those of a potential consort and he says he finds himself absorbed in "the absolute nature of reality" (p. 134), interpretations from outside the system are also possible: this is just sexual energy; this is just plain old lust. Chagdud, however, remains firmly within a Tibetan Buddhist and tantric worldview as he relates fantastic phenomena without apology. Instead of translating his experiences for Westerners into more familiar terms, his world is one replete with *dakinis, terma,* divinations, empowerments, and experiences of "uncontrived awareness" (p. 93). Of course, placing such things in an English-language text inevitably involves a kind of translation—a kind of carrying across from one worldview to another—even as it invokes the old tales of marvels and mysticism. Even so, there is something undomesticated in his tale, something unrecuperable, something "hybrid," in Homi Bhabha's sense of the term: a disavowal of prevailing relations of power, which resist "outsiders" attempts to contain it.[11] These moments of otherness, these things that I cannot get a hold of, reside not in his *use* of "alien" symbols but rather in the utter conviction and ease with which he accepts the interpretations of events that these symbols allow.

One ready example appears in his description of his mother. While in their autobiographies both the Dalai Lama and Thubten Jigme Norbu focus on their mother's wonderful *human* qualities, Chagdud Tulku describes his mother as

> one of Tibet's great wisdom *dakinis*—female emanations who spontaneously benefit beings by their activities. Terton Jigmed Khakyod Wangpo had prophesied her birth as an emanation of the longevity deity White Tara and an incarnation of Yeshe Tsogyal, Tibet's most valued female practitioner and the spiritual companion of Padmasambhava. . . . Dawa Drolma [his mother] . . . has crossed the threshold of death, traveled in realms of existence beyond those visible to us as humans and returned to tell about it. (pp. 4–5)

It would be possible to read such a description as a kind of mystification—an incantation of specialized terms designed to alienate and impress the uninitiated listener. I read the passage, however, as a sign of the largely untranslated, undomesticated aspects of the book. In another example, Chagdud mentions how he came to learn local history. "Some of the history of Chagdud Gonpa and the Chagdud incarnations I had heard before, some I learned from the monks who escorted me through Nyarong, some were spontaneously revealed within my mind" (pp. 71–2). All through his account he encounters extraordinary phenomena that lead him on the path—a one-legged old man who mysteriously tells him of a secret mountain retreat, dragons and tigers who appear in dreams to warn him, whisperings of places he has never heard of—"America," a voice says in a dream—that will later figure in his life (p. 207).

The inseparability of his experience and his belief is also suggested by his account of the journey into exile. The travelers have had to get rid of all extra baggage; this act of renunciation throws Chagdud into a liminal state:

> It was while crossing this pass that I came to the melancholy realization that this was the end of my life as I had known it. My possessions, my relatives, my monastery, my country—layer by layer these had been stripped away. I felt as if I had entered the *bardo,* the intermediate state between death and rebirth where one experiences existence as completely insubstantial and miragelike. Like a wayfarer in the *bardo,* I knew that this journey would end only in an inconceivably different existence. (p. 153)

Reading this, I have the sense not that Chagdud Tulku *thought* about the *bardo* state and then interpreted his experience in those terms (as a neophyte Tibetan Buddhist in the West might), but that he *experiences* his life as a kind of *bardo*. For him, there is no distance between the symbol and its interpretations. And, as I see it, that's what it means to inhabit a worldview—rather than to take one on, or to learn one.

In this way, when I read his book, I implicitly encounter the limits of my own interpretive systems. While usually I simply inhabit them as natural—as just the way things are—when I enter into the world created in Chagdud's book I feel, at moments anyway, the utter relativity of my convictions, the utter lack of foundation in the things I take as reality.

But what more would we expect from this tantric master? The ability to challenge received categories, the ability to press past established boundaries, the continual effort to push us beyond who we think we are—all of these mark the work of a crazy wisdom adept. Like both Milarepa and Drukpa Kunley of the Kagyu lineage, Chagdud inherits the tradition of the crazy wisdom master, a kind of trickster figure that recurs within the Tibetan tradition. For while one strand of Tibetan culture elevates the monastic tradition, passed on by a lineage of masters and scholars and expressed in the figure of the celibate monk, another strand champions a very different figure—the antinomial *naljorpa* or *yogi,* who teaches more by his extreme actions than by reference to chapter and verse. Thus, for example, when Milarepa's sister visits him in the cave where he meditates and is troubled by his nakedness, she weaves him a cloth. Instead of making a robe or cloak with it, however, Mila sews a hood for his head and sheaths for his fingers, feet, and penis. When she is ashamed by this display of his genitals, he rebukes her, saying

> Knowing what real shame is, I remain faithful to my vows and precepts. . .
> Since I consider all parts of my body to be of equal worth, I made these
> sheaths. . . . If you blush at my organ, blush equally at your own. If for you it
> is better to get rid of an object you consider shameful, get rid of your own.[12]

Similarly, the sixteenth-century *siddha* Drukpa Kunley—whose name refers to Chagdud's own Drukpa Kagyu school—frequently instructed people by forcing them to encounter their own limitations and hypocrisies. In one story, Drukpa Kunley's mother begs him to take a wife. When he brings home an ancient old crone from the market place, his mother tells him to take her back, saying, "I could do her work better than she." Kunley relents, replying, "If you can do her work for her, I'll take her back." That night, Kunley gets into bed with his mother and demands that she "perform a wife's duties." At first his mother refuses, but when he persists, she gives in, saying it's okay as long as he won't tell anyone. When he hears this, Kunley gets out of bed and the next day heads to the market where he announces to the world, "Hey listen, you people! If you persist, you can seduce even your own mother!" Despite his mother's efforts to keep her moral failings private, her hypocrisy and weakness are all too apparent to Kunley, and he does not hesitate to expose them. And when he did so, "her faults were eradicated, her sins expiated, and her troubles and afflictions removed."[13]

But radical as they might seem, both Milarepa and Drukpa Kunley are firmly entrenched in the Tibetan tradition. As in the case of Bogle's self-reflection, the question arises: can a conventionalized trickster still effectively trick? If an iconoclast is institutionalized, can he or she still challenge the institution? Within the Tibetan tradition, these two strains of the scholarly monk and the iconoclastic trickster serve as kind of dialectical counters to each other, counters which through their oscillating movement encourage creativity and reflection *within* the system but do not, finally, eradicate it. Indeed, without the symbolic system that produced them, both the monk and the trickster would be meaningless.

When Milarepa is challenged by a *geshe* to explain the logic of a Buddhist text, the yogi sings out, among other things: "Having assimilated the teaching in the stream of my consciousness, I forgot to engage in doctrinal politics. . . . Having embraced the spirit rather than the letter, I forgot how to play with words."[14] Like Mila, Chagdud challenges institutions without questioning the ultimate truth of the dharma. With a Sakya mother and a Geluk father, the Kagyu lama versed in Nyingma teachings cannot be bothered with the finer points of sectarian politics. Thus, when a Geluk monk deprecates the Kagyu school, the Kagyu lineage-holder proclaims:

> You think what you think, of course, but for me the dharma is like a ball of sugar, sweet wherever you taste it. Like milk, it tastes the same no matter where you stand to drink it. Like gold, it is gold no matter how you slice through it. The Sakya, the Gelug, the Kagyu and the Nyingma are all dharma, essentially the same. (p. 65).

In his matter-of-fact presentation of the fantastic, in his juxtaposition of the all-too-human and the far-out divine, and in his embracing of the mixed, the complex, and the unsettled, Chagdud Tulku's book offers a different version of the marvelous Tibetan—a Tibetan we have seen before and who still eludes us, a Tibetan who can both confirm the old tales and shake us up.

Indeed, at several points in the narrative, Chagdud Tulku's story seems designed to reanimate the dharma—to make the old stories more than just stories. For as Trungpa, another crazy wisdom master, has argued, it is possible to get materialistic about even spirituality. Despite sporadic glimpses of "the fallacy of the concept of 'I,' the fallacy of the ego as a reference point for reality" (p. 85), there is always the danger of being egotistical about egolessness. To teach these old lessons, Chagdud Tulku frequently uses himself as an example. In one instance, after experiencing a profound sense of calm after a lama urges him to "meditate more," Chagdud Tulku throws himself into meditation with ferocity. But that is precisely the problem, as is recognized by a grimy old monk of little status: the monk tells him he was "meditating with attachment to conceptless stability, and this attachment had resulted in heavy, flawed meditation." Rather than being affronted, Chagdud takes the reprimand as a blessing: "So I had been powerfully blessed twice in two days, once by the revered Sechhen Kongtrul [who told him to meditate more], once by that ragged, disreputable lama who cut short my wrong turn of mind" (p. 78). What Chagdud is pointing to here is that attachment to titles and high-ranking lamas will not in itself take you anywhere: sometimes your best teacher is the teacher you hate, the teacher you look down on, the stupidest person you know. For it is often such figures who can show you your own face.

In another story of self-encounter, Chagdud describes his return to Tibet in 1987. By then he is a 57–year-old lama with numerous accolades, an American wife, a throne-holding son, and a growing dharma center in Oregon; nonetheless, he is again confronted by his attachment both to his teacher and to his sense of himself. His old lama, Tulku Arig, who first ordained Chagdud into the monastic life, speaks harshly to him, demanding "Why did you go that way?" The question throws the now–mature lama into confusion: Is he asking why I abandoned my monastic vows? Does he want to know why I left Tibet? To add further tension to the meeting, the old lama dismisses his pupil abruptly and chastises him for wasting his time. Chagdud is initially disturbed and thinks deprecatingly about his former teacher: "Does he still hope to gain some greater realization in the little time he has left?" After further consideration, however, what the scene finally conveys to Chagdud is in the spirit of a Tibetan Buddhist cautionary tale. "And suddenly I saw my own hope and fear, clinging to his physical presence as the lama, when truly, as a master of the Great Perfection teachings, he, his mind and his dharma teachings knew no boundaries of time and space. When I realized this, my mind relaxed into its natural awareness" (pp. 226–7). The old lama, in effect, throws his student's self-image back to him, forcing him to ask: Who am I? Who is this "I" that asks who am I? What am I looking for? Or that, at least, is how Chagdud Tulku, with his fluency in Buddhist symbols, reads the scene. The old lama's refusal to accept his disciple's self-presentation has the effect of undermining the *tulku's* conception of self: he asks himself gain if perhaps his teacher is criticizing his American wife or his decision to go to the West. Looking into his wife Jane's eyes, however, he finds again that state of pervasive, enlightened mind that is the essence-less ground of Chagdud's tantric Tibetan Buddhist world. Once again, he recalls, "[my] hopes and fears fell away and I experienced the spacious expanse of pure awareness" (p. 227). This awakening is accomplished by means of the standard ploy of showing the student himself. In this way, the cautionary tale itself can be seen as utterly conventional. Within the worldview that Chagdud Tulku constructs for his readers, however, this encounter with the emptiness of self is one of the primary lessons to learn, relearn, and yet not attach to.

As an inhabitant of—or shall I say traveler within—a thoroughgoing Buddhist worldview, Chagdud Tulku cannot capture the dharma; he can only try to activate it. In a similar fashion, he cannot confine the dharma to a single place: if it is really true, if it is really real, it will be meaningful in Tibet, in China, in the United States, and in Brazil, where he now lives. Thus, in the final image of the autobiography, Chagdud Tulku describes a site in China "where centuries before one of the Buddha's most profound practice lineages had passed from master to master, then was carried to India, Tibet and, eventually, to America" (p. 238). For one inside the system—a *nangpa*—the universal teachings are also the ones that travel.

Tibetan Women in the Western Buddhist Lineage: Rinchen Dolma Taring and Dorje Yudon Yuthok

HEROINES

The Buddha dharma that travels is the one that now makes its home in Brazil, Switzerland, India, Tibet, the United States and elsewhere. As Western practitioners of the dharma explore the nature of the Buddhist tradition in which they have taken refuge, some have made efforts to separate the "essential" from the "cultural," or to "revitalize" Buddhism in order to make it more appropriate for Western and modern settings. Western feminists, in particular, have attempted to decipher whether the patriarchal ways in which Buddhist institutions have been formed are integral to the tradition or if they are something that might be exorcised.

Women within the Tibetan Buddhist tradition occupy an ambiguous position. While on the one hand there are teachings and teachers who espouse the notion that any one, in any body, is capable of attaining full enlightenment, historically and culturally things have not worked out so happily. And while female deities populate the Buddhist cosmology and enlightened figures like Yeshe Tsogyel suggest that gender is no obstacle to realization, renowned women teachers and nuns have been few and far between. The Tibetan saying, "If you want to be a servant, make your son a monk; if you want to have a servant, make your daughter a nun," suggests the subordinate role that female renunciates have occupied in Tibetan society.[1] Furthermore, unlike other Mahayana traditions, the Tibetan Buddhist tradition lacks a lineage of fully ordained nuns or bhikshunis.[2] And while it is frequently touted that in comparison to other Asian women, Tibetan women possess an unprecedented amount of independence,[3]

Tibetan women traditionally have occupied a lower status than their male counterparts.

All of this has combined to encourage Western female practitioners of Tibetan Buddhism to rethink and sometimes "reinvent" their tradition. In her book *Buddhism After Patriarchy,* Rita M. Gross, for example, offers a "feminist revalorization of Buddhism" that "repairs" its sexism and attempts to bring it "much more in line with its own fundamental values and vision than was its patriarchal form."[4] In her article, "Tibetan Buddhist Women Practitioners, Past and Present: A Garland to Delight Those Wishing Inspiration," Janice Willis has fashioned for women a "special lineage of renowned women practitioners"—a lineage of "more than thirty-two exemplary and inspirational women practitioners" that includes nuns, tantric adepts, as well as lay devotees.[5] Two women listed in Willis's lineage are contemporary laywomen whose life stories have been told in autobiographies in English. These include Rinchen Dolma Taring and Ama Adhe. While Willis does not discuss Ama Adhe's story at length (I discuss Adhe below), she does elaborate on the meaning of Rinchen Dolma Taring's life and her potential as a model for female practitioners of Tibetan Buddhism. In a very direct way, then, this Tibetan's autobiography in English is offered as a (New Age) *namtar,* one that might instruct and inspire. It offers the story of a Tibetan laywoman who has both studied and taught unflaggingly, an exile who has devoted herself both to the welfare of Tibetan children and to her Indian neighbors.

While Willis chooses to focus on the details of Taring's life as related by Canyon Sam, who visited Dolma in Rajpur, she does point her readers to Taring's "truly classic autobiographical account."[6] Indeed, if one wants to explore Willis's lineage of female practitioners, the English account is the only textual evidence of the life of Rinchen Dolma Taring. What will readers find there? How could this Tibetan aristocratic exile be a model for American women and others in the international community of female Buddhist practitioners? What stories of subjectivity and travel are told there?

To begin considering those questions we might look at the title of Taring's book, *Daughter of Tibet.* In one version of the birth of the Tibetan people, an ogress couples with a monkey: is Taring, then, the daughter of this Tibet? Or is she the daughter of the land, an essentialized product of that place, a place now distant and lost to her? Perhaps because both of Taring's parents had died by the time she turned ten, she can be seen as a kind of orphan—a child raised by Tibet itself. But what version of Tibet is this parent? And what kind of child did it spawn?

As in the case of Jetsun Pema, another woman who moved in aristocratic circles, the figure created by this Tibet was educated abroad, fluent in English, and one to whom the name "Mary" was attached. She is strong, independent, forthright, and determined, a perfect model, one might guess, for a Western feminist. And as Hugh Richardson writes in the foreword, "Mary-La" writes from the heart in a way that is representative not only of Tibetan women of a certain class but of all Tibetans:

> Hers is the unmistakable Tibetan voice, quiet, moderate, yet determined. It reveals the deep kindness and sympathy for want and distress, characteristic of all Tibetan women and, also, the special influence and authority enjoyed, gently and unostentatiously, by the ladies of the Lhasa nobility.[7]

Despite its apparent representativeness, the book is marked by the unmistakable personality of its author; as Richardson writes, "The directness of this book, combined with calm unexcitability, verging on understatement, and the devout, warm, humanity mark it clearly as Mary-La's. No one else could have written it. It is herself."[8] This is no representation: this is straight from the heart, unadulterated Tibetan, pure Mary-La.

Born Rinchen Dolma into the noble Tsarong family in 1910, Taring describes Lhasa in the 1910s and 1920s as a place not isolated from the rest of the world but connected to it by "Huntley and Palmer's biscuits and 'King George' chocolates."[9] After her father, a senior lay member of the Kashag, is murdered in a political shake-up (p. 22) and her mother dies (p. 38), young Taring is sent to Darjeeling at the urging of David MacDonald, the half-Sikkimese British trade agent for Yatung and Gyantse whose family ran an English school in Yatung. (MacDonald had also been part of the Younghusband Mission.) As the first Tibetan girl to be sent to school abroad, the Tsarong child is eager to begin her schooling early, and copies "down the English letters from empty biscuit tins and chocolate boxes to show off to my friends that I knew how to write English even before going to Darjeeling" (p. 50). Once she arrives at the Methodist Mount Hermon school, in a gesture that is the mirror image of Bogle's abandonment of his "European Habit,"[10] Taring exchanges her Tibetan clothes for European ones (p. 75) and her Tibetan name for an English one:

> At [the MacDonald's] school they called me Dolma, which is the Tibetan name for the Indian goddess Tara and means "Protector." Then Annie [MacDonald's daughter] asked me if I would like to be renamed "Mary" before I went to Darjeeling, Mary being the Lord Jesus's mother's name. To me it sounded like Dolma, as Christ's mother is also a protector, so I accepted it and have since been known as Mary to all my friends. (p. 56)

And while at this school, Mary, like Jetsun Pema after her and many others educated in Christian schools, attends Christian services. As she writes:

I went to church regularly with the other girls, took scripture lessons and respected Christ. Yet I kept my faith in the Lord Buddha and in Dolma as my karma deity—the goddess who had been my protector in all previous incarnations. Mother used to say that once you are protected by your own deity neither devils nor witches can harm you. She also taught me that when we pray we must pray not only for ourselves and our loved ones in this life, but for all living beings. So at church, and during prayers at school, I used to repeat, "I pray to the Virtuous Protector, Protect all living beings from frightening destruction and death." (p. 58)

For those educated in a monotheistic system in which one's singular soul is invested in one omnipotent god, Taring's flexible accommodation of Christ into her pantheon may seem inappropriate. But as Anne Klein notes, such pluralism is not unusual within the Tibetan tradition[11] and might even suggest a variety of subjectivity that is not so fixed in unities and oppositions as that common in the West. In this way, if Taring is to be accepted as a model for Western Buddhist women, her flexibility here may indeed offer an antidote to the dogmatism and emotional conflicts attendant to conversion to another religion. In any case, Taring's own mixed position, like Jetsun Pema's, offers an alternative to the notion of the Tibetan-only, strictly-Buddhist version of the authentic Tibetan.

Before Mary can finish school, however, she is sent home, where her English skills can be applied to the commercial interests of her family, and where she is married. Historically, Tibetans have engaged in flexible forms of marriage; both polygamy and polyandry are practiced—sometimes within a single household.[12] As Taring's two older sisters are already married to Tsarong,[13] she becomes his third wife, with the expectation that she might leave the marriage when she finds a suitable husband. She has her first child, a girl, in 1926 at the age of 16. Soon, though, a proposal of marriage comes from the Taring family for her older sister, and after Tsarong determines that Mary is herself interested in the Taring boy she had known at school, both she and her sister join the Taring family. The political importance of these arrangements should be underscored here; marriage is a way to connect these powerful families of the Tibetan nobility, and women (and less often men) are exchanged in these proceedings. The Tibetan practice of giving *nurin*—or "breast-price"—at the time of marriage is a kind of cash payment for the bride, ostensibly to her mother for suckling her. Furthermore, as Taring writes, "[though] no fixed amount was expected, . . . the bride judged her value by the number of presents and the amount of *Nurin* received" (p. 89). While similar exchanges characterize marriage practices around the world, it is practices like these that Western feminist Buddhists identify as cultural and expendable rather than integral to the Tibetan Buddhist worldview.

But if Taring is a lay heroine of sorts, the vicissitudes of her own relationships and reproductive life may be central to her later desire to renounce the world, and later still, to devote herself to working for others. As Irawati Karve writes of the Hindu tradition, men seem to need to be reminded of the impermanent nature of the samsaric life as it is manifested in the body; such reminders are designed to inspire renunciation. Women are more likely to have a different sense of the body:

> A woman brings into this world a shapeless mass of flesh, feeds the hungry being every three or four hours [from her own body], washes its soiled clothes, and cleans its body; and when gradually the bundle of flesh begins to take on color and form and smiles at her, she feels herself the happiest being on earth. Such a mother knows quite well what the human body is made of, and a description is not likely to engender renunciation in her mind.[14]

As Karve suggests, many women's lives are intimately bound up with the vicissitudes of birth, living, and dying, and Taring's is no different. Having left her first daughter with the Tsarong family, Taring goes on to have six more children, and

> [w]henever my nieces or any of the maid-servants were having babies I nursed them and many babies were born into my hands. But my chief interest was studying Buddhism and trying to understand the false or illusory nature of all things. This is such a difficult study that I invited famous lamas to the house and learned from them. (p. 148)

Taring retains the desire to renounce the worldly life and devote herself to Buddhism amidst her life in Lhasa, where she teaches English to her daughters and other children (p. 148), acts as interpreter for the 1947 visit of Lowell Thomas to Tibet (p. 80), and keeps up a busy social life which at one point includes Heinrich Harrer (p. 153). When she visits the famous teacher Ani Lochen, who was then over 100, she asks the nun to pray that Taring will eventually be able to "live in the mountains and lead a religious life." The reply that the old nun gives her may be reassuring to Western Buddhist women:

> She said it would never be possible for me to do this, but explained that the true religious life consists in watching your mind, as mind controls all our sensory powers. She said, "There is no need to isolate yourself. If you know, all places are paradise. There are truly religious people, well purified, among

all people everywhere. If you practice the teaching of the Lord Buddha in your daily life it is not necessary to go into the mountains. Be kind to all living beings, then I am sure you will achieve what you wish." (p. 166)

That Taring's daily life will include the uncertainties and turbulence of Chinese occupation, her coerced participation in a Chinese-organized women's group, and eventually exile, is not yet part of the story. But it is from these engagements that Taring emerges as a heroine, both for her willingness to speak out on behalf of women and her continuing desire to live a spiritual life.

One scene in particular seems designed to speak to equality-minded men and women. The situation is a gathering of the Lhasa Patriotic Women's Association. Asked to speak about the lives of "ordinary women," Taring talks for four hours to the four hundred Chinese women soldiers assembled there. She pronounces that "Tibetan women have always enjoyed equal rights with men, except that no women work in government offices." Going on to note that although it is customary for women to show respect to their husbands, women are intricately involved in almost every aspect of daily life. Make no mistake, you Chinese soldiers: Tibetan women can "shoot and fight and there have been women soldier heroines in our history." We can "work in the fields, do most of the dairy jobs, care for animals, blow the bellows of blacksmiths, weave, sew, cook, paint, draw, and sometimes go trading or look after shops in towns"—we can even get drunk if we want to. And be sure of this too: "Never in history have Tibetan women suffered any physical or mental torture, like the women of some other countries—for example, China, with its terrible custom of binding the feet of little girls, with the big toes turned in and the feet pointed and forced into tiny black shoes, so that women could never walk fast;" neither have we had to hide in *purdah,* as Muslim women have, nor throw ourselves on our husbands' funeral pyres, as in Hindu culture. Working together alongside our menfolk, we have accomplished a worldly union of male and female aspects: "The husband provides the effort and his wife the intelligence; and effort and intelligence combined produce the most fruitful results in every form of work" (pp. 185–6).

Designed as a presentation to Chinese women, Taring's self-presentation here bolsters the notion that Tibetan women before Chinese occupation enjoyed a degree of independence unique in the Asian world. And certainly, the image of the defiant Taring throwing back to these Chinese women an account of their own history of oppression is a delightful bit of resistance against her would-be liberators. She is depicted as a woman with a strong sense of self and self-worth, a woman recognizable and palatable to Western feminists like myself, a role model, an exemplar. Indeed, it was women like Taring who organized protests in Lhasa in March 1959, leading up to the famous large demonstration of the Patriotic Women's Association (W. P. A.) on March 12:

> The Lhasa women had made many anti-Chinese posters and when I joined them they were lined up around the Barkor shouting slogans—"From today Tibet is independent!" and "China must quit Tibet!" Our women were more fierce than our men. It was frightening to walk through the Barkor, where Chinese soldiers with machine-guns were watching us from the roofs. All the shops were shut and no one was on the streets except the shouting women. (pp. 226–7)

The situation in Lhasa is desperate by this time; a sizeable Chinese force has entered the city, and there are fears that the Chinese want to kill the Dalai Lama. Summoned to Norbulingka, the Dalai Lama's summer palace, by his sister Tsering Dolma in order to report on the women's activities, Taring disguises herself in an old chuba and bids a sad farewell to her grandchildren, taking her servant Tashi with her. Once at the Norbulingka, where her husband, a member of the Dalai Lama's entourage, is also staying, she deliberates as to whether she should go into exile. Her husband is determined to stay with the Dalai Lama as his only English interpreter, but Taring decides to try to make her way to Drepung and from there back home. She never makes it. Upon hearing that Norbulingka is being shelled, she decides that the only alternative is to go to India, so she sets out with Tashi and makes her way into exile with the assistance of Khampa freedom fighters.

Taring's decision to head to India on her own is a turning point in the autobiography but one that she does not adequately prepare her readers for. Taring reports that she feels compelled to go to avoid being captured. In letters to her family she writes:

> I assured them that if I got through safely the rest of my life would be devoted to seeking the truth and that my prayers and love would be with them for ever. I said that the sun can come out of the clouds and asked them never to lose courage and faith, because by struggling through hardship our karma develops itself. I reminded them that none of us can escape our karma and asked them, if they were still alive, to pray always and consider that this was what our karma had to lead to. (p. 232)

Although Taring interprets her decision to go to India in light of Buddhist notions of karma, the main trend of the autobiography has not prepared readers for such an emphasis. Instead, given the emphasis on her independence and strong personality, it is hard not to read this departure as an abandonment of her family—as a kind of selfish gesture. I neither want to make Taring live up to my ideal of what a "good mother" should be nor confine her to a notion of the dutiful Asian woman; but as a reader, I am unprepared for her actions; the narrative does not account for them. Furthermore, Taring's subsequent announcement that she wants to renounce everything might seem like something of a surprise, if it did not accord so well with the myth of epiphany I have analyzed in Part One. For when she is traveling *out* of Tibet, Taring represents herself as a kind of mirror image of Younghusband: she has an epiphany which reorients her sense of herself and the world.

While staying in Shabje Thang, Bhutan, Taring borrows books from the local temple—*The Will of Kunsang Lama,* and the poems of Milarepa. With these Taring interprets her grief at parting from her family:

> . . . I gained much understanding of religion through finding so many precious books and having time to concentrate on them. I appreciated what a great opportunity this was to realise the teaching of the Lord Buddha, through the grief that I was enduring. Now I could see for myself that all things are impermanent. I thought of our beautiful possessions and of how hard we had tried to accumulate wealth. Yet when the time came, according to our karma, for us to part with everything—even our children—it happened just like that. Now the pain was making me think much and I understood that one must come to the state where one is meant to be. Although children are born to us they each have their own karma and must bear it alone. I feel that parents are like fruit trees, from which the fruit is separated when it ripens. (p. 252)

Through these encounters with texts, Taring—like Lobsang Gyatso, Kipling, and Younghusband—gains a new sense of her life. The doctrine of karma gives Taring a way to understand the experience of motherhood and its attendant loss, giving her a heightened sense of the reality of the Buddha's teaching and what it means for her sense of herself:

> At Shabje Thang I experienced the reality of the Lord Buddha's teaching that only love can conquer hatred, that goodwill towards all beings is the essence of religion and that we must trust in the Truth—which is best as it is, though it may be bitter and we may not be able to understand it. I saw that Self is a transient vision and that the way to real happiness is the path of unselfishness. I found that my own suffering could be lessened by thinking of the suffering of others. (p. 253)

When he was leaving Lhasa Younghusband wrote that he "was insensibly infused with an almost intoxicating sense of elation and goodwill. . . . Never again could I think evil, or ever again be at enmity with any man."[15] The epiphanic moment gives both subjects a way of understanding their lives, a way of making them into a meaningful stories. While Taring would not become a nun, the story told in the rest of her autobiography outlines the shape her realization takes in practice. When she sees her husband again in India, he reminds her of Ani Lochen's teaching that the truth can be sought through service to others (p. 264). Working with other refugees in India, she experiences the reality of this teaching; the rest of her life is dedicated to teaching, to using her English to help other Tibetan exiles, and to working on behalf of orphan refugee children.

The figure that emerges in *Daughter of Tibet* may appeal to Western Buddhist feminists. Drawn to renunciation, Taring discovers a lay spiritual path that allows her to live out a Buddhist ideal through service, thus satisfying the desire both for a spiritual life and for work in the world—something Younghusband himself sought. Exemplifying the qualities of independence, selfhood, and personality, Taring embodies certain Western feminist ideals. That the Buddhism valorized by the English-educated, Christian-schooled Taring is a philosophical Buddhism rooted in selfless service as it is represented in texts is not to be missed; hers is not the Buddhism of oracles, red threads, and protecting deities—at least not as she presents it here. It is a kind of stripped-down Buddhism. Indeed, at the close of her book, Taring looks forward to the next generation of Tibetans who "will not be fooled by superstitions and delusions; they will be more knowledgeable." Like the Protestant Buddhism created by Colonel Olcott and Anagarika Dharmapala in Ceylon (Sri Lanka) and the rationalized Buddhism sometimes offered by the current Dalai Lama, Taring's version of Buddhism is one that valorizes the rational and ecumenical:

> Lord Buddha himself has said that whether we have great teachers or not the Truth is there—and no one can alter it, neither can anyone improve it. This Truth which the Lord Buddha preached is now being sought all over the world and when religions are compared the principle of Truth is seen to be the same in each one. All religions remind us to do good and by following our various religions we can help one another gain happiness. (p. 273)

This version of Buddhism attempts to include all religious "truths" under what the Buddha has already taught. Such a colonizing gesture by one whose country has been colonized strives to make Buddhism into a religion always already present in the larger world in which Tibetans now find themselves. Buddhism then becomes just the truth. Because the creed she offers is presented as universal, and because Rinchen Dolma Taring is a figure whose persona in *Daughter of Tibet* connects to Western feminist ideas about independence and self-realization, Western readers might apprehend her as an admirable other. Without such a figure, shaped and reshaped by epiphany, we might be in foreign territory indeed.

WOMEN'S WORK

Which is perhaps what happens to readers of Dorje Yudon Yuthok's *House of the Turquoise Roof.* Although the translator and editor of this autobiography, Michael Harlin, strives to represent Yuthok as a feisty old lady who knows her own mind, the figure that comes across in the autobiography is one who is utterly un-self-reflective, a persona who seems shaped by happenstance rather than one whose personality drives the story. More a chronicle of customs and family relations than a story of the narrator's internal life, the book is a kind of curriculum vitae of the life of an aristocratic woman.

In his preface to the book, Tenzin N. Tethong writes, "It is not the story of a woman's liberation, but her life does shed light into the status of women in Tibet, their position in society and the rights they enjoyed"[16]— which is to say, not many. With this book, we are not offered stories to live by. For one: while it is clear that Yuthok occupies a high status position, commanding estates, servants, and considerable sums of money, she seems to move within this world unreflectively. The emotional background for her decisions is not emphasized in this narrative: things just seem to happen. For example, because we learn so little about her internal or spiritual life, it comes as something of a surprise when she reveals at one point that "I was seriously contemplating becoming a nun."[17] In another chapter, she describes her acquaintance with Yuthok Tashi Dhondup and we are treated to a detailed discussion of their courtship and marriage. Readers steeped in the conventions of English-language autobiographies are not fully prepared, then, when the narrator later offhandedly reveals that she lived with her husband before marriage. Whether this is the result of poor editing or lack of reflection is hard to say: the effect, however, is to make Yuthok, as an autobiographical subject and narrator, seem rather clueless. While it may be possible to use Yuthok's oscillation between the desire for renunciation and the desire for marriage to mark the two conventional roles offered to Tibetan women—nun or wife—Yuthok (and her editor) cannot remark on that; instead, the protagonist moves on only to get caught up in the same conflict later in life. In the second case, after learning that her husband has had affairs with other women, she is hurt, but soon begins her own affair with the historian Tsepon Shakabpa. Troubled by all this turmoil and subterfuge, she takes the vows to become a nun while on pilgrimage in India, though soon resumes both her relationship with her husband and her affair with Shakabpa. Yuthok's resources for interpreting her actions seem to be few: she can become a nun or she can find her identity through sexuality, but she seems unable to recognize her situation as produced through certain cultural values. While it is certainly novel (and welcome) that Yutok writes of her sexual life so frankly, these events are presented with such a lack of self-reflection that they make her seem a fool, a kind of pawn within the proscribed world of the Tibetan aristocracy.

Given that Yuthok's book fails to give Western readers the self-reflective personality we have come to expect in autobiographies, one might well wonder if, in a strange way, this book might not actually give readers a figure who expresses something of what Karma Lekshe Tsomo calls the "other-centered" focus of Himalayan Buddhist women—which involves a tendency not so much to "play down" one's own needs and interests but to not give them much account at all.[18] In a strange sense, then, what fails as a Western-type autobiography may in fact be a successful portrayal of the identity of a female Tibetan aristocrat, an autobiography representative of a particular class and position but not yet translated into palatable Western terms and genres. Could it be, then, that in this list of customs and events, we have the real thing—a real Tibetan woman?

For while I fault Yuthok's autobiography for not being self-reflective, perhaps it is exactly this quality that makes it representative of at least one kind of Tibetan class and worldview. As Anne Klein writes, "Far more than in the modern West, in Asian cultures one lives within a well-articulated social matrix intricately connected with one's own projects and sense of identity."[19] Yuthok presents a figure that is enmeshed in the relations created by family, marriage, and position. It may very well be that the kind of self-awareness I am asking of Yuthok is a kind unavailable to her, the mark of a notion of individuality that was almost completely foreign to an older generation of Tibetans. In her book *The Great Bliss Queen*, Klein writes, "Tibetans, like many Asians who have grown up outside strong Western influence, do not cultivate individuality" through the expression of their "idiosyncratic traits, personal choices, and unique accomplishments."[20]

But even if Yuthok's lack of self-reflectiveness may show us a different kind of subjectivity, should we read this "failure" in self-expression as the mark of a successful Buddhist sensibility? In her discussion of Himalayan Buddhist women, Tsomo attempts to convert the expectations placed on women into Buddhist ideals. Tsomo notes that "[i]n Himalayan Buddhist cultures a woman should be serene and subdued, humble and not arrogant, calm rather than harried, patient rather than angry, kind rather than uncaring, other-centered rather than self-centered, content rather than greedy"; she suggests that these are "the same traits valued in a Buddhist practitioner."[21] In this way, Tsomo asserts that, in effect, laywomen ideally embody all the Buddhist ideals usually ascribed only to monastic men. But whether someone who never struggled with the self at all can win liberation by default, as it were, is an important question. And whether women's resignation to the expectations placed on them and to their "subordinate status" is a sign of their strength or of their acquiescence to dominant ideology would seem to matter very much. [22] For this reason, because Taring makes her struggles known, because she is forthright and self-reflective, and, finally, expressly rationalist Buddhist in orientation, she, and not Yuthok, more readily occupies the position of heroine for feminist, Western Buddhist practitioners. Within the house of mirrors that makes up Tibetan self-presentation in the diaspora, it is Taring's image that is likely to please more onlookers.

CHAPTER 7

Political Prisoners:
Palden Gyatso and Ama Adhe

BEARING WITNESS

In discussing the urgency of the Tibetan political situation, Robert Thurman has suggested that, for contemporary human rights activists, Tibetans are today's baby seals. Although the atrocities experienced by many political refugees and prisoners from Tibet are real enough, it is nonetheless troubling to see "the Tibetan question" become a *cause celebre*. In becoming popular, the "Tibetan cause" too easily becomes a commodity, one that will fall out of favor like last year's must-have toy. Nonetheless, a recent "poster child" of the Tibetan independence movement, as one scholar of Tibetan Buddhism phrased it to me, is Palden Gyatso, a toothless, elderly Gelukpa monk who spent over 30 years in prison in Chinese-occupied Tibet. This unassuming monk came into exile expressly to bear witness to what he had seen, carrying with him a bag of torture instruments used on Tibetan political prisoners, the ones the Chinese government claims are not in prison at all, the ones China claims are not tortured.

But accounts of the horrible sometimes push the limits of credulity. As James E. Young writes of Holocaust diarists, "The words in a translated and reproduced Holocaust diary are no longer traces of the crime, as they were for the writer who inscribed them; what was evidence for the writer at the moment he wrote is now, after it leaves his hand, only a detached and free-floating sign, at the mercy of all who would read and misread it."[1] As in the reception of Holocaust diaries, a weird thing can happen when one encounters grotesque torture instruments and reads accounts of unspeakable atrocities in Tibet: one cannot help wondering if they might not be fakes. And, then, one has to wonder, if they are fakes, perhaps the whole thing is a lie, a misrepresentation—and all that we know about Chinese oppression and Tibetan resistance goes down the tubes. For the story of Communist Chinese oppression of Tibet is an "event at the limits"—an event, which as Saul Friedlander writes of the Holocaust, "tests our traditional conceptual and representational categories."[2] Accounts of the inhumane treatment of political prisoners—the brutal struggle sessions (*thamzing*); the near-starvation of prisoners who, in order to survive, are forced to eat grass, shoe leather, even human flesh; unlivable conditions in which prisoners are not allowed to relieve themselves or sleep; the systematic execution of unreformables—all of these stories stretch, if not our ability to believe, then our willingness to do so. Indeed, what is perhaps most disturbing about Tibetan accounts of Communist atrocities is the utter conviction with which most torturers carry out their duties. The "banality of evil" that was the mark of Nazi Germany, as Hannah Arendt described it, is fully evident in these accounts, and in many ways the fact that this brutality has acquired a kind of "everyday" character makes it all the more appalling.[3]

Tibetan efforts to represent something of these atrocities appear in a number of Tibetan autobiography in English. But as in the case of the Chinese torture instruments brought into exile by Palden Gyatso, which might strangely lead us to doubt him, these efforts to bear witness in writing inevitably contain their own undoing. Any attempt to represent the "truth" (if it is more than a list of dates and names) inevitably involves interpretation. There are always gaps between the event and its representation. As Young writes in reference to writing from the Holocaust:

> The possibility that, once committed to paper, a witness's testimony could be perceived as a fabrication of reality and not the trace of it he had intended, would seem to mock a witness's very *raison d'être*. And to compound the dilemma, the more insistently a survivor-scribe attempts to establish the "lost link" between his text and his experiences in the text, the more he inadvertently emphasizes his role as maker of the text, which ironically—and more perversely still—further undermines the sense of unmediated fact the writer had attempted to establish. Both the writer's perceived absence from the text and his efforts to relink himself to it thus seem to thwart—and thereby inflame still further—the testimonial impulse.[4]

As in Young's discussion here, this study of autobiography has already suggested that if we analyze these accounts as texts, there are gaps separating the narrated subject (the protagonist), the speaking subject (the narrator), and the author. My reading of Palden Gyatso's *The Autobiography of a*

Tibetan Monk explores how the book deals with these gaps. While the book is hardly a literary autobiography, it does employ several compelling narrative strategies, strategies that address the gaps between witness and event, between signifier and signified, between the spoken and speaking subjects. In taking on these questions of rhetoric and interpretation, I have not "forgotten the horror behind the words,"[5] nor do I wish to deny the brute facts of Communist Chinese oppression in Tibet; instead, I want to consider the way these events are represented, how they address readers, and the kinds of selves they construct.

As he relates it in his *Autobiography of a Tibetan Monk,* Palden Gyatso tells his story because he was asked to tell it—many times. One time the request came from the Dalai Lama—"You should write your story," he says; at other times the request came from people who felt Palden should bear witness to the brutality and horror he had experienced firsthand in Chinese prisons in Tibet. Indeed, Palden Gyatso's very exile is driven by this urge to tell his story.

> When the suggestion was made that I should write my story, I was embarrassed and puzzled by people's interest. It was not that I had no desire to tell my story; on the contrary, one of the main reasons for my escape from Tibet was to be able to speak to the world. I had spent thirty years in prison and during that time I had experienced and witnessed unimaginable horrors. Every prisoner lives with the hope that somehow, once the world learns of their suffering, there will be a rush to help those who have fallen into the pit of hell.

But because Palden comes from a tradition of autobiography that focuses on the exploits of spiritually realized beings, it seems difficult for him to figure out just what "his story" might be, as he has few models on which to base it:

> In Tibet we have a long tradition of writing biographies of great lamas and figures who attain a high degree of spirituality. These books are known as Namthar. They are never merely good stories, but are intended to impart spiritual teachings and are read as guides to life. The power of these books is recognised by all. "When we read the Namthar of the great warrior King Gesar," the Tibetan saying goes, "even a beggar would be moved to pick up a sword; when we read the biography of the great hermit Milarepa, even a prince would wish to renounce the world."[6]

But the *namtar* cannot really be a model for him; Palden Gyatso's purposes are different: he wants to bear witness. So after the Dalai Lama asks for his story, as Tsering Shakya, his editor and translator recalls, Palden Gyatso put together "a first draft of his book in a faded notebook. Like most Tibetan books of this type, it consisted of the dates and names of those who had perished. Palden had written this as a testimony and record of those who did not live to tell their own stories."[7] In other words, Palden Gyatso has produced an annal of sorts, but not yet a story—not yet an interpretation of events.

In a strange way, these many demands for Palden's story recall the efforts of his Chinese and Tibetan jailers, who (as represented in his autobiography) repeatedly ask him to "tell his story." Hauling him into an interrogation room, threatening him with beatings, they would demand that he tell his life story, beginning at age eight. From the perspective of his would-be reformers, such storytelling was intended to reveal the mind of the prisoner; as they saw it, his contradictions, confessions, and reinterpretations of himself along party lines revealed the extent to which the prisoner had been reformed. That such life story telling was coercive is hardly to be disputed. But the question begs to be asked: are there ways in which the interests of the Dalai Lama, Tsering Shakya, and Western readers also "coerce" a particular kind of story? Or are there ways in which Tsering Shakya's rendering of Palden Gyatso's story addresses and goes beyond even those pressures to tell a different kind of story—one unlike other Tibetan autobiographies in English?

The specific shape of the story that Palden Gyatso records only really begins to take shape in exile. It is largely through interaction with other political refugees that his story becomes emplotted. As he writes:

> Shortly after my arrival [in Dharamsala], I was given the task of interviewing other new arrivals to record their testimonies. I could not believe how many of us had the same story to tell. There was not a single individual without a story of horror and brutality, and I realised that all subjugated people share the common experience of bruised bodies, scattered lives and broken families.

Unable to use Tibetan *namtar* as a model, the refugees develop other plots and forms. In effect, Palden Gyatso's reception of their stories shapes his sense of the stories that can be told. At the same time, he encounters foreigners who are eager to hear his story. In cosmopolitan Dharamsala, where "people from Japan, America, Israel and Europe [mingle] in the two narrow, muddy streets which form the main market of McLeod Ganj"—a contact zone bringing together Indian nationals, Tibetan refugees, and a host of interested foreigners—Palden's story takes further shape. He notes that in Dharamsala:

> I befriended many foreigners from countries I never knew existed, including a young English woman called Emily and a Dutch woman called Francisca, who regularly visited my hut to talk to me. It was during the course of those conversations that the story of my life began to unfold. I realised that because I had been lucky enough to survive, I was also duty bound to bear witness to the suffering of others.[8]

Palden's story takes shape first as a kind of collective oral narrative told in Tibetan—an oral narrative reminiscent of a *namtar;* it is further developed by his contact with European interlocutors. And with this story, Palden Gyatso begins to travel abroad.

In London, he meets, Tsering Shakya, the Tibetan historian who has lived there for decades. And there Shakya begins to interview him in order to fill out Palden's life story. But the monk does not make the job easy and initially resists speaking about himself. Shakya describes their process:

> I hired a room and Palden visited me each day for the next three months. The moment he entered the room, I started the tape machine and recorded every conversation. In the end we accumulated more than 120 tapes, some 300 hours of reminiscences. I had each tape transcribed in Tibetan and those transcripts became the basis of the book.

Again, Palden is made to speak, to fill out the details of his life story, to construct an oral narrative. Shakya continues:

> First I asked Palden to take me through his life story, to sketch out the chronology and the background. Then I asked him for more information about each incident, and about his thoughts and feelings. He spoke frankly and openly, yet it was evident that he was deeply distressed and embarrassed by the unaccustomed attention. And while it was my task to encourage him to speak of his views and feelings, his own natural humility made him shy away from speaking about himself.[9]

Perhaps because he had been unable to speak freely for years, Palden was prevented from speaking for himself; perhaps a certain culturally- and religiously-produced humility was at work; perhaps a fear of being interrogated made Palden reticent. In any case, it was only through dialogue that the written story was constructed; it was only through such give and take that Shakya can help Palden construct an image of himself—construct a author/protagonist, and speaker—around which to base the English-language autobiography. It was only through such question and answer that an "I" could be constructed with which to begin the narrative: "I was born beneath a rainbow."[10]

By his own account, part of Palden Gyatso's reticence in telling his story stems from a sense about what the proper subject of a life story should be. While traditional *namtars* might be said to teach readers and listeners about the nature of suffering (*dug-ngal* in Tibetan) and the spiritual path that leads one out of it, Palden Gyatso's story of suffering focuses largely on the suffering that one person inflicts on another—that one group of people inflicts on another—rather than the more Buddhistic suffering of impermanence, the kind that is inherent in existence. Thus, in the final lines of the book he notes:

> All I can do is bear witness and set down what I saw and heard and what the strange journey of my life has been. Suffering is written now in the valleys and mountains of Tibet. Every village and monastery in the Land of Snows has its own stories of the cruelty inflicted on our people. And that suffering will go on until the day Tibet is free. (p. 232)

Tsering Shakya is careful to argue in his preface that "Tibet was no Shangri-La," but the final lines seem to recuperate that image.[11] Though the agent who inflicts cruelty on Tibetans is not named, the suggestion is that once the Chinese are out of Tibet, suffering will end. In this way the conclusion recalls the old myth of Tibet as a peaceful place, where all the citizens are happy and free. While there is certainly an enormous difference between the kinds of stories Palden can offer foreign friends or in his book and the ones he can tell his jailers, this inclusion of the image of Tibet as a peaceful utopia—uncharacteristic as it is within the body of the narrative—can be read not so much as a conjuring of the Tibetan Shambala but as a concession to the power of Western myths about Tibet, an assent to Bogle's image of Tibet as a place "defended by . . . barren mountains" where "peace and contentment" reign, a nod to Hilton's Shangri-La, an acknowledgement of the Dalai Lama's Zone of Ahimsa.[12]

Bearing witness, then, inevitably involves more than simple presentation of the facts; it is always rhetorical—it is always produced in contexts. And, as Young points out, there is always the danger that the text produced by a "survivor-scribe" will be "perceived as the fabrication of reality," as just another interpretation, a fiction, "and not the trace of [reality] he had intended."[13] One of the strategies by which Palden Gyatso's book works to avoid the suspect nature of the written text is to repeatedly represent him as a speaker rather than a writer. In the West, as Derrida has argued, primacy is given to the spoken word.[14] Thus, in the judicial system in the United States and Western Europe, witnesses do not write their testimony—they speak it. A written word is the result of a gesture in the past, but the spoken word is understood as unadulterated; because the unrecorded spoken word can only be heard in the present, it is often understood as conveying something of presence. Lending credence to Palden Gyatso as witness, his autobiography offers numerous images of him speaking—to his jailers and interrogators, to the Dalai Lama, to foreigners, to Tsering Shakya. Indeed, the culminating scene in the book shows Palden speaking in Geneva, Switzerland, where he offers his testimony to no less an esteemed body than the United Nations Commission on Human Rights. There, dressed in a monk's robes before a packed house of initially disinterested listeners, he offers his story yet again. And as he speaks he notices that members of the Chinese delegation gradually turn their attention to him:

> That gave me such a rousing sense of my freedom and I wished all my fellow prisoners had been there to witness it, for we had all dreamed of being able to confront our tormentors face to face and have them listen to our testimony. I was the first Tibetan prisoner to have had the opportunity to speak before the United Nations, so I knew that I was not just speaking for myself but for all Tibetans still in prison and for all Tibetans who had ever been in prison. The delegates heard only my voice, but behind my voice lay the suffering of thousands of prisoners who had not survived to bear witness as I have. (p. 232)

The power of the scene—and it is a kind of triumph and a narrative climax—depends on Palden's ability to finally speak out, to say what he was not allowed to say in Tibet. It also depends on the conceit that Palden is not so much writing as speaking—he *speaks out;* readers are invited to see him *face to face* with his oppressors; he *testifies* on behalf of all suffering Tibetans. That the book cannot be a speech, of course, is clear enough; it can only be a sign of that speech, a representation of experiences as they appeared to Palden Gyatso retrospectively, in exile. The representation of Palden Gyatso as *speaker* helps to bracket, for the moment, the suspicions cast on the written account and the compromised status of the book as interpretation.

If the book gains credence from its emphasis on Palden as speaker, it also gathers persuasive power by what seems to be an opposing impulse: the impression it gives that what Palden tells *is* a story—a version of events. Such relativity is missing in other accounts. For example, while Tsering Dorje Gashi's *New Tibet* is touted by its translator as offering "a different story," the tale at hand is a familiar one, one in which Communists are single-minded villains and Tibetan nationalists are courageous heroes.[15] Gashi recounts the almost unspeakable brutality that Tibetan students and other minorities faced in the Chinese Communist schools designed to train them. But even though Gashi is careful to include stories in which Tibetans also appear as perpetrators and not just victims, the repetitive drive to tell the truth, to show the "reality" of Chinese oppression of Tibet in all its gory details, finally pushes against the limits of representation. In Gashi's memoir there is no room to move. While in terms of the "facts" I do not distrust his account, his overdetermined representations of events make me doubt this survivor-scribe. I see "representation" and not the thing represented. His insistence on a narrative strategy of long quotations of "he said/she said" raises my suspicions about his reliability; his utter conviction, finally, fails to persuade. The narrator does not trust me as a reader to make my own interpretation, so I, in turn, do not trust him. In Gashi's tale, the desire to represent—without the reflective admission that there are other stories to be told—thwarts "the testimonial impulse."[16]

Unlike Gashi's testimonial, Palden Gyatso's book offers not only his account of events but also includes scenes in which the story he wants to tell is repressed, deliberately misconstrued, refuted, or simply ignored by others. Readers then are allowed a sense of choosing which version of events they want to side with; the choice is limited, of course, and we have already come to trust Palden as speaker. But even this much openness in the text is worth noting. Palden Gyatso's book, while it also has a political message to convey, does so by allowing for other accounts of things. On the final page of the book, he offers someone else's interpretation of his life— a version that counters and subverts the one he offers to readers. After Palden spoke in Geneva, the Chinese ambassador to Britain wrote to a national newspaper, and argued that instead of being a victim,

> Palden Gyatso was a criminal who persisted in anti-government activities. The crimes he committed include activities aimed at overthrowing the government, escaping from prison and theft. Palden Gyatso's story of how he was tortured by prison guards is untrue. Torture is forbidden in Chinese prisons. (p. 272)

By including such counter-narratives, Palden Gyatso suggests again the utter incommensurability of the official Chinese view of Tibet with the view of pro-independence Tibetan exiles. In this case, however, due to the force of the narrative that precedes this statement, the ambassador's characterization of Palden Gyatso as a criminal and his assertion that "torture is forbidden" in Chinese prisons lends persuasiveness to the truth-character of Palden Gyatso's testimony. He signs his name to the book that represents his voice and thus asserts the coterminousness of speaker, protagonist, torture victim, narrator, and narrated. And in that sense the book is not only about bearing witness but also about the construction of self, the coming to possession of one's subjectivity.

One way the book accomplishes this recovery of self is through scenes in which Palden Gyatso is asked to identify with his name. "Palden Gyatso" was not his given name or his family name; it was the name he received when he entered the monastic community, at which time he abandoned his given name "Ngodrup." When the name Palden Gyatso is fixed by Chinese Communist officials on undecipherable identification papers, it is difficult for the narrator to locate himself in the characters:

> One day we were lined up and issued with a piece of paper. The writing on the paper was Chinese and none of us understood it. We were told that we should keep this piece of paper with us at all times and show it to any visiting officials. Months later a young Tibetan from Gyantse translated the Chinese for me. The writing on the paper said, "Name: Palden Gyatso. Age: 27. Class: son of a rich landlord. Political background: not yet investigated." (p. 64)

Palden Gyatso's inability to completely recognize himself in his identity papers is echoed at other moments when he measures himself against his oppressors' definitions of him. "[M]y name was called," he writes, and hailed by police interrogators, he responds, though inevitably the figure they require—a criminal, an accomplice—does not accord with his own sense of himself. Though they want him to implicate his guru, Gyen Rigzin Tenpa, Palden Gyatso knows no crime his teacher has committed. Holding steadfastly to the guru-student bond, he cannot offer an account that will satisfy the police. His name is called, again. Answering to it, he stands up and receives his sentence (p. 77). On another occasion, his name is called —"Who is Palden Gyatso?" (p. 106)—and he must gather his bedroll, his leg irons rattling, and prepare to be shifted to the infamous Drapchi prison. His name is called—"Palden Gyatso"—and he watches as the faces of the other prisoners around him relax; they will not be the ones who are beaten this time. Palden Gyatso stands up and walks to the middle of the room to face the accusation that he is an "evil reactionary" who persists in superstitious Buddhist rituals, acts for which he is bound and severely beaten by his fellow prisoners (pp. 133–5). When, after over 20 years of imprisonment, he is released and allowed to return to the now-derelict monastery Drepung, a voice outside his room asks, "Who are you? What is your name?" and he must give this name to a police squad—a group that cannot see anything but "criminal" and "traitor" in it. "Palden Gyatso," he says. Searching his room, they discover the evidence of "splittist sentiments" for which they seek and take him yet again into detention (pp. 176–7).

But Palden does not only own up to his name to be punished for it. As the autobiography progresses, his assent to his name brings different results. When he is released for the last time in 1992 and plans for escape into exile are underway, a man knocks on his door in the middle of the night, asking, "Are you Palden Gyatso?" This time responding to his name does not mean more interrogations, more beatings. Instead, his response procures for him the bag of instruments of torture used in Chinese prisons that he will take out of Tibet, the weapons that are intended to prove the truth of his tale (p. 227). When, for the last time in the book, he speaks his name before the United Nations Commission on Human Rights—"My name is Palden Gyatso. I became a monk when I was ten years old" (p. 232)—it is as if he finally owns this name—an identification that previously brought him so much misery. In taking up his name in the final pages of the book, Palden Gyatso moves from object to subject—from being the object in a disempowered dialogue with oppressive and fanatical rulers and jailers (both Chinese and Tibetan) to being a subject in dialogue with those who value his story differently; he becomes a subject who can imagine the possibility of speaking for himself, a subject who can speak until he is finished. The scene in Geneva has the effect of placing the speaker Palden Gyatso in dialogue with readers who see him as a victim of an oppressive regime— who might see in his story a tale of resistance and strength, a call to action. My name is Palden Gyatso, and this is what I have seen. My name is Palden Gyatso and I speak because others cannot. My name is Palden Gyatso and even if ambassadors deny the story I tell, this is my story. This is my story.

Postscript

On one of several speaking tours in the United States, Palden Gyatso also came to my college. He spoke for two hours to an overflow crowd. I had already finished most of my work on his autobiography, but even then I had this sense of disbelief—the desire not to believe what he had to say. Students who came expecting to learn about Tibetan Buddhism from this monk were treated with translated tales of torture. One student commented that she hated listening to it all but felt that if he could endure all that he spoke of, then she had to stay. He took out his dentures to show us how all his teeth had fallen out, and moved an electric cattle prod around his face and body to show the precise way the torture had been conducted. While displaying these instruments of torture in this way, Palden Gyatso did not flinch. It was as if he had completely expurgated the physical memory and emotional traces of his suffering. When he was finished, he rolled the prods and chains in cloth, treating them as carefully as he would a loose-leaf Tibetan holy book.

On this visit, Palden Gyatso stayed with my family. When Palden Gyatso first arrived at our house and saw our children—aged two and five at the time—he reached out for them, gathering the five-year-old near and holding him close. It was as if he had just stepped into the sun after a long time in the dark. It was as if he were holding a bunch of fresh flowers after a long time among the dead.

FREEDOM MAMA

Palden Gyatso may currently be the most visible Tibetan to tell his story of persecution and suffering, but he is not the only one. One of the earliest Tibetan accounts of life in a Chinese prison was told in John Avedon's *In Exile from the Land of Snows,* which related the chilling tale of Dr. Tenzin Choedrak, one of the Dalai Lama's personal physicians. Another example, David Patt's *A Strange Liberation: Tibetan Lives in Chinese Hands,* pairs the story of Tenpa Soepa, a government official, with the story of Adhe Tapontsang (Ama [Mother] Adhe), a woman from Kham who worked with the resistance in the early years of Chinese occupation. And in a strange turn of events and representations, Ama Adhe's story is also told in *The Voice that Remembers: The Heroic Story of a Woman's Fight to Free Tibet.* Published five years after Patt's account, this version of Adhe's life, edited by Joy Blakeslee, relates in further detail much of the material recounted in Patt's book. And while both books manage to convey something of the desperation, hunger, and brutality experienced by this courageous woman, the existence of these two books tells another story.

As Patt notes in the introduction, "Ama Adhe decided early on in her captivity that if she lived, she would live to tell her story. Throughout her captivity she watched carefully and as she says, 'engraved the memories on my heart.' She is so determined to tell her story to the world that she has earned the Tibetan nickname of 'Rangzen Ama-la,' 'Freedom Mama.'"[17] What perhaps underlies Patt's words here is the knowledge that just after she gave her story to him during weeks of interviews in Dharamsala, she then told her story for Blakeslee, another American, who traveled to Dharamsala in part to honor a friend's memory by doing something for the Tibetans her friend had loved. Indeed, as Patt recalled in correspondence with me, he met Blakeslee at the Pathankot train station (the closest one to Dharamsala) as he was leaving and she was arriving. That both Americans would be led to Adhe is perhaps not surprising: her story is dramatic, she was eager to tell it, and the Tibetan government-in-exile was eager to have it told. It is also important that she is a woman among the many Tibetan men who have told their stories. And because, as Patt puts it, Tibetans "are constantly deluged by Western do-gooders who promise to do this or that for the Tibetans"[18]—some of which bear fruit, most of which don't—it is understandable if no doubt unsettling for both authors that Ama Adhe would tell her story for many who were willing to listen. Indeed, she tells it again in a moving cameo in Mickey Lemley's film "Compassion in Exile," a documentary about the Dalai Lama and the Tibetan struggle for freedom.[19]

For many readers like myself who are ingrained in the habit of reading autobiographies as a kind of presentation of life, the existence of two autobiographies for one person, published within a few short years, may violate the sense of the "person" as a unified being, and thus seem to cheapen Ama Adhe's tale, dividing the fullness of her life. But there are precedents for writing more than one autobiography, even in American letters. Furthermore, within the Tibetan tradition, a different sense of self is at work. There is no unity of self here, as I have argued in the case of the Dalai Lama; the self—the ego—is a problem to be dealt with. Beyond that, the very violation and incarceration of Ama Adhe's body—the attempt to pin her down like the demoness on whose supine body Lhasa was established, the very attempt to control the speech and contain the mind of this political prisoner—helps to explain this outpouring of words from exile, this excess of expression, this adamant insistence on the significance of *her* story—for she has survived, "a witness to the voice of my dying compatriots."[20] As she says in Blakeslee's book, when her jailers released her they insisted that she "speak to no one of my life's experiences."[21] That she would speak to as many people as possible is a sign of her adamant resistance and more than simple "self"-expression.

Like a lama with many disciples, like a monk with many patrons, Ama Adhe's story cannot just be reserved for one listener. Although publishing two accounts of one's life story is somewhat unusual (the Dalai Lama doubled his age before he did so), Ama Adhe's multiple life story tellings can also be understood within the remodeled system of Tibetan patronage. While I do not wish to reduce the telling of the tale to a simple mercenary strategy, publishing her story "for the world" is one way that Tibetans can gain Western donors and supporters. As the Dalai Lama writes in his foreword to Blakeslee's edition, not only will readers learn "the true extent of the suffering of the Tibetan people and the attempts that have been made to eliminate their culture and identity," they might also "be inspired to lend their support to the just cause of the Tibetan people."[22] It would be easy to be cynical about this appeal for support, which in the context of the capitalist United States can seem to commodify Tapontsang's victimhood; in fact, at times, it is hard for me not to be cynical—not to feel disappointed that Wisdom Publications overlooked Patt's more succinct and lively tale when it published Blakeslee's version of Tapontsang's story. I hang in the balance among several sentiments: the gut feeling that a person should really only publish one autobiography at a time; sympathy for a desperate cause; and the willingness to recognize the operation of patronage even in the selective world of American publishing.

The stories told in the autobiographies of Palden Gyatso and Ama Adhe are particularly sobering examples of what life has been like for some Tibetans under Chinese occupation. Other Tibetan autobiographies in English also have this desire to bear witness, to tell the truth, to let the world know what has happened, what is happening. While such stories have done much to publicize "the Tibetan situation," the prevalence of such documents has led to a lopsided view of Tibetan-ness. As Vincanne Adams' argues in "Karaoke in Modern Tibet, Lhasa," not all Tibetans are preoccupied with throwing off the yoke of Chinese oppression.[23] Indeed, many Tibetans—whether in Tibet, India, Switzerland, or some other place—devote their time to other occupations: making money, raising families, working. And, of course, many Tibetans have accommodated themselves to Chinese rule, taking up positions within the Communist hierarchy, acting as jailers and policemen within Tibet, living their lives under Chinese rule. When I traveled to Tibet in 1987 and stayed in the modest home of some villagers near Ganden monastery, I noted the display both of Buddhist deities and of Communist leaders. When I later told a Swiss-Tibetan exile about this scene, he could only see it as a result of coercion; he read the presence of the image of the Chinese leaders as a kind of disguise—its own kind of protection. But it seemed to me that the coexistence of these two images was evidence of a different kind of Tibetan mindset, one that had accommodated Chinese rule and Buddhist traditions. Despite the efforts of pro-independence activists to make Chinese and Tibetan, Communist and

Buddhist into oppositional terms, some Tibetans' experience of the Chinese presence in the Tibetan Autonomous Region, especially outside of Lhasa, may not accord with that construction. There have been few, however, to "bear witness" to that experience in the West.

One exception to this is Tashi Tsering.

CHAPTER 8

Resisting Exile: Tashi Tsering

The first indication that we are in different territory with this auto-biography is suggested in the listing of its authors. For the first author of the book subtitled *The Autobiography of Tashi Tsering* is listed as Melvyn Goldstein rather than Tashi Tsering himself; the second author is William Siebenschuh, and the third is Tashi Tsering. Mel Goldstein has long been known as something of an enigma within Tibetan Studies: he was able to study in Tibet when few other Western scholars could; he has dared to be critical of the Tibetan government-in-exile; and he has frequently been accused of harboring pro-Chinese sentiments. (When I first entered the field and moved 30 miles away from Goldstein in Cleveland, a friend who is an established anthropologist of Tibetan culture warned me to stay away from him, intimating that he was no friend of Tibetans and no friend of ours.) It is perhaps not surprising, then, that Goldstein would break from the established tradition of emphasizing Tibetan authorship in such autobiographies in English and put his own name first, as Tashi Tsering's primary interviewer. The second author, William Siebenschuh, is a scholar of English biography and autobiography who was enlisted in the project when Goldstein could not finish it. That the subject and narrator of the book, Tashi Tsering, appears only third in the list of authors may be an accident of the English alphabet; it is also indicative of the many ways that this book works against prevailing norms of Tibetan self-presentation. Tashi Tsering's life story as told in *The Struggle for Modern Tibet* is a dramatic intervention in Tibetan self-presentations in English, working against stereotypes, assumptions, and prevailing norms in several ways. In the following analysis, I outline a number of these departures and suggest what they mean for representations of Tibetans in the West.

In many of the autobiographies encountered so far, the subject is often presented as having to be coaxed to tell his or her story. (Adhe is an exception to this.) Aware of the *namtar* tradition that focuses on exemplary and enlightened beings, raised in a cultural milieu that does not emphasize the importance of individuality in a Western sense, many Tibetan autobiographers are represented as resisting the request to tell their story. Not so with Tashi. As Goldstein recounts:

> On one of my trips [to Tibet], Tashi surprised me by asking if I could help him publish a book about his life. He thought foreigners needed to know about common Tibetans—that is, Tibetans who were not aristocrats or monastic prelates or incarnate lamas. He felt his life story could play a useful role in assisting both Westerners and young Tibetans born in exile to understand the real—the non-Shangri-la—Tibet.[1]

While not the first to want to work against the Shangri-La myth (Tsering Shakya writes of a similar desire in his introduction to Palden Gyatso's autobiography), Tashi Tsering tells a story unique in the genre. Having moved into exile in India in 1957, shifted to the United States to study in the 1960s, Tashi Tsering actually abandons his scholarship, his small Tibetan community in Seattle (including his wife), and his exile status to return to Chinese-occupied Tibet in the hopes that he might be able to work on behalf of ordinary Tibetans there: "The more I thought about it, the surer I became that the Chinese invasion of Tibet provided a once-in-a-lifetime opportunity for Tibetans and that I wanted to become part of the process of change."[2] Instead of devotedly following the path and the wishes of the Dalai Lama, Tashi feels so determined to follow this path that he will not even be dissuaded by Gyalo Thondup, the Dalai Lama's brother, with whom he had worked in India and for whom he had collected the stories of recent refugees in India in 1959. Tashi's acute sense of inequities within the traditional Tibetan system drives him to seek a different path and marks yet another way that his story departs from others offered by Tibetans in English.

Palden Gyatso's autobiography, we might recall, begins with the enigmatic sentence, "I was born beneath a rainbow."[3] Tashi Tsering's story has quite a different beginning but echoes Palden's accounts of life in prison: Tashi's name is called; he describes himself as "weak with fear;" he steps forward to receive a beating. Then he is "lashed across [his] bare buttocks with long thin switches" until his skin splits open.[4] But instead of recounting brutal treatment by Chinese oppressors, Tashi relates a recurring nightmare he has about a beating he received at the hands of another Tibetan—the director of the dance troupe in which he performed—the Dalai Lama's special dance troupe. Rather than the usual criticisms of the Chinese system, Tashi's story begins with an account of a "centuries-old Tibetan punishment" and a critique of Tibetan brutality within the traditional "feudal" system in Tibet, a system which forces his parents to send him from his village to Lhasa in payment of a sort of tax, a society that forces him to become the homosexual partner of a powerful Lhasa monk, a hierarchical system that thwarts almost every effort that the low-status village boy makes to become literate. And because he feels that he will always remain an outsider to a society dominated by monastic and aristocratic elites, when the Chinese move into Lhasa in 1952, young Tashi becomes intrigued by how they operate—how practical, economical and egalitarian they seem—and what this might mean for Tibet:

> I became fascinated by the way they did things, which were so different from our own. They fished in the rivers with worms on a hook and set out to become self-sufficient in food by using dog droppings and human waste they collected on the Lhasa streets for the new fields they opened in a swampy area along the river. These were things we never would have thought of doing and, to be honest, found revolting. The Chinese wasted nothing; nothing was lost. So despite the revulsion, I was also overall fascinated by the extent of their zeal for efficiency and their discipline. They would not take a needle from the people. (p. 40)

Rather than demonizing the Chinese, Tashi sees much to admire in their economy and practicality, even if their practices violate cherished Tibetan notions of what is proper. On the other hand, Tashi finds the Lhasan bureaucracy (of which he is part) slow, inefficient, and corrupt. Comparing the Chinese system to the Tibetans', Tashi finds:

> The Chinese worked tirelessly and with a sense of dedication and purpose. Soon after arriving, they opened the first primary school in Lhasa and a hospital as well as other public buildings. I had to admit that I was impressed by the fact that they were doing things that would directly benefit the common people. It was more change for the good in a shorter period of time than I had seen in my life—more change, I was tempted to think, than Tibet had seen in centuries. (p. 41)

While others such as Lobsang Gyatso also criticize the Tibetan aristocracy, such a view of the Chinese Communists is unique among Tibetan self-presentations. Instead of decrying the destruction of Tibet's unique culture at the hands of the Chinese, Tashi looks forward to the possibilities of

Chinese rule, seeing it as a chance for common people like him to finally improve their lives.

When Tashi becomes an exile in 1957, then, it is not out of political reasons; neither did he flee Tibet for his life. In effect, Tashi's exile is an accident of his efforts at self-improvement and his drive for literacy. Traveling to India under the pretense of trade, Tashi remains in the area of Kalimpong and Darjeeling in order to learn English, first by working with a tutor and then by enrolling as an older student in the well-known international school, St. Joseph's. From there he befriends an American who arranges his matriculation at Williams College; from there another friend gets him into the University of Washington.

While many Tibetan autobiographies place allegiance to the Dalai Lama at the center of the subject's orientation, even a meeting with the Dalai Lama becomes fuel for Tashi's questioning. Before Tashi departs for the United States for the first time in 1960, he is granted an audience with the Dalai Lama, who urges him, "Be a good Tibetan. . . . Study hard. And use your education to serve your people and your country." But Tashi has the sense that his understanding of these things may be quite different from that of the revered leader:

> I fully intended to study hard, as the Dalai Lama had urged. And I wanted badly to be considered a good Tibetan and use my education to serve my people and my country. I just wished I could be more certain that those powerful words and phrases—"good Tibetan," "my country"—meant the same things to both of us. At that point it was hard to say for sure and easy to assume the best, and so I did. (p. 65)

The journey his life eventually takes seems to be a continual rethinking of what it means to serve his people and to be a good Tibetan. Indeed, his debates with Gyalo Thondup about his desire to study in the United States center around the very question of Tibetan identity and what makes a "real" Tibetan:

> One day it got so bad that some strong words passed between us and he called me a bad Tibetan, by which he meant, I believe, that I disagreed with him. But I thought to myself that I was every bit as good a Tibetan as he was! (p. 62)

In this way, the book raises complex questions: "Who speaks for Tibet?" and "Who represents Tibet?" For if Tashi is not a typical Tibetan nationalist, neither is he the usual faithful Buddhist. Although as a young man he was convinced that "Tibetan Buddhism was the greatest religion in the world" (p. 43), his later study of politics and Marxism in the United States make him more of a secular intellectual. While studying at an American liberal arts college, Tashi comes up with a new self-definition:

> It was during this period that I think I really began to think of myself as a new, "modern" Tibetan. I was no longer blinded by the self-serving religious ideology that had so effectively masked the total domination of a small religious and aristocratic elite over the mass of poor peasants and held back all attempts at change. I thought it was time for some kind of revolution in Tibet, too, although I didn't wish for any of the violence or the bloodshed of the sort I had been reading about. (pp. 76–7)

Although Tashi's self-definitions as a modern, intellectual, secular, and critical Tibetan do not fit the standard model of the authentic Tibetan outlined in this study, his sense of his Tibetan-ness is strong, so much so that his desire to be part of the dismantling of the old system and the creation of a new one leads him to the unusual step of becoming an ex-exile. While he is at the University of Washington in 1963, he determines, despite considerable opposition, to return to Chinese-occupied Tibet in order to serve his people.

This is a unique move in Tibetan self-presentation, if not in Tibetan exile history. The book works—often quite directly—to stake out a position for Tashi that is different from that inscribed in other Tibetan autobiographies in English. As Goldstein notes, Tashi's is the "non-Shangri-La Tibet"—and his is a book that consciously positions itself against the "several Tibetan 'Pollyanna' books" already in print.[5] But the shape Tashi's life takes in China will not be wholly unfamiliar to readers of Tibetan autobiographies in English. The story he tells is one of struggle, hardship, and deprivation. Accused of being an anti-revolutionary in 1967 and during the Cultural Revolution, Tashi suffers as many did during that horrific time of upheaval, and is eventually imprisoned from 1970 to 1973 under appalling conditions. Allowed to return to Tibet on his release, Tashi makes his way to his village, where all around he sees the signs of the effects of that pogrom:

> Though the visit to the village itself was not as shocking as the sight of my parents, it was equally disturbing. From the minute I returned to Guchok, it was easy to see that the old village was poorer than it had been in my youth. I learned that it had been turned into a commune in the early 1960s, and it was easy to see the unhappy results. When I was a boy, though the village had not been a center of wealth or prosperity, it had functioned quite well under the old system. (pp. 150–1)

If the old Tibetan system bred inequality, the new one created poverty and degradation. What differentiates Tashi's story from Palden Gyatso's and Ama Adhe's, however, is his interpretation of that deprivation. While such conditions lead others to seek exile, Tashi remains committed to his purpose, finding hope in the Chinese government's later efforts to redress the excesses of the Cultural Revolution. Asserting that he is not a Communist, Tashi criticizes the Chinese system in order to become a critical participant within it. That it takes Tashi Tsering over 14 years to actually begin to do something with his education is the shocking and depressing aspect of his life story, a fact over which he expresses little bitterness.

Despite Tashi's strong desire to work in Tibet for Tibetan people, between 1964 and the early 1980s, most of his time is actually spent in Szechuan at the Tibetan Minority Institute, in Xi'an, or in prison. One of the projects Tashi completed at the end of this period was the ambitious project of publishing an English-Tibetan-Chinese dictionary. In the early 1980s, he is finally allowed to move to Lhasa with his wife Sangye-la, where in addition to his work on his dictionary and at Tibet University, he opens an English-language school for Tibetans—initially without official consent. With the considerable profits from this school, Tashi builds a primary school in his home village, a project to spread literacy that blossomed into the creation of over thirty primary schools at the time of publication of his book in 1997. The boy who eagerly left his village at the age of 10 becomes an exile, returns, is imprisoned, but eventually lives to fulfill his dream of helping his people, strikingly through the very thing that first led him out of the village, to India, and to the United States: literacy and education. The prodigal son returns.

But not without side-trips to the United States. For despite the continuing image of Tibet as a place where Tibetans are deliberately isolated from the outside world, Tashi travels several times to the United States. And on one journey there in 1994, Tashi has the chance to see the Dalai Lama again—this time in Michigan rather than Tibet or India—and this time with the conviction of his experience. Thirty years have passed since he has last spoken to the Dalai Lama, and Tashi ponders the directives given to him then: "'Be a good Tibetan,' [the Dalai Lama] had said. 'Study hard. And use your education to serve your people and your country.' Would he think that I had done so? What did I think myself?" (p. 199). In Tashi's account of that meeting, he cannot just sit in awe of the high lama, nor can he confine his discussion to neutral topics. Instead, he offers to the Dalai Lama—and to the reader—his sense of the shape Tibetan activism should take:

I told him how much I respected his commitment to nonviolence, but I also suggested that we—meaning Tibetans—needed to know how to oppose the Chinese when their policies seemed unreasonable and also to learn how to live with them. I had confidence in my opinions. I felt great reverence, but I no longer saw myself as a supplicant. Instead I felt I was someone who had something to say. I told the Dalai Lama that he had an extraordinary opportunity. He was in a unique position to strike a deal with the Chinese that could be beneficial to both themselves and to Tibetans. "Both the Chinese and the Tibetans would listen to you," I said emphatically. I wanted him to unite our people once again, to end the government-in-exile and return to Tibet. (p. 199)

Rather than locating himself in opposition to the exile Tibetans, Tashi asserts a unity of all Tibetans—in exile or in Tibet—in opposition to the Chinese: "[W]e—meaning Tibetans—needed to know how to oppose the Chinese." For Tashi, one can be a Tibetan and cooperate with the Chinese when it is beneficial and oppose them when it is not. The notion that the authentic Tibetan must be Buddhist and in exile is not for him: it is enough to love Tibet—to love its land and its people, as the Dalai Lama's first autobiography has it. "To me Tibet was not just an idea, an abstraction; it was a place—my home. It was the mountains, river, flinty landscapes, and the villages I knew as a child" (p. 87).

Tashi's more complex sense of the diversity within Tibetan-ness leads him to ask questions not unlike those I propose at the start of Part Two:

Who? or What? I sometimes ask myself now is the Tibet I am trying to help? Who represents Tibet? The Dalai Lama? The old elite now living in exile who made people like me wait outside the door when it came time to discuss important issues? The more progressive intellectuals in Tibet, or those in exile in India, America, and Europe? Is Tibet the Tibetan librarian I met in Austin, Texas, who would scarcely even talk to me because he thought I was a communist? Is Tibet the soldier who interrogated me at the Changwo prison and wanted to be even more Chinese than the Chinese, or the villagers in Guchok who were so quick to suspect my motives when I wanted to build them a school, or the brave woman who trusted me when I was classified as a political criminal and gave me a job when I desperately needed one? The older I get, the harder it is to find simple answers. . . . (p. 201)

It may be the case that Tashi's questions mirror those of Western intellectuals of the anti-Shangri-La variety. In my own case, it is impossible to see whether his questions echo mine or my questions echo his. In the realm of Tibetan self-presentations in the West, we are in a complexly intertwined world of exchange, dialogue, performance, and mirroring, where no idea can pretend to be original, where participants are continually offering to each other stories that respond to other representations and are taken up by those others in ways that are both predictable and unforeseeable. Tashi Tsering's autobiography offers a story that people need to hear, that some want to hear, that a few have already told, though in different genres. It is a story that throws a monkey wrench into the works of Tibetan self-presentation in the West—a tale that by its self-reflectiveness seems to offer the story of a "real" person, one accessible to readers versed in the representation of personality. If it is a New Age *namtar*, it is one that instructs and inspires by inserting itself into the genre of Tibetan autobiography in English, and thereby unsettling the version of Tibetan-ness represented there.

In many ways, it is refreshing to read a story that departs from the usual tales of idyllic Tibet, and it is certainly welcome to hear the story of a lay, working-class Tibetan who lives under the Chinese system, rather than one who demonizes it from afar. But in an interesting way, Tashi's story also depends on other Tibet self-presentations. Instead of being "just the truth," it is written in opposition to them. While offered as a story that serves to dismantle the myth of idealized Tibetans and glorified old Tibet, it relies on those stories to find its footing. If many Tibetan self-presentations cannot fully escape the Western myths that construct and idealize Tibetans, Tashi's story only makes sense in their wake. If Tibetans have "seamfully" mirrored Western fantasies in their self-presentations, as Lopez puts it, Tashi's story does not escape that: it offers us the anti-Shangri-La Tibet, one similar to the anti-mythic Tibet represented by Peter Bishop, Donald Lopez, Vincanne Adams, Oliver Schell, Laurie Hovell McMillin, and, of course, Melvyn Goldstein. In a sense, then, the life Tashi's story represents is one shaped in part by these other Western interests. Just as Tashi had to reshape the refugees' stories on the Indian border, his story is shaped, in part, by Western interlocutors. In this way, "the struggle for modern Tibet," it seems, is also at one level a textual struggle, one that Goldstein, Siebenschuh, and Tashi Tsering wage through a series of reversals—an account of a beating by Tibetans rather than Chinese, the story of a return to Tibet rather than an escape, the representation of a secular Tibetan rather than a Buddhist one, among others. Tashi Tsering's book directly intervenes in the struggle over Tibetan representation—who gets to do it? who speaks for Tibet?—and to be fair, it offers to complicate the representation of Tibetans to the West. But when the book relies on reversals, the overall effect is blunted. For Tibet cannot simply be the opposite of its image. Its multiform, complex reality will have to be more than the mirror image of what we have already been shown. It will have to be something else, and not just contrary. And because the strength of the Shangri-La myth is so strong, it will take more than one autobiography—conceived as a coherent, directional development of a life and brilliant as it is—to shift things. It will take, I think, other textual and political struggles.

Postscript: One More Story

In the preceding pages I have chosen to tell stories that explore the diversity of Tibetan self-presentation, that seek to expose Western myths about Tibetans; I have sought out a way of encountering these autobiographies that recognizes "syncretic" generic forms and the hybridic cultural ways of many Tibetan self-presentations rather than one that hides those same qualities. My analysis of Tibetan autobiographies has proceeded through pairing: I compared the travels of two of the Dalai Lama's siblings, considered the stories offered by two Gelukpa monks, looked at the Dalai Lama's two autobiographies, the stories of two other *tulkus,* the tales of aristocratic women, the accounts of two political prisoners, and then moved on to the unique story of Tashi Tsering. There are no doubt gaps in my analyses— things I do not see and do not look for—as well as other self-presentations which I could analyze. The stories I tell in my interpretations do not emerge from a monolithic theoretical apparatus; instead, my method is more open-ended and searches for movement in these tales—the ways they can be read as both mobilizing and undermining stereotypes, myths, and fantasies, the ways they can be read to move us as readers from usual points of view. It may be that the places my interpretations move us are sites that are already trampled, sites that are indistinguishable from the old romantic ground. Like the Tibetan autobiographers whose stories I have read against, summarized, mangled, and, in a sense, rewritten, I do the best I can to tell a story, but I cannot finally control how it will be received. But I can tell one more story.

My son Liam, who is crazy for horses, was given two different horses on a stick when he turned four years old, a wooden one with vinyl ears, and a cloth one with fake fur and brushable mane. While in the car one day he tells me he doesn't like the wooden one. Trying to encourage him to see the good points of the wooden one, which his great-uncle Clyde made for him, I tell him that it has "real ears."

"No, it doesn't. They're pretend," he says.

"Maybe your ears are not real either," I say playfully.

"Yes, they are," he replies.

Looking at his little brother in the rearview mirror, I say, testing Liam, "Jack's ears are pretend."

"No, they're not. They're real," he says even more adamantly. Then I go too far in my teasing, but I've been reading theory on autobiography and subjectivity all day: "My ears aren't real." (One actually has had some surgical reconstruction.) I go on: "*None* of me is real. I'm all pretend." "ALL PEOPLE ARE . . . NOT PRETEND!" he shouts at me. Clearly, I've hit a nerve. And it strikes me how well my four-year-old knows the distinction between real and pretend, between the representation of something and its referent out there in the world. Despite his continual forays into make-believe, the distinctions between real and pretend, especially when it comes to people—especially his mother—are very important. And necessary.

In some ways, this exchange with my son exemplifies the dilemmas of self-presentation I face in offering this analysis—the problems all self-presenters face. Longing for expression, we end up with representation. Desiring to be perfectly understood, we can only be interpreted. Eager to speak for ourselves, we end up echoing others. Tibetans longing to tell the truth to Westerners tell stories. They tell stories.

APPENDIX

Full Transliteration of Tibetan Words[1]

amban	am ban	khandro	mkha' 'dro
amchi	em chi	khandro-ma	mkha' 'dro ma
Amdo	A mdo	khata	kha btags
bardo	bar do	Kundun	skun mdun
Bonpo	bon po	lama	bla ma
Böpa	bod pa	Lhasa	lha sa
cham	'cham	lo sar	lo gsar
Chenrezig	spyan ras gzigs	Loseling	blo gsal gling
chipa	phyi-pa	Milarepa	mi la ras pa
chö	gcod	mi-ser	mi ser
cho-yon	mchod yon	Mo-La	rmo lags
chuba	chu pa	momo	mog mog
Dorje Phamo	rdo rje phag mo	namtar	rnam-thar
Drepung	'bras spungs	nangpa	nang pa
dug ngal	sdug bsngal	naljorpa	rnal 'phyor pa
Ganden	dga' ldan	ngagpa	sngags pa
gelong	dge slong	nurin	nu rin
Geluk	dge lugs	Nyingma	rnying ma
geshe	dge bshes	Öpame	'od dpag med
go-nyi	mgo gnyis	Panchen Lama	pan chen
Inji	in ji		bla ma
jinda	sbyin-bdag	pema	pad ma
Jokhang	jo khang	Potala	po ta la
Kagyu	bka' brgud	rangnam	rang rnam
Kashag	bka' shag	Rinpoche	rin po che
Kham	khams	Sakya	sa skya

Sera	se ra	Trijang	khri byang
sungdu	srung mdud	Rinpoche	rin po che
Tashilhunpo	bkra shis	Tsongkhapa	tsong kha pa
	lhun po	tulku	sprul sku
terma	gter ma	tunmo	gtun-mo
terton	gter ston	toshö	mtho shos
thamzing	'tha 'dzing	Xigatse	gzhis ka rtse
thangka	thang ka	Yeshe Tsogyel	ye shes
tongpa nyi	stong pa nyi		mtsho rgyal

Notes

PREFACE

1. George Bogle, The British Library, Add. Ms. 19283, p. 60. The lama first shows him a compass that Bogle surmises is of French origin. "He then made his people bring a Hand Organ which he had lately received from Chyte Sing, much out of Order, and a Camera Obscura with views of London, about which he asked me many pertinent questions. . . . After this he desired me to walk about the Room, which he understood was our Custom.—'As for me, says he, here I sit from Morning to Night thus;'—at the same time crossing his Hands before him, closing his Eyes, and primming himself up in the Figure of an Image."

2. The use of the term "English" here refers both to the self-identifications of the writers and to the language in which they write. Even the lone Scotsman in the group, George Bogle, was known to refer to himself as English. See Hugh Richardson, "George Bogle and his Children," *High Peaks, Pure Earth: Collected Writings on Tibetan History and Culture* (London: Serindia, 1999), p. 470.

3. Edward Said, *Orientalism* (New York: Vintage, 1979), p. 92.

4. See Peter Bishop, *The Myth of Shangri-La: Tibet, Travel Writing and the Western Creation of Landscape* (Berkeley: University of California, 1989); Vincanne Adam, "Karaoke in Modern Lhasa," *Cultural Anthropology,* vol. 11, no. 4 (1996), pp. 510–546; Frank Korom, ed., *Constructing Tibetan Culture* (Quebec: World Heritage Press, 1997); and Oliver Schell, *Virtual Tibet: Searching for Shangri-La From the Himalayas to Hollywood* (New York: Metropolitan, 2000).

5. See Laurie Hovell, "Horizons Lost and Found: Travel, Writing and Tibet in the Age of Imperialism," Syracuse University Ph.D. dissertation, 1993.

PART ONE

CHAPTER I

1. See also James Hilton, *Lost Horizon* (New York: Pocket Books, 1960 [1933]), Jean-Jacques Annaud, *Seven Years in Tibet* (Columbia, 1997), Frank Capra, *Lost*

Horizon (Columbia, 1937), and Frederick Lenz, *Surfing the Himalayas* (New York: St. Martin's Press, 1997).

2. James Joyce has been largely attributed with developing a literary notion of epiphany. See Harry Levin, *James Joyce: A Critical Introduction* (Norfolk, Conn.: New Directions, 1960 [1941]), pp. 28–29.

3. Peter Matthiessen, *The Snow Leopard* (New York: Penguin, 1978), p. 212, emphasis in original. Subsequent citations are noted by page number in the text.

4. Charlotte Watson, "The Search For Shangri-La," *Great Destinations* (Supplement to the *Minneapolis Star Tribune),* October 1987, p. 6.

5. These include Patrick French, *Younghusband: The Last Great Imperial Adventurer* (London: Harper Collins, 1994), pp. 204–5 and Pico Iyer "Lost Horizons," *New York Review of Books,* January 15, 1998, p. 14.

CHAPTER 2

1. Thomas Holdich, *Tibet, The Mysterious* (New York: F. A. Stokes, 1906), p. 92.

2. Schuyler Camman, *Trade through the Himalayas* (Princeton: Princeton University Press, 1951), p. 35.

3. Peter Bishop, *The Myth of Shangri-La: Tibet, Travel Writing and the Western Creation of Landscape* (Berkeley: University of California, 1989), p. 36.

4. See Clements R. Markham, *Narratives of the Mission of George Bogle to Tibet and of the Journey of Thomas Manning to Lhasa* (New Delhi: Manjusri, 1971 [1876]). Others who have used Bogle's manuscripts include Woodcock, Hugh Richardson, and Alistair Lamb.

5. All of the manuscripts to which I refer are those held at the British Library. Others are held at the Mitchell Library in Glasgow.

6. George Bogle, Mss. Eur. E226/67. The numbers here and below refer to the catalog number of the manuscripts held at the British Library. I have included the dates of the original manuscripts when they were available. In all excerpts from Bogle's papers I have opted not to clutter the quotations by marking misspellings, grammar errors, or inconsistencies with "sic."

7. Bogle, Mss. Eur. E226/77c, 25 August 1774.

8. Bogle, Mss. Eur. E226/18. See also E226/80.

9. Bogle, Mss. Eur. E226/80, undated, though probably November 1774.

10. This Alexander Hamilton is to be confused neither with the Orientalist scholar nor with the American revolutionary.

11. Bogle, Mss. Eur. E226/80, 27 November 1774.

12. David Snellgrove and Hugh Richardson state that Bogle married a Tibetan lady who was a relation of the Panchen Lama; see Snellgrove and Richardson, *A Cultural History of Tibet* (New York: Praeger, 1968), p. 226. Woodcock notes that Bogle is reported to have had two daughters with an Asian woman who were raised in Scotland by his sister Martha. Bogle's will also provided support

for a "Bebee Bogle," and Woodcock surmises that this is probably his mistress (p. 169). See George Woodcock, *Into Tibet: The Early British Explorers* (New York: Barnes and Noble, 1971), p. 167. I could find no evidence of this relationship in the documents at the British Library, though one letter from Alexander Hamilton to Bogle notes that "GB has a son and heir appt." in Dinagephore [probably Patna], 9 December 1775 (Mss. Eur. E226/86e).

13. David Kopf, *British Orientalism and the Bengali Renaissance* (Berkeley: University of California, 1969), p. 21.

14. In many British accounts of this period, the Panchen Lama is frequently referred to as Teshoo or Teshu Lama—"Tashi" Lama of Tashilhunpo monastery.

15. Bogle, Mss. Eur. E226/80.

16. The common transliteration of this name is "Pema." Markham has Paima.

17. Qtd. in Woodcock, *Into Tibet: The Early British Explorers* (New York: Barnes and Noble, 1971), p. 41.

18. Born on November 26, 1746, the youngest son in an upper middle-class family in Glasgow, George Bogle was educated at Haddington and Glasgow, and attended the University of Edinburgh. After making the prescribed Grand Tour through France, he joined his brother's business in London, a counting house called Bogle and Scott. When this business failed, George, age 23, entered the East India Company as a writer, the lowest civil position. On a tour to assess revenue rates in Bengal, Bogle impressed Hastings and was shortly made envoy to Tibet.

19. Warren Hastings, Mss. Eur. E226/6. See Markham, *Narratives,* p. 8.

20. These texts were probably donated by Markham himself in 1874–75; they are catalogued as Mss. Eur. E226.

21. These are catalogued as Additional Manuscripts: the report is 19283; a letter to Hastings is included in 29233, and his letters to D. Anderson are collected in 45421 and 45432, f112.

22. Markham, *Narratives,* pp. v–vi.

23. Bogle, Mss. Eur. E226/19.

24. Markham, *Narratives,* p. 121.

25. For example, sections from Bogle's letter to his father (Mss. Eur. E226/77c) are included in the account of Bhutan, Markham, *Narratives,* pp. 14–17.

26. Bogle, Mss. Eur. E226/86b, 17 May 1775. Another letter from an English friend named Mustapha written to Bogle on 22 December 1772, before his journey to Tibet, supports this idea (Mss. Eur. E226/75).

27. Bogle, Mss. Eur. E226/18, 27 December 1774. Bogle writes that his life at Tashilhunpo "was monastick to the greatest degree."

28. Markham, *Narratives,* p. clv.

29. Bogle, Add. Ms. 19283.

30. Bishop, *The Myth of Shangri-La,* p. 36.

31. Woodcock, *Into Tibet,* p. 22.

32. Bogle, Mss. Eur. E226/77c, 25 August 1775, from Tassisudon. See Markham, *Narratives,* p. 15.

33. Bogle, Mss. Eur. E226:77c, emphasis in original.
34. From a letter to his father, Mss. Eur. E226/77c. See Markham, *Narratives,* p. 24.
35. Hayden White, *Tropics of Discourse: Essays in Cultural Criticism* (Baltimore: Johns Hopkins, 1978), p. 73.
36. This appears in Bogle's journal, Mss. Eur. E226/18, 11 November 1774. E226/18 seems to be a finished account in Bogle's hand. E226/18 bears Markham's pencil notes for his edition. See Markham, *Narratives,* p. 85.
37. Ibid.
38. Bogle, Mss. Eur. E226/18, 12 December 1774. See Markham, *Narratives,* pp. 94–5.
39. Bogle, Add. Ms. 19283. This note is omitted from Markham's text.
40. Bogle, Mss. Eur. E226/16. This appears in his journal, dated 24 October 1774. See Markham, pp. 67–8.
41. Matthew Kapstein, "A Pilgrimage of Rebirth Reborn: The 1992 Celebration of the Drigung Powa Chenmo," *Buddhism in Contemporary Tibet,* ed. Melvyn Goldstein and Matthew Kapstein (Berkeley: University of California Press, 1998), p. 107.
42. Bogle, Mss. Eur. E226/16.
43. Bogle, Mss. Eur. E226/16, from his journal, 27 October 1774. See Markham, *Narratives,* pp. 69–70.
44. Bogle, Mss. Eur. E226/16.
45. Markham has "Chumalhari" (*Narratives,* p. 70).
46. Bogle, Mss. Eur. E226/16.
47. Bishop, *The Myth of Shangri-La,* p. 36.
48. Bogle, Mss. Eur. E226/16, from his journal, 28 October 1774. See Markham, *Narratives,* p. 72.
49. Bogle, Mss. Eur. E226/18, from Bogle's journal, 18 December 1774. See Markham, *Narratives,* p. 99.
50. Bogle, Mss. Eur. E226/39.
51. Bogle, Mss. Eur. E226/39 is the only folio that bears such editorial marks in Bogle's hand.
52. Bogle, Mss. Eur. E226/39, 2 February, 1775. See Markham, *Narratives,* p. 107.
53. Bogle, Mss. Eur. E226/19.
54. Bogle, Mss. Eur. 226/18, from his journal, dated 5 January 1775. Their father was Chanzo Coosho [Chanzo Kushog], brother of the Panchen Lama.
55. Bogle, Mss. Eur. E226/18, from his journal, dated 27 December 1774.
56. Bogle, Mss. Eur. 226/18, from his journal, dated 12 December 1774. See Markham, *Narratives,* p. 96.
57. Ibid.
58. Ibid.
59. Bogle, Mss. Eur. E226/76, 8 January 1775.
60. Bogle, Mss. Eur. E226/18, 28 February 1775. In Mss. Eur. E226/39, the phrase "which showed his Sagacity" is crossed out, again bearing out the general tendency in this journal to minimize ironic comments. See Markham, *Narratives,* p. 111.

61. Bogle, Mss. Eur. E226/77c, from a letter to his father, dated 25 August 1774.
62. Bogle, Mss. Eur. E226/16, 28 October 1774. See Markham, *Narratives*, p. 72.
63. John Bell, *Travels from St. Petersburg, in Russia, to diverse parts of Asia* (Glasgow: Printed for the author by R. and A. Foulis, 1763).
64. Bogle, Mss. Eur. E226/77l, 8 January 1775.
65. Bogle, Mss. Eur. E226/18, 27 December 1774.
66. The two spoke Hindustani.
67. Bogle, Mss. Eur. E226/77L, 8 January 1775.
68. Ibid.
69. Bogle, Mss. Eur. 226/18, 23 November 1774. See Markham, *Narratives*, pp. 83–4.
70. Bogle, Mss. Eur. 226/18, 23 November 1774. See Markham, *Narratives*, p. 84.
71. Ibid.
72. See Bogle, Mss. Eur. E226/80, for example.
73. Ibid.
74. Bogle, Mss. Eur. E226/18, 23 November 1774. See Markham, *Narratives*, p. 87.
75. See Philip Almond on Victorian interpretations of nirvana, in *The British Discovery of Buddhism* (Cambridge: Cambridge University Press, 1988), pp. 102–110.
76. Bogle, Mss. Eur. E226/27 undated, emphasis added. See Markham, *Narratives*, p. 180.
77. Bogle, Mss. Eur. E226/18, 25 February 1775. See Markham, *Narratives*, p. 110. This account was translated into Tibetan with the help of an interpreter. Fragments of this account are contained in E226/65.
78. Bogle, Add. Mss. 19283. See Markham, *Narratives*, p. 143.
79. Ibid.
80. Bogle, Add. Ms. 19283.
81. Bogle, Mss. Eur. E226/80, 30 November 1774.
82. Bogle, Mss. Eur. E226/18, 17 January 1775. See Markham, *Narratives*, pp. 106–7.
83. For a discussion of *Lo-sar* rituals, see Norbu Chophel, *Folk Culture of Tibet* (Dharamsala: Library of Tibetan Works and Archives, 1983), p. 40; for similar Sherpa rituals, see Sherry Ortner, *Sherpas Through Their Rituals* (New York: Cambridge University Press, 1978), pp. 128–156.
84. Bogle seems to be combining two King James Bible passages on Satan in what he presents as quotation. The first part of the phrase paraphrases Satan's reply to God as to his whereabouts in Job 1:7 and 2:2. Satan says he has come "from going to and fro in the earth and from walking up and down in it." The second part echoes 1 Peter 5:8: "Be sober, be vigilant: because your adversary the devil, as a roaring lion, walketh about, seeking whom he may devour."
85. Markham, *Narratives*, p. cxliii.
86. Qtd. in Sara Suleri, *The Rhetoric of English India* (Chicago: University of Chicago, 1992), p. 64.
87. Bogle, Mss. Eur. E226/18, 18 February 1775. See Markham, *Narratives*, p. 109.
88. Bogle, Mss. Eur. E226/18, 23 November 1774. See Markham, *Narratives*, p. 88.
89. See Victor Turner, "Pilgrimages as Social Processes," *Dramas, Fields, and Metaphors:*

Symbolic Action in Human Society (Ithaca: Cornell University Press, 1974), pp. 166–230.

90. Bogle, Add. Ms. 19283. See Markham, *Narratives,* p. 163.

91. Hastings arranged for a Tibetan Buddhist temple to be built on the banks of the Hooghly, opposite Calcutta.

92. Bogle, Add. Ms. 19283. See Markham, *Narratives,* p. 167.

93. Ibid.

94. Bogle, Add. Ms. 19283. See Markham, *Narratives,* p. 170.

95. See Martin Green, *Dreams of Adventure, Deeds of Empire* (New York: Routledge, 1980), pp. 8–10.

96. Bogle, Add. Ms. 19283. See Markham, *Narratives,* p. 197.

97. Bogle, Add. Ms. 19283, emphasis added. See Markham, *Narratives,* p. 171.

98. Bogle, Mss. Eur. E226/18, 8 April 1775.

99. Bogle, Mss. Eur. E226/18, 11 March 1775.

100. Bogle, Mss. Eur. E226/18, 28 March 75, emphasis added. See Markham, *Narratives,* p. 118. Markham notes that the Pyn Cooshos both died in the spring of 1776.

101. Markham, *Narratives,* p. 177, emphasis added.

102. Ibid, cxliii.

103. Bogle, Mss. Eur. E226/18, 17 January 1775.

104. Bogle, Mss. Eur. E226/25, 10 March 1775, Markham, *Narratives,* p. 177.

105. Bogle, Add. Ms. 45421, 26 October 1775.

106. The references are to Thomas Hervey's *Meditations Among the Tombs* (Paisley [Scotland]: Weir, Tate, and Brown, 1744), Edward Young's *The Complaint: or, Night-thoughts on Life, Death, and Immortality* (London: R. Dodsley, 1742), and to the work of John Bunyan.

107. Hamilton refers to Bogle's recitation of the poem while at Tashilhunpo. See Add. Ms. 19283 and Markham, *Narratives,* p. 168 and Bogle, Mss. E226/77c. Hamilton has misquoted Gray's poem. The pertinent stanza is this: "Beneath those rugged elms, that yew tree's shade,/ Where heaves the turf in many a moldering heap,/ Each in his narrow cell forever laid,/ The rude forefathers of the hamlet sleep." *The Poetical Works of Thomas Gray,* ed. John Mitford (Boston: Little, Brown, and Co., 1853), p. 96.

108. Hamilton, Mss. Eur. E226/86f, 26 December 1775.

109. Bogle uses a Muslim term for a religious ascetic (Mss. Eur. E226/77c.).

110. Bogle, Add. Ms. 45421, 4 November 1776.

111. Qtd. in Woodcock, *Into Tibet,* p. 180.

112. Bogle, Mss. Eur. E226/14, 15 October 1774. See Markham, *Narratives,* p. 64.

CHAPTER 3

1. The phrase is Edward Said's. See *Culture and Imperialism* (New York: Knopf, 1993), p. 143.

2. Charles Long, "The Study of Religion: Its Nature and its Discourse," *Significations* (Philadephia: Fortress, 1986), p. 25.

3. Marlon B. Ross, "Romantic Quest and Conquest: Troping Masculine Power in the Crisis of Poetic Identity," *Romanticism and Feminism,* ed. Anne K. Mellor (Bloomington: Indiana University Press, 1988), pp. 26–7.

4. Samuel Turner, *An Account of an Embassy to the Court of the Teshoo Lama in Tibet* (New Delhi: Manjushri, 1971 [1800]), p. 80. Subsequent citations are noted by page number in the text.

5. See Marjorie Nicholson, *Mountain Gloom, Mountain Glory* (Ithaca: Cornell University Press, 1957).

6. Bogle, Mss. Eur. E226/18, December 1774. See Clements Markham, *Narratives of the Mission of George Bogle to Tibet and of the Journey of Thomas Manning to Lhasa* (New Delhi: Manjusri, 1971 [1876]) p. 98.

7. Charles Long, "Towards a Post-colonial Method in the Study of Religion," *Religious Studies News,* "Spotlight on Teaching," vol. 3., no. 2 (May 1995), p. 5.

8. Ashis Nandy, *The Intimate Enemy: Loss and Recovery of Self Under Colonialism* (New Delhi: Oxford University Press, 1984), p. 2 and p. xv.

9. Graham Sandberg, *The Exploration of Tibet* (Delhi: Cosmo Publications, 1987 [1904]), p. 110.

CHAPTER 4

1. M. H. Abrams, *Natural Supernaturalism: Tradition and Revolution in Romantic Literature* (New York: Norton, 1971), p. 13.

2. Peter Bishop, *The Myth of Shangri-La: Tibet, Travel Writing and the Western Creation of Landscape* (Berkley: University of California, 1989), p. 46.

3. Qtd. in Clements Markham, *Narratives of the Mission of George Bogle to Tibet and of the Journey of Thomas Manning to Lhasa* (New Delhi: Manjusri, 1971 [1876]), p. clx.

4. Qtd. in Markham, *Narratives,* p. 228.

5. George Woodcock, *Into Tibet: The Early British Explorers* (New York: Barnes and Noble, 1971) p. 208.

6. Thomas Manning, "Journey of Mr. Thomas Manning to Lhasa," in Markham, *Narratives,* p. 217. Subsequent citations are noted by page number in the text.

7. Francis Younghusband, *India and Tibet* (London: John Murray, 1910), p. 250.

8. Bogle, Mss. Eur. E226/25, 10 March 1775. See Markham, *Narratives,* p. 177.

9. Manning uses the Chinese term for the regent, who is Demo Rinpoche II.

10. Donald S. Lopez, Jr., "New Age Orientalism: The Case of Tibet," *Tricycle* (Spring 1994), p. 40.

11. These include both Europeans (missionaries, scientists, adventurers) and Indians in the employ of the Raj. For an exhaustive discussion of these travelers, see Bishop (1989), as well as Peter Hopkirk, *Trespassers on the Roof of the World* (Oxford: Oxford University Press, 1982), and Derek Waller, *The Pundits: British Exploration of Tibet and Central Asia* (Lexington: University of Kentucky, 1990).

12. Donald S. Lopez, Jr., *Prisoners of Shangri-La: Tibetan Buddhism and the West* (Chicago: University of Chicago Press, 1998), pp. 5–6.

CHAPTER 5

1. Philip Almond, *The British Discovery of Buddhism* (Cambridge: Cambridge University Press, 1988), p. 13.

2. Ibid., p. 12.

3. The Fourth Panchen Lama gave Hodgson a complete set of the Tibetan religious corpus known as the *Kagyur* and *Tengyur.*

4. Brian Houghton Hodgson, *Essays in the Languages, Literatures, Religion of Nepal and Tibet Together with Further Papers on the Geography, Ethnology, and Commerce of these Countries* (New Delhi: Manjusri, 1972 [1874]), p. 99.

5. Ibid., p. 41, emphasis in original. Subsequent citations appear in the text.

6. Ibid., p. 65 and p. 66. See Theodore Duka's biography *Life and Works of Alexander Csoma de Körös* (New Delhi: Manjusri, 1971 [1885]) and Donald S. Lopez, Jr.'s discussion of Csoma de Körös in "Foreigner at the Lama's Feet," *Curators of the Buddha* (Chicago: University of Chicago Press, 1995), pp. 256–259.

7. Almond, *The British Discovery,* p. 37.

8. Edward Said, *Orientalism* (New York: Vintage. 1978), p. 93.

9. Almond, *The British Discovery,* p. 13.

10. For more on the term "Lamaism," see "The Name" in Lopez's *Prisoners of Shangri-La* (Chicago: University of Chicago, 1998), pp. 15–45.

11. L. Austine Waddell, *The Buddhism and Lamaism of Tibet* (New Delhi: Heritage, 1979 [1895]), p. viii. Subsequent citations are noted by page number in the text.

12. Bogle qtd. in Waddell, *The Buddhism and Lamaism,* p. 237.

13. Ibid., p. 238.

14. Turner qtd. in Waddell, *The Buddhism and Lamaism,* p. 239.

15. Bruce Campbell, *Ancient Wisdom Revived* (Berkeley: University of California Press, 1980), p. 49.

16. L. Austine Waddell, *Lhasa and Its Mysteries* (New York: Dover, 1988 [1904]), pp. 409–410.

17. Rudyard Kipling, *Something of Myself* (Cambridge: Cambridge University Press, 1990), p. 35.

CHAPTER 6

1. For more on the ways in which texts can be "consumed," see T. S. McMillin's "The Consumption of Emerson," in *Our Preposterous Use of Literature* (Champaign: University of Illinois, 2000).
2. Rudyard Kipling, *Kim* (New York: Penguin, 1989 [1901]), p. 281. Subsequent citations are noted by page number in the text.
3. George Bogle, Mss. Eur. E226/19.
4. Clements Markham, *Narratives of the Mission of George Bogle to Tibet and of the Journey of Thomas Manning to Lhasa* (New Delhi: Manjusri, 1971 [1876]), p. 177.
5. Ibid., p. 171.
6. Barry V. Quall's *The Secular Pilgrims of Victorian Fiction* explores how pilgrimage and conversion are re-shaped for secular use in the Victorian novels of Carlyle, Dickens, Charlotte Bronte, and George Eliot (Cambridge: Cambridge University Press, 1982).
7. Kipling, *Something of Myself* (Cambridge: Cambridge University Press, 1990 [1937]), pp. 39–40, emphasis in original.
8. Qtd. in Quall's, *The Secular Pilgrims,* p. 1.
9. Ashis Nandy, *The Intimate Enemy: Loss and Recovery of Self Under Colonialism* (New Delhi: Oxford University Press, 1984), p. 64. Subsequent citations are noted by page number in the text.
10. For more on Kim's healing, see J. M. S. Tompkins' "Kipling's Later Tales: The Theme of Healing," *Modern Language Review* 45 (1950), pp. 18–32.
11. The cog and wheel machinery is vaguely reminiscent of the chakras, or centers, associated with Hatha Yoga and Tantrism. See Mircea Eliade, *Yoga, Immortality and Freedom* (Princeton: Princeton University Press, 1958).
12. Francis Hutchins, *The Illusion of Permanence: British Imperialism in India* (Princeton: Princeton University Press, 1967).
13. Nandy, *The Intimate Enemy,* pp. 33–4.

CHAPTER 7

1. Patrick French, *Younghusband: The Last Great Imperial Adventurer* (London: Harper Collins, 1994), pp. 89–90.
2. Francis Younghusband, *India and Tibet* (London: John Murray, 1910), p. vii. Subsequent citations are noted by page number in the text.
3. French, *Younghusband,* p. 277.
4. For example, see Mary Louise Pratt, *Imperial Eyes: Travel and Transculturation* (New York: Routledge, 1991), p. 6.
5. French, *Younghusband,* p. 137.
6. L. Austine Waddell, *Lhasa and Its Mysteries* (New York: Dover, 1988 [1904]), p. 2.
7. Qtd. in Younghusband, *India and Tibet,* p. 24.

8. French, *Younghusband,* pp. 213–214.

9. French, *Younghusband,* pp. 214–215.

10. Walt Whitman, Stanza 1, "Song of Myself," in *Leaves of Grass* (Brooklyn, NY: [s.n.], 1855). The first edition of this poem was untitled; the title "Song of Myself" was added in 1881.

11. French, *Younghusband,* p. 24.

12. George Seaver, *Francis Younghusband: Explorer and Mystic* (London: John Murray, 1952), p. 113. Seaver was Younghusband's first biographer.

13. Qtd. in French, *Younghusband,* p. 109.

14. French, *Younghusband,* p. 160.

15. Qtd. in Charles Long, "The Study of Religion: Its Nature and its Discourse," *Significations* (Philadelphia: Fortress, 1986), p. 16.

16. Monier Monier-Williams, *Buddhism, In Its Connexion with Brahmanism and Hinduism* (London: John Murray, 1889), pp. 4–5.

17. Ibid., p. 263, p. 281. This notion is echoed by June Campbell in *Traveller in Space* (New York: Braziller, 1996).

18. Waddell, *Lhasa and Its Mysteries,* p. 573.

19. Bogle in Clements Markham, *Narratives of the Mission of George Bogle to Tibet and of the Journey of Thomas Manning to Lhasa* (New Delhi: Manjusri, 1971 [1876]), p. 84.

20. Victor Turner, "Betwixt and Between: The Liminal Period in *Rites de Passage,*" *The Proceedings of the American Ethnological Society* (Seattle: University of Washington Press, 1964), pp. 4–20.

21. Perceval Landon, *The Opening of Tibet: An Account of Lhasa and the Country and People of Central Tibet and of the Progress of the Mission sent there by the English Government in the Year 1903–4* (New York: Doubleday, 1905).

22. Seaver, *Francis Younghusband,* p. 374; French, *Younghusband,* p. 281.

23. Rudyard Kipling, *Kim* (New York: Penguin, 1989 [1901]), p. 337. Said suggests that the lama's "encyclopedic vision of freedom strikingly resembles Colonel Creighton's Indian Survey, in which every camp and village is duly noted." *Culture and Imperialism,* pp. 142–3.

24. Phillip Almond, *The British Discovery of Buddhism* (Cambridge: Cambridge University Press, 1988), p. 104. See also Guy Richard Welbon, *The Buddhist Nirvana and its Western Interpreters* (Chicago: University of Chicago Press, 1968).

25. Monier-Williams, *Buddhism,* p. 35

26. Waddell, *The Buddhism and Lamaism,* p. 110

27. Waddell, *The Buddhism and Lamaism,* p. 6

28. Almond, *The British Discovery,* p. 1.

29. Edwin Arnold, *Light of Asia* (Adyar: Theosophical Society, 1980 [1879]), p. 112.

30. Qtd. in Younghusband, *The Heart of a Continent* (New York: Scribner's, 1896), p. 387; this passage is from William Wordsworth, "Lines Composed a Few Miles above Tintern Abbey, on Revisiting the Banks of the Wye during a Tour, July 13, 1798," (lines 93–102), in *The Complete Poetical Works of William Wordsworth: together with a description of the country of the lakes in the north of England,* ed. Henry Reed (Philadelphia: J. Kay, 1837).

31. French, *Younghusband,* pp. 204–5.
32. Qtd. in Seaver, *Francis Younghusband,* p. 249.
33. Bogle, Mss. Eur. E226/18, 27 December 1774.

PART TWO

CHAPTER 1

1. This baseball-watching situation recalls the excitement at a Tibetan monastery in Bhutan during the World Cup soccer finals depicted in *The Cup,* a film directed by the Tibetan Buddhist lama, Khyentse Norbu (New Line, 1999).
2. The first Tibetan autobiography written in English appears to be Tsewang Y. Pemba's *Young Days in Tibet* (London: J. Cape, 1957).
3. I adapt this term from Vincanne Adams's discussion of the authentic Sherpa in *Tigers of the Snow and other Virtual Sherpas* (Princeton: Princeton University Press, 1996). Hereafter I will drop the scare quotes.
4. Ibid., p. 82.
5. For collections of several Tibetan life histories in one volume, see Sandy Johnson, *The Book of Tibetan Elders: The Life Stories and Wisdom of the Great Spiritual Masters of Tibet* (New York: Riverhead, 1996) and Vyvyan Cayley, *Children of Tibet: An Oral History of the First Tibetans to Grow Up in Exile* (Balmain, Australia: Pearlfisher, 1994).
6. Janet Gyatso, *Apparitions of the Self: The Secret Autobiographies of a Tibetan Visionary* (Princeton: Princeton University Press, 1998), p. 111.
7. For English versions of these namtars, see Lobsang P. Lhalunpa's *The Life of Milarepa* (New York: Arkana, 1979), Keith Dowman's *The Divine Madman: The Sublime Life and Songs of Drupka Kunley* (Dawn Horse: Middletown, Calif., 1980), Dowman's *Sky Dancer: The Secret Life and Songs of the Lady Yeshe Tsogyel* (Ithaca: Snow Lion, 1996), and Janice Willis's *Enlightened Beings: Life Stories from the Ganden Oral Tradition* (Boston: Wisdom, 1994). The phrase "full liberation" is from Willis.
8. Willis, *Enlightened Beings,* p. 3.
9. Janet Gyatso, *Apparitions of the Self,* p. 103.
10. Ibid., p. 101.
11. Ibid., p. 265.
12. Georges Gusdorf, "Conditions and Limits of Autobiography," trans. and ed. James Olney, in *Autobiography: Essays Theoretical and Critical,* ed. Olney (Princeton: Princeton University Press, 1980), p. 30.
13. Philippe Lejeune, "The Autobiographical Pact," *On Autobiography,* ed. Paul John Eakin, trans. Katherine Leary (Minneapolis: University of Minnesota, 1989), p. 4.
14. Palden Gyatso, "Prologue," *Autobiography of a Tibetan Monk* (New York: Grove Press, 1997), no page number.
15. At least two Tibetan autobiographies in English were first published in Tibetan:

Tsering Dorje Gashi's *New Tibet: Memoirs of a Graduate of the Peking Institute of National Minorities* (Dharamsala: Information Office of His Holiness the Dalai Lama, 1980) and Jamyang Norbu's *Warriors of Tibet: The Story of Aten and the Khampas' Fight for the Freedom of their Country* (London: Wisdom, 1979).

16. Dawa Norbu, *Red Star over Tibet* (New York: Ebony, 1987).

17. Jamyang Sakya and Julie Emery, *Princess in the Land of Snows: The Life of Jamyang Sakya in Tibet* (Boston: Shambala), p. xi.

18. Heinrich Harrer, "Preface," *Tibet is My Country: Autobiography of Thubten Jigme Norbu, Brother of the Dalai Lama as told to Heinrich Harrer* (London: Wisdom, 1986), p. 18.

19. Dorje Yudon Yuthok, *House of the Turquoise Roof,* trans. and ed. Michael Harlin (Ithaca, Snow Lion, 1990, [revised 1995]), p. 16.

20. Exceptions to this include Dawa Norbu's *Red Star Over Tibet* in which he presents himself as a secular intellectual (New York: Envoy, 1987) and Melvyn Goldstein, William Siebenschuh, and Tashi Tsering, *The Struggle for a Modern Tibet: The Autobiography of Tashi Tsering,* (New York: M. E. Sharpe, 1997).

21. This phrase was first suggested to me by a Tibetan exile in Switzerland.

22. This is also suggested by the career of Gongkar Gyatso, a Tibetan artist trained in the Tibetan Autonomous Region of China, as described in Clare Harris's *In the Image of Tibet: Tibetan Painting after 1959* (London: Reaktion, 2000).

23. Jetsun Pema with Gilles van Grasdorff, *Tibet: My Story, An Autobiography* (Boston: Element, 1997), p. 217.

24. A 27-year-old male, interview by author in English, tape recording, Horgen, Switzerland, June 1996.

25. Ibid.

26. Donald S. Lopez, Jr., *Prisoners of Shangri-La: Tibetan Buddhism and the West* (Chicago: University of Chicago Press, 1998), p. 200.

27. Ibid., p. 201.

28. George Bogle, Ms. Eur. E226/18. See Clements Markham, *Narratives of the Mission of George Bogle to Tibet and of the Journey of Thomas Manning to Lhasa* (New Delhi: Manjusri, 1971 [1876]), p. 95.

29. In an interview in the September 1999 issue of *Vanity Fair,* Rupert Murdoch said of the Dalai Lama, "I have heard cynics who say he's a very political old monk shuffling around in Gucci shoes" (no. 470, p. 321).

30. See Johannes Fabian's *Time and the Other: How Anthropology Makes its Object* (New York: Columbia University Press, 1983).

31. Orville Schell, *Virtual Tibet: Searching for Shangri-La From the Himalayas to Hollywood* (New York: Metropolitan, 2000), p. 78.

32. Sandy Johnson, *The Book of Tibetan Elders: Life Stories and Wisdom from the Great Spiritual Masters of Tibet* (New York: Riverhead, 1996), p. 5. See also Peter Gold's *Navajo and Tibetan Sacred Wisdom: The Circle of Spirit* (Rochester, Vt.: Inner Traditions, 1994).

33. Johnson, *The Book of Tibetan Elders,* p. 20.

34. Adams, "Karaoke in Modern Tibet, Lhasa," pp. 510–546.

35. Robert Thurman, *Essential Tibetan Buddhism* (San Francisco: Harper San Francisco, 1995), p. 10; Lopez, *Prisoners of Shangri-La,* p. 200.

36. Lejeune, "The Autobiographical Pact," *On Autobiography,* p. 11, emphasis in original.

37. One exception to this is a reader's comments on Jetsun Pema's autobiography, which is described as a "poorly written, scattered story lacking depth and clarity. . . . Her story lacks the glue that makes anecdotal material into a book, a public figure into a writer" (Amazon.com: A Glance: An autobiography, July 3, 1999).

38. Janet Gyatso suggests that within the Tibetan tradition, editing by a second person often poses no threat to their status as *rangnam,* noting that "works that are considered autobiography are often completed and sometimes edited by the subject's disciple" (*Apparitions of the Self,* p. 103).

39. Two exceptions to this are *Princess in the Land of Snows* and *The Struggle for Modern Tibet,* which list two or more authors.

40. Lejeune, "The Autobiography of Those Who Do Not Write," *On Autobiography,* ed. by Paul John Eakin, trans. Katherine Leary (Minneapolis: University of Minnesota Press, 1989), p. 194.

41. When I tested the system by offering my own comments, they appeared unedited and almost instantly on the website.

42. Amazon.com: Customer comments: Freedom in Exile: The Autobiography of the Dalai Lama, July 3, 1999.

43. Ibid.

44. Amazon.com: Customer comments: The Autobiography of a Tibetan Monk, July 3, 1999.

45. Ibid.

46. Amazon.com: Customer comments: Freedom in Exile: The Autobiography of the Dalai Lama, July 3, 1999.

47. Ibid.

48. Harrer, "Preface," *Tibet is My Country,* p. 15.

49. Pema, *Tibet: My Story,* p. xii.

50. Goldstein, et al., *The Struggle for Modern Tibet,* pp. 56–7.

51. P. Christiaan Klieger, *Tibetan Nationalism: The Role of Patronage in the Accomplishment of a National Identity* (Meerut [India]: Archana, 1992), p. 19.

52. Lopez, *Prisoners,* p. 206.

53. Klieger, *Tibetan Nationalism,* p. 16. See also Adams, *Tigers of the Snow,* pp. 164–5.

54. For more on this chapter in Tibetan-U.S. relations, see John Knaus, *Orphans of the Cold War: America and the Tibetan Struggle for Survival* (New York: Public Affairs, 1999) and Tsering Shakya, *Dragon in the Land of Snows* (New York: Columbia University Press, 1999).

55. Donald Lopez told me that when he appeared on National Public Radio's "Talk of the Nation" to discuss *Prisoners of Shangri-La: Tibetan Buddhism and the West,* he was told that he would be paired with someone "from the other side." Lopez imagined someone who spoke the party line of the Chinese govern-

ment; instead, he was matched with a Tibetan spokesman from the International Campaign for Tibet, an organization devoted to keeping the Tibet issue alive in the United States. The scenario suggests that to critique Western representations of Tibet is equivalent, for some, to criticizing the entire Tibetan struggle for self-determination. (Cited with permission.)

56. Amazon.com: Customer comments: Freedom in Exile: The Autobiography of the Dalai Lama, July 3, 1999.

57. Janet Gyatso, *Apparitions,* p. 189.

58. Lejeune, "The Autobiographical Pact (Bis)," p. 131.

59. Lopez, "New Age Orientalism: The Case of Tibet," *Tricycle,* Spring 1994, p. 42.

60. Lopez, *Prisoners,* p. 7.

CHAPTER 2

1. Jetsun Pema with Gilles van Grasdorff, *Tibet: My Story, an Autobiography* (Boston: Element, 1997), p. xi.

2. Pema, *Tibet: My Story,* p. 213. Pema also notes that when as a teenager she corresponded with her brother, Lobsang Samten, he wrote to her in an English transcription of Tibetan because she had forgotten the Tibetan script (p. 59).

3. "Traveling Cultures," *Cultural Studies,* ed. Lawrence Grossberg, et al. (New York: Routledge, 1992), p. 108.

4. Matthew Kapstein, "A Pilgrimage of Rebirth Reborn: The 1992 Celebration of the Drigung Powa Chenmo," *Buddhism in Contemporary Tibet,* ed. Melvyn Goldstein and Matthew Kapstein (Berkeley: University of California Press, 1998), p. 117.

5. Jamyang Sakya and Julie Emery, *Princess in the Land of Snows: The Life of Jamyang Sakya in Tibet* (Boston: Shambala), p. 50.

6. Janet Gyatso, *Apparitions of the Self: The Secret Autobiographies of a Tibetan Visionary* (Princeton: Princeton University Press, 1998), p. 121.

7. Pema, *Tibet: My Story,* p. 217.

8. Ibid., p. 219.

9. Orville Schell, "Virtual Tibet: Where the mountains rise from the sea of our yearning," *Harper's,* April 1998, p. 39. Subsequent citations are noted by page number in the text.

10. James Hilton, *Lost Horizon* (New York: Pocket Books, 1960 [1933]), p. 72.

11. Donald S. Lopez, Jr., *Prisoners of Shangri-La: Tibetan Buddhism and the West* (Chicago: University of Chicago Press), p. 86.

12. Heinrich Harrer, "Preface," *Tibet is My Country: Autobiography of Thubten Jigme Norbu, Brother of the Dalai Lama as told to Heinrich Harrer* (London: Wisdom, 1986), p. 18.

13. Lopez, *Prisoners,* pp. 93–94.

14. Lobsang Gyatso, *Memoirs of a Tibetan Lama,* ed. Gareth Sparham (Ithaca: Snow Lion, 1998), p. 95.

15. Geshe Rabten, *The Life and Teaching of Geshe Rabten: A Tibetan Lama's Search for Truth,* trans. and ed. B. Alan Wallace (London: George Allen and Unwin, 1980), pp. 73–74.
16. Norbu, *Tibet is My Country: Autobiography of Thubten Jigme Norbu, Brother of the Dalai Lama as told to Heinrich Harrer* (London: Wisdom, 1986), p. 233.
17. Ibid., p. 230.
18. Tenzin Gyatso, *Freedom in Exile: The Autobiography of the Dalai Lama* (New York: Harper Perennial, 1990), p. 54.
19. Norbu's connection to the C.I.A. is also suppressed in his text. See John Kenneth Knaus's *Orphans of the Cold War: American and the Tibetan Struggle for Survival* (New York: Public Affairs, 1999).
20. Norbu, *Tibet is My Country,* p. 255.
21. Clifford, "Traveling Cultures," p. 97.
22. Norbu, *Tibet is My Country,* p. 241.
23. Ibid., p. 244.
24. Levi-Strauss quoted in Clifford, "Traveling Cultures," p. 96.
25. Norbu, *Tibet is My Country,* p. 235. The foreigner in question is Robert Ekvall, son of former Christian missionaries in Amdo and a noted anthropologist of Tibet.
26. Harrer, "Preface," p. 13.
27. Norbu, *Tibet is My Country,* p. 241.

CHAPTER 3

1. Gareth Sparham, "Introduction," *Memoirs of a Tibetan Lama* (Ithaca: Snow Lion, 1998), p. 7.
2. Geshe Rabten, *The Life and Teaching of Geshe Rabten: A Tibetan Lama's Search for Truth* (London: Allen and Unwin, 1980), p. 54. Subsequent citations are noted by page number in the text.
3. In 2001 Wallace was a lecturer in the Department of Religious Studies at the University of California at Santa Barbara.
4. In a kind of endorsement of authenticity, the Dalai Lama has written prefaces for three other autobiographies discussed here: Blakeslee's autobiography of Ama Adhe, as well as those of Palden Gyatso and Jamyang Sakya.
5. The Dalai Lama, "Foreword," *The Life and Teaching of Geshe Rabten: A Tibetan Lama's Search for Truth* (London: Allen and Unwin, 1980), no page number.
6. B. Alan Wallace, "Preface," *The Life and Teaching of Geshe Rabten: A Tibetan Lama's Search for Truth* (London: Allen and Unwin, 1980), no page number. "*Geshe*" is a title that denotes an advanced degree within the Geluk tradition.
7. Lejeune, "The Autobiographical Pact (Bis)," *On Autobiography* (Minneapolis: University of Minnesota, 1989), p. 128.
8. See Part Two, chapter 4.
9. Sparham in Gyatso, "Introduction," p. 7. Subsequent citations are noted by page number in the text.

10. James Olney, "Autobiography and the Cultural Moment," *Autobiography: Essays Theoretical and Critical* (Princeton: Princeton University Press, 1980), p. 25.

11. See Stephen Batchelor, "Letting Daylight into Magic: The Life and Times of Dorje Shugden," and Donald S. Lopez, Jr., "Two Sides of the Same God," *Tricycle,* Spring 1998, pp. 60–66 and 67–82 respectively, and Georges Dreyfus, "The Shuk-den Affair: History and Nature of a Quarrel," *Journal of the International Association of Buddhist Studies* 21:2 (1998), pp. 227–270.

12. Lobsang Gyatso, *Memoirs of a Lama* (Ithaca: Snow Lion, 1998), p. 11. Subsequent citations are noted by page number in the text.

13. Janet Gyatso, *Apparitions of the Self: The Secret Autobiographies of a Tibetan Visionary* (Princeton: Princeton University Press, 1998), p. 105.

14. Ibid., p. 111.

15. Bogle, Ms. Eur. E226/18, 27 December 1774.

16. Kipling, *Something of Myself* (Cambridge: Cambridge University Press, 1990 [1937]), pp. 39–40.

17. Tenzin Gyatso, *Ethics for a New Millennium* (New York: Riverhead, 1999), p. 188.

18. See Richard Gombrich and Gananath Obeyesekere, *Buddhism Transformed: Religious Change in Sri Lanka* (Princeton: Princeton University Press, 1988).

19. Walpola Rahula, *What the Buddha Taught* (London: Gordon Fraser, 1978), p. 8.

20. Donald S. Lopez, Jr., *Prisoners of Shangri-La: Tibetan Buddhism and the West* (Chicago: University of Chicago Press, 1998), p. 19.

21. See Lopez, "The Prison," *Prisoners,* pp. 181–207.

22. Ritu Sarin and Tenzin Sonam, "The Reincarnation of Khensur Rinpoche," White Crane Films, 1991.

CHAPTER 4

1. The term Dalai is Mongolian for "ocean" and is a translation of "Gyatso," part of this monk's name.

2. A 27–year-old woman, interview by author in English, tape recording, Rikon, Switzerland, June 1996.

3. A 46–year-old layman, interview by author in English, tape recording, Winterthur, Switzerland, June 1996.

4. Tenzin Gyatso (Dalai Lama XIV), *My Land and My People: The Original Autobiography of His Holiness the Dalai Lama of Tibet* (New York: Warner, 1997 [1962]), p. v.

5. Tenzin Gyatso (Dalai Lama XIV), *Freedom in Exile: The Autobiography of the Dalai Lama* (New York: Harper Collins, 1990), p. xiii. Subsequent citations are noted by page number in the text.

6. He notes in *Freedom in Exile* that he was assisted by David Howarth, an English writer, p. 169.

7. Daniel Goleman, "We Must Change Our Lives," *New York Times Book Review,* September 30, 1990, Sunday, Late Edition-Final Section 7, p. 3.

8. Philippe Lejeune, "The Autobiography of Those Who Do Not Write," *On Autobiography,* ed. by Paul John Eakin, trans. Katherine Leary (Minneapolis: University of Minnesota Press, 1989), p. 195.

9. Janet Gyatso, *Apparitions of the Self: The Secret Autobiographies of a Tibetan Visionary* (Princeton: Princeton University Press, 1998), p. 107.

10. This phrase is Janet Gyatso's, *Apparitions,* p. 265.

11. Clifford Geertz, "Religion as a Cultural System," *Interpretation of Cultures* (New York: Basic Books, 1973), pp. 110–111.

12. Alexandra David-Neel, *Magic and Mystery in Tibet* (New York: Kendall, 1932).

13. See Donald S. Lopez, Jr., *Prisoners of Shangri-La: Tibetan Buddhism and the West* (Chicago: University of Chicago Press, 1998), pp. 181–207.

CHAPTER 5

1. Chagdud Tulku, *Lord of the Dance* (Junction City, Calif.: Padma, 1992), p. 10. Subsequent citations are noted by page number in the text.

2. Chögyam Trungpa, *Born in Tibet* (London: Unwin, 1979 [1966]), p. 67. Subsequent citations are noted by page number in the text.

3. Wilber, "Introduction," *Lord of the Dance* (Junction City, Calif.: Padma, 1992), p. xiii.

4. See Campbell, *Traveller in Space* (New York: Braziller), 1996.

5. See Chögyam Trungpa's *Cutting Through Spiritual Materialism* (Berkeley: Shambala, 1973), *The Myth of Freedom* (Berkeley: Shambala, 1976), and *Crazy Wisdom* (Boston: Shambala, 1991).

6. David Snellgrove, *Four Lamas of Dolpo* (Cambridge: Harvard University Press, 1967), p. ix.

7. See David Germano, "Remembering the Dismembered Body of Tibet," in *Buddhism in Contemporary Tibet,* ed. Melvyn Goldstein and Matthew Kapstein (Berkeley: University of California, 1998), pp. 53–94.

8. Marco Polo, *The Book of Ser Marco Polo the Venetian concerning the Kingdoms and Marvels of the East,* trans. and ed. Sir Henry Yule (New York: Scribner's, 1903), p. 301.

9. Ibid., p. 92.

10. Geertz, "Religion as a Cultural System," *Interpretation of Cultures* (New York: Basic Books, 1973), p. 112.

11. See Bhabha's classic "Signs Taken for Wonders: Questions of Ambivalence and Authority under a Tree Outside Delhi, May 1817," *"Race," Writing, and Difference,* ed. Henry Louis Gates, Jr. (Chicago: Chicago University Press, 1985), pp. 163–184.

12. Lobsang P. Lhalungpa, *The Life of Milarepa* (New York: Arkana, 1977), p. 139.

13. Keith Dowman, *The Divine Madman: The Sublime Songs and Drukpa Kunley* (Middletown, Calif.: Dawn Horse Press, 1980), pp. 8–9.

14. Lhalungpa, *The Life of Milarepa,* pp. 154–5.

NOTES

CHAPTER 6

1. Lopez, "Introduction," *Religions of Tibet in Practice* (Princeton: University of Princeton, 1997), p. 21.
2. The Dalai Lama has said that he would like to see such a lineage established in the Tibetan tradition. See "Opening Speech of His Holiness the Dalai Lama," *Daughters of the Buddha,* ed. Karma Lekshe Tsomo (Ithaca: Snow Lion, 1988), p. 44.
3. See for example Karma Lekshe Tsomo's "Change in Consciousness: Women's Religious Identity in Himalayan Buddhist Cultures," in *Buddhist Women Across Cultures: Realizations,* ed. Karma Lekshe Tsomo (Albany: State University of New York Press, 1999), p. 175.
4. Rita M. Gross, *Buddhism After Patriarchy: A Feminist History, Analysis, and Reconstruction of Buddhism* (Albany: State University of New York Press, 1993), p. 3. For a discussion of the divergent ways in which women were constructed in early Buddhism, see Alan Sponberg, "Attitudes toward Women and the Feminine in Early Buddhism," in *Buddhism, Sexuality, and Gender,* ed. José Ignacio Cabezón (Albany: State University of New York Press, 1992) pp. 3–36.
5. Willis, "Tibetan Buddhist Women Practitioners, Past and Present: A Garland to Delight Those Wishing Inspiration," *Buddhist Women Across Cultures: Realizations,* ed. Karma Lekshe Tsomo (Albany: State University of New York Press, 1999), pp. 146–7.
6. Ibid., p. 154.
7. Hugh Richardson, "Foreword," *Daughter of Tibet* (New Delhi: Allied Publishers, 1970), p. xiv.
8. Ibid., p. xv.
9. Rinchen Dolma Taring, *Daughter of Tibet* (New Delhi: Allied, 1970), p. 50. Subsequent citations are noted by page number in the text.
10. Bogle, Ms. Eur. E226/18.
11. Anne Klein, *Meeting the Great Bliss Queen: Buddhists, Feminists, and the Art of the Self* (Boston: Beacon, 1995), p. 31.
12. For more on Tibetan systems of marriage, see Nancy Levine, *The Dynamics of Polyandry: Kinship, Domesticity, and Population on the Tibetan Border* (Chicago: University of Chicago Press, 1988).
13. A favored and controversial member of the court of the 13th Dalai Lama, Chensal Namgang took the surname Tsarong when he married into Taring's family.
14. "'On the Road': A Maharashtrian Pilgrimage," trans. D. D. Karve and Franklin Southworth, in *The Experience of Hinduism: Essays on Religion in Maharashtra,* ed. Maxine Berntsen and Eleanor Zelliot (Albany: State University of New York Press, 1988), p. 163.
15. Francis Younghusband, *India and Tibet* (London: John Murray, 1910), p. 326.
16. Tenzin N. Tethong, "Preface," *House of the Turquoise Roof* (Ithaca: Snow Lion, 1990), p. 9.
17. Dorje Yudon Yuthok, *House of the Turquoise Roof* (Ithaca: Snow Lion, 1990), p. 128.

18. Karma Lekshe Tsomo, "Change in Consciousness," *Buddhist Women Across Cultures: Realizations*, p. 174.
19. Klein, *Meeting the Great Bliss Queen,* p. xvii.
20. Ibid., p. 26.
21. Tsomo, "Change in Consciousness," p. 175.
22. For a feminist analysis of Tibetan women and gender relations, see Charlene E. Makley's "Meaning of Liberation: Representations of Tibetan Women," *The Tibet Journal,* vol. xxii, no. 2 (Summer 1997), pp. 4–29.

CHAPTER 7

1. James E. Young, *Writing and Rewriting the Holocaust: Narrative and the Consequences of Interpretation* (Bloomington: Indiana University Press, 1988), p. 24.
2. Saul Friedlander, "Introduction," *Probing the Limits of Representation: Nazism and the Final Solution,* ed. Saul Friedlander (Cambridge: Harvard University Press, 1992), p. 3.
3. Hannah Arendt, *Eichmann in Jerusalem: A Report on the Banality of Evil* (New York: Penguin, 1964).
4. Young, *Writing and Rewriting the Holocaust,* p. 25.
5. The quotation is Friedlander's; he argues that despite their interest in formal and abstract questions, the contributors to *Probing the Limits of Representation* have not "forgotten the horror behind the words" (p. 1).
6. Palden Gyatso, "Prologue," *Autobiography of a Tibetan Monk* (New York: Grove Press, 1997), no page number.
7. "Preface," Tsering Shakya, *Autobiography of a Tibetan Monk* (New York: Grove Press, 1997), no page number.
8. Palden Gyatso, "Prologue."
9. Shakya, "Preface," no page number.
10. Palden Gyatso, *Autobiography of a Tibetan Monk,* p. 3. Subsequent citations are noted by page number in the text.
11. Palden Gyatso, "Prologue," no page number.
12. See Bogle, Ms. Eur. E226/25, 10 March 1775, and Clements Markham, *Narratives of the Mission of George Bogle to Tibet and of the Journey of Thomas Manning to Lhasa* (New Delhi: Manjusri, 1971 [1876]), p. 177.
13. Young, *Writing and Rewriting the Holocaust,* p. 25.
14. Jacques Derrida, *Of Grammatology,* trans. Gayatri Chakravorty Spivak (Baltimore: Johns Hopkins University Press, 1974).
15. Samphel, "Translator's Note," in Tsering Dorje Gashi, *New Tibet: Memoirs of a Graduate of the Peking Institute of National Minorities* (Dharamsala: Information Office of HHDL, 1980), p. 1.
16. Young, *Writing and Rewriting the Holocaust,* p. 25.
17. David Patt, *Strange Liberation: Tibetan Lives in Chinese Hands* (Ithaca: Snow Lion, 1992), p. 33.

NOTES

18. Personal correspondence, August 1999. Cited with permission.
19. Mickey Lemle, "Compassion in Exile," Betacam, 1992.
20. Dalai Lama, "Foreword," *The Voice that Remembers: A Tibetan Woman's Inspiring Story of Survival* (Boston: Wisdom, 1997), p. vii.
21. Adhe Tapontsang, "Prologue," *The Voice that Remembers: A Tibetan Woman's Inspiring Story of Survival* (Boston: Wisdom, 1997), p. 3.
22. Ibid., p. 4.
23. Adams, "Karaoke in Modern Tibet, Lhasa," in *Cultural Anthropology* (Vol. 11, no. 4, 1996), pp. 510–546.

CHAPTER 8

1. Melvyn Goldstein, "Preface," *The Struggle for Modern Tibet: The Autobiography of Tashi Tsering* (Armonk, NY: M. E. Sharpe, 1997), p. viii.
2. Melvyn Goldstein, William Siebenschuh, Tashi Tsering, *The Struggle for Modern Tibet: The Autobiography of Tashi Tsering* (Armonk, NY: M. E. Sharpe, 1997), p. 79. Subsequent citations are noted by page number in the text.
3. Palden Gyatso, *Autobiography of a Tibetan Monk* (New York: Grove Press, 1997), p. 3.
4. Goldstein, et al., p. 4.
5. Goldstein, "Preface," pp. viii–ix.

APPENDIX

1. With a few exceptions, I have not included the spellings of proper names.

Index